Where the Gods Are

THE ANCHOR YALE BIBLE REFERENCE LIBRARY is a project of international and interfaith scope in which Protestant, Catholic, and Jewish scholars from many countries contribute individual volumes. The project is not sponsored by any ecclesiastical organization and is not intended to reflect any particular theological doctrine.

The series is committed to producing volumes in the tradition established half a century ago by the founders of the Anchor Bible, William Foxwell Albright and David Noel Freedman. It aims to present the best contemporary scholarship in a way that is accessible not only to scholars but also to the educated nonspecialist. It is committed to work of sound philological and historical scholarship, supplemented by insight from modern methods, such as sociological and literary criticism.

John J. Collins
General Editor

THE ANCHOR YALE BIBLE REFERENCE LIBRARY

Where the Gods Are

Spatial Dimensions of Anthropomorphism in the Biblical World

MARK S. SMITH

 Yale   NEW HAVEN

UNIVERSITY   AND

PRESS   LONDON

Yale University Press books may be purchased in quantity for educational, business, or promotional use. For information, please e-mail sales.press@yale .edu (U.S. office) or sales@yaleup.co.uk (U.K. office).

Set in Adobe Caslon and Bauer Bodoni types by Newgen North America. Printed in the United States of America.

Library of Congress Control Number: 2015954508
ISBN 978-0-300-20922-8 (cloth : alk. paper)

A catalogue record for this book is available from the British Library.

This paper meets the requirements of ANSI/NISO Z39.48–1992 (Permanence of Paper).

10 9 8 7 6 5 4 3 2 1

In memory of Franz Rosenthal,
teacher and beloved friend

We long for place; but place itself longs.
—Anne Michaels, *Fugitive Pieces*

Love makes you see a place differently.... And if you learn to love one place, sometimes you can also learn to love another.
—Anne Michaels, *Fugitive Pieces*

Contents

Acknowledgments

For work on this book, I have turned to many wonderful scholars for their insightful writings as well as their comments. My wife, Elizabeth Bloch-Smith, has been a tremendous help and wonderful critic. Her suggestions on many material and literary matters have been invaluable. Dan Fleming, Alex Jassen, and Elliot Wolfson, departmental colleagues at New York University, were also very helpful. The libraries of New York University and the École Biblique in Jerusalem were of immense service. This book benefited from the work and advice of many scholars cited in these pages: Susan Ackerman, Spencer Allen, Corrine Carvalho, David Goldenberg, Ron Hendel, Bernd Janowski, Othmar Keel, Marjo C. A. Korpel, Martin Leuenberger, Baruch Levine, Ted Lewis, Christl Maier, P. Kyle McCarter, Dennis Olson, Dennis Pardee, Wayne Pitard, Aaron Schart, Karel van der Toorn, Christoph Uehlinger, and Ziony Zevit. I especially note the contributions of Spencer Allen, Esther Hamori, Benjamin Sommer, and Andreas Wagner, as their works have been touchstones for Chapters 1 and 5. I particularly appreciate their generous spirit in discussing their work with me.

Several chapters in this book were the subjects of a doctoral seminar in the spring term of 2014 at New York University. The students in this course aided me tremendously, and I thank them: Dylan Johnson, Michael Stahl, Zachary Margulies, all of New York University; and Carolyn Klaasen of Union Theological Seminary. In addition, Liz Bloch-Smith, Andrea Weiss, and Evelyne Martin (visiting from the University of Bern) presented their work in the seminar. We had the additional benefit of the participation of Raik Haikl (visiting from the University of Tübingen). My profound thanks go to all these fine scholars. I am also grateful to the members of the Old Testament Colloquium and of the Colloquium for

Biblical Research for their help and many acts of kindness. I thank Anchor Yale Bible Reference Library for accepting this work and its board members for their valuable suggestions. I am particularly grateful to my editor, John Collins, my copy editor, Jessie Dolch, and my production editor, Susan Laity, for their great help. I thank Julie Deluty, Rachel Smith, and Michael Stahl for their proofreading and work on the indexes.

This book draws on material published elsewhere: "The Three Bodies of God," *JBL* 134 (2015): 471–88; "Like Deities, Like Temples (Like People)," in *Temple and Worship in Biblical Israel*, ed. John Day, LHB/OTS 422 (London: T & T Clark, 2005), 3–27; "Ugaritic Anthropomorphism, Theomorphism, Theriomorphism," in *Göttliche Körper—Göttliche Gefühle: Was leisten anthropomorphe und anthropapathische Götterkonzepte im Alten Orient und im Alten Testament?*, ed. Andreas Wagner, OBO 270 (Fribourg: Academic Press; Göttingen: Vandenhoeck & Ruprecht, 2014), 117–40; "Counting Calves at Bethel," in *"Up to the Gates of Ekron": Essays on the Archaeology and History of the Eastern Mediterranean in Honor of Seymour Gitin*, ed. Sidnie White Crawford with Amnon Ben-Tor, J. P. Dessel, William G. Dever, Amihai Mazar, and Joseph Aviram (Jerusalem: W. F. Albright Institute of Archaeological Research/Israel Exploration Society, 2007), 382–94; "The Problem of the God and His Manifestations: The Case of the Baals at Ugarit, with Implications for Yahweh of Various Locales," in *Die Stadt im Zwölfprophetenbuch*, ed. Aaron Schart and Jutta Krispenz, BZAW 428 (Berlin: de Gruyter, 2012), 205–50; and "The Concept of the 'City' ('Town') in Ugarit," in *Die Stadt im Zwölfprophetenbuch*, ed. Aaron Schart and Jutta Krispenz, BZAW 428 (Berlin: de Gruyter, 2012), 107–46. I thank the publishers for their kind permissions to use these materials.

Finally, it gives me pleasure to dedicate this book to the memory of Franz Rosenthal. In the early 1980s at Yale, I studied Aramaic dialects and Comparative Semitics with Rosenthal. He was a model of broad and precise learning as well as clear reasoning and correction. He was also a generous soul. After learning of my upcoming trip to Chicago for my wedding in the spring of 1982, he surprised me with a check in the amount of the airfare. He also took the initiative twice to visit with me when we were both in Jerusalem (when he was receiving academic awards). After I returned to Yale in 1986 as a young faculty member, he shared many dinners with Liz and me and our three children. They particularly remember Franz (as they called him) for the candy he often gave them and for their running through the sprinkler in his backyard. I appreciated his dry sense of humor (he told me that scholars are hostages to their children). After I left Yale in 1993, we visited with him as trips back to New Haven permitted. At this time, I learned much more about his life. Thanks to William Foxwell Albright's letters, which I read in the late 1990s, I discovered when Albright first learned of Rosenthal's escape from Germany in 1938 and arrival in the United States in 1940 (via Sweden and England). Like many who found refuge in the United States, Rosenthal served his new country during the war. I shared with Rosenthal what I was learning from Albright's letters, and he enjoyed hearing about Albright's interest. From Rosenthal's "Half an Autobiography" (which he never published but shared with many), I later learned about his parents, whom he supported for many years in the United States, and about his older brother, Karl Günther Rosenthal, who provided the cost of his exit visa from Germany and later was deported to Auschwitz. Franz Rosenthal died on 8 April 2003, at the age of eighty-eight. As I complete this work today (31 August 2014), I observe the one hundredth anniversary of Franz Rosenthal's birth.

Abbreviations

The following appear in this volume for publications and grammatical terms. Ancient sources not listed here have been abbreviated according to *The SBL Handbook of Style* (ed. Patrick H. Alexander et al.; Peabody, MA: Hendrickson, 1999).

Publications

ABD	*Anchor Bible Dictionary.* Ed. David Noel Freedman. 6 vols. New York, 1992
ABRT	*Assyrian and Babylonian Religious Texts.* J. Craig. 2 vols. Leipzig, 1885, 1887
ADAJ	*Annual of the Department of Antiquities of Jordan*
AHw	*Akkadisches Handerwörterbuch.* Wolfram von Soden. 3 vols. Wiesbaden, 1965–1981
AIL	Ancient Israel and Its Literature
AJSR	*Association for Jewish Studies Review*
AnBib	Analecta biblica
ANEP	*The Ancient Near East in Pictures Relating to the Old Testament.* Ed. James B. Pritchard. 2nd ed. Princeton, 1994
ANET	*Ancient Near Eastern Texts Relating to the Old Testament.* Ed. James B. Pritchard. Princeton, 1969
AOAT	Alter Orient und Altes Testament
ASOR	American Schools of Oriental Research
AYB	Anchor Yale Bible
BASOR	*Bulletin of the American Schools of Oriental Research*
BDB	Francis Brown, S. R. Driver, and Charles A. Briggs. *A Hebrew and English Lexicon of the Old Testament.* Oxford, 1907

BETL	Bibliotheca Ephemeridum Theologicarum Lovaniensium
BHS	*Biblia Hebraica Stuttgartensia*. Ed. Karl Elliger and Wilhelm Rudolph. Stuttgart, 1983
Bib	*Biblica*
BZAW	Beihefte zur Zeitschrift für die alttestamentliche Wissenschaft
CAD	*The Assyrian Dictionary of the Oriental Institute of the University of Chicago*. Chicago, 1956–
CBQ	*Catholic Biblical Quarterly*
CBQMS	Catholic Biblical Quarterly Monograph Series
CEBT	Contributions to Biblical Exegesis and Theology
CHANE	Culture and History of the Ancient Near East
CIS	*Corpus inscriptionum semiticarum*. Paris, 1881–
CMHE	*Canaanite Myth and Hebrew Epic: Essays in the History of the Religion of Israel*. Frank Moore Cross. Cambridge, 1973
ConBOT	Coniectanea Biblica: Old Testament Series
COS	*The Context of Scripture*. Ed. William H. Hallo and K. Lawson Younger, Jr. 3 vols. Leiden, 1997–2002
CT	Cuneiform Texts from Babylonian Tablets in the British Museum, 1896–
CTA	*Corpus des tablettes en cuneiforms alphabétiques découvertes à Ras Shamra-Ugarit de 1929 à 1939*. Ed. Andrée Herdner. Paris, 1963
DCH	*Dictionary of Classical Hebrew*. Ed. David J. A. Clines. 9 vols. Sheffield, 1993–2014
DDD	*Dictionary of Deities and Demons in the Bible*. Ed. Karel van der Toorn, Bob Becking, and Pieter W. van der Horst. 2nd rev. ed. Boston, 1999
DNWSI	*Dictionary of North-West Semitic Inscriptions*. J. Hoftijzer and K. Jongeling. 2 vols. Leiden, 1995
DSSR	*The Dead Sea Scrolls Reader*. 2nd ed., revised and expanded. Ed. Donald W. Parry and Emanuel Tov, in association with Geraldine I. Clements. 2 vols. Leiden, 2014 (continuous pagination between the two volumes)

DULAT	*A Dictionary of the Ugaritic Language in the Alphabetic Tradition. Part One [(ʾa/i/u–k]; Part Two [l–z].* Gregorio del Olmo Lete and Joaquín Sanmartín. Trans. Wilfred G. E. Watson. 3rd rev. ed. 2 vols. Leiden, 2015 (continuous pagination between the two volumes)
EA	El Amarna texts, numbering as found in Anson F. Rainey, *The El-Amarna Correspondence: A New Edition of the Cuneiform Letters from the Site of El-Amarna Based on Collations of all Extant Tablets.* Ed. William Schniedewind and Zipora Cochavi-Rainey. 2 vols. *HdO* 110. Leiden, 2015
EI	*Eretz Israel*
Emar	Daniel Arnaud. *Recherches au pays d'Aštata. Emar VI.3: Textes de la bibliothèque transcriptions et traductions.* Paris, 1987. Cited by text number (#) or by page number.
EvT	*Evangelische Theologie*
FAT	Forschungen zum Alten Testament
FRLANT	Forschungen zur Religion und Literatur des Alten und Neuen Testaments
HAR	*Hebrew Annual Review*
HdO	*Handbuch der Orientalistik*
HSM	Harvard Semitic Monographs
HSS	Harvard Semitic Studies
IEJ	*Israel Exploration Journal*
JAOS	*Journal of the American Oriental Society*
JBL	*Journal of Biblical Literature*
JCS	*Journal of Cuneiform Studies*
JHS	*Journal of Hebrew Studies*
JQR	*Jewish Quarterly Review*
JSOT	*Journal for the Study of the Old Testament*
JSOTSup	Journal for the Study of the Old Testament Supplement Series
JSQ	*Jewish Studies Quarterly*
KAI	*Kanaanäische und aramäische Inschriften.* Herbert Donner and Wolfgang Röllig. 2nd ed. Wiesbaden, 1966–1969

KBo	*Keilschrifttexte aus Boghazköi.* Leipzig, 1916–1923; Berlin, 1954–
KTU	*Die keilalphaberischen Texte aus Ugarit, Ras Ibn Hani und anderen Orten.* Ed. Manfried Dietrich, Oswald Loretz, and Joaquín Sanmartín. 3rd ed. AOAT 360/1. Münster, 2014
KUB	Keilschrifturkunden aus Boghazköi. Berlin, 1921–
LAI	Library of Ancient Israel
LAPO	Littératures anciennes du Proche-Orient
LHB	Library of the Hebrew Bible
MC	Mesopotamian Civilizations
NABRE	New American Bible Revised Edition
NEAEHL	*The New Encyclopedia of Archaeological Excavations in the Holy Land 5: Supplementary Volume.* Ed. Ephraim Stern. Jerusalem/Washington, D.C., 2008
NETS	*A New English Translation of the Septuagint.* Ed. Albert Pietersma and Benjamin G. Wright. New York, 2007
NJPS	*TANAKH The Holy Scriptures: The New JPS Translation According to the Traditional Hebrew Text.* Philadelphia, 1988
NRSV	New Revised Standard Version
OBO	Orbis Biblicus et Orientalis
OLP	*Orientalia Lovaniensia Periodica*
ORA	Orientalische Religionen in der Antike
OTL	Old Testament Library
OTP	*Old Testament Pseudepigrapha.* Ed. James H. Charlesworth. 2 vols. New York, 1983, 1985
OTS	Old Testament Studies
PE	Eusebius. *Praeparatio Evangelium,* cited according to Harold A. Attridge and Robert A. Oden, *Philo of Byblos. The Phoenician History: Introduction, Critical Text, Translation, Notes.* CBQMS 9. Washington, D.C., 1981
PEQ	*Palestine Exploration Quarterly*
PPD	Charles R. Krahmalkov. *Phoenician-Punic Dictionary.* OLA 90. Leuven, 2000

PRU III	*Le palais royal d'Ugarit. Volume III.* Jean Nougayrol. Mission de Ras Shamra VI. Paris, 1955
PRU IV	*Le palais royal d'Ugarit. Volume IV.* Jean Nougayrol. Mission de Ras Shamra IX. Paris, 1956
RB	*Revue biblique*
RCU	Dennis Pardee. *Ritual and Cult at Ugarit.* Ed. Theodore J. Lewis. WAW 10. Atlanta, 2002
RdQ	*Revue de Qumrân*
RES	*Répertoire des études sémitiques*
RIH	Ras Ibn Hani
RS	Ras Shamra
RSO	Ras Shamra—Ougarit
RTU	Nick Wyatt. *Religious Texts from Ugarit: The Words of Ilimilku and His Colleagues.* Biblical Seminar 53. Sheffield, 1998
SAA	State Archives of Assyria
SBL	Society of Biblical Literature
SBLDS	Society of Biblical Literature Dissertation Series
SBLMS	Society of Biblical Literature Monograph Series
SBLRBS	Society of Biblical Literature Resources for Biblical Study
SBLSCS	Society of Biblical Literature Septuagint and Cognate Studies
SEL	*Studi epigrafici e linguistici sul Vicino Oriente antico*
SMEA	*Studi Micenei ed Egeo-Anatolici*
TA	*Tel Aviv*
TDOT	*Theological Dictionary of the Old Testament.* Ed. G. Johannes Botterweck and Helmer Ringgren. Trans. John T. Willis et al. 8 vols. Grand Rapids, 1974–2006
TZ	*Theologische Zeitschrift*
UBC 1	*The Ugaritic Baal Cycle: Volume 1. Introduction with Text, Translation and Commentary of KTU 1.1–1.2.* Mark S. Smith. VTSup 55. Leiden, 1994
UBC 2	*The Ugaritic Baal Cycle: Volume 2. Introduction with Text, Translation and Commentary of KTU 1.3–1.4.* Mark S. Smith and Wayne T. Pitard. VTSup 114. Leiden, 2009

UBL	Ugaritisch-biblische Literatur
UF	*Ugarit-Forschungen*
Ugaritica V	*Ugaritica V.* Jean Nougayrol, Emmanuel Laroche, Charles Virolleaud, and Claude F. A. Schaeffer. Mission de Ras Shamra XVI. Paris, 1968
UNP	*Ugaritic Narrative Literature.* Ed. Simon B. Parker. WAW 9. Atlanta, 1997
VAT	Vorderasiatische Abteilung Tontafel. Vorderasiatisches Museum, Berlin
VT	*Vetus Testamentum*
VTSup	Supplements to Vetus Testamentum
WAW	Writings from the Ancient World
WAWSup	Writings from the Ancient World Supplement Series
WMANT	Wissenschaftliche Monographien zum Alten und Neuen Testament
WO	*Die Welt des Orients*
WZKM	*Wiener Zeitschrift für die Kunde des Morgenlandes*
ZAW	*Zeitschrift für die alttestamentliche Wissenschaft*

Grammatical Terms and Other Sigla

D-stem	Verbal stem in Semitic languages with doubled second root-letter, including the Hebrew Piel
Dt-stem	*t*-infix/prefix form (reciprocal/reflexive) of the *D*-stem, including the Hebrew Hithpael
N-stem	Medio-passive verbal stem corresponding to the Hebrew Niphal
BH	Biblical Hebrew
MB	Middle Babylonian
NA	Neo-Assyrian
NB	Neo-Babylonian
OB	Old Babylonian
SB	Standard Babylonian

DN(s)	divine name(s)
GN(s)	geographical name(s)
PN(s)	personal name(s)

| LXX | Septuagint |
| MT | Masoretic Text |

D	Deuteronomist source or redaction in the Pentateuch
H	Holiness source or redaction in the Pentateuch
J	Yahwist (putative source in the Pentateuch)
P	Priestly source or redaction in the Pentateuch

| // | parallel passages |
| * | theoretical forms (such as roots) |

Where the Gods Are

Introduction

The Place of Anthropomorphism

1. Being There

For more than a decade I have been thinking about deities in relation to place and space. I attend both churches and synagogues in Philadelphia, where I live, and I regularly revisit the churches of my childhood. My early religious life took place in my family home in Washington, D.C.; our family parish of Blessed Sacrament; and my school at Saint Anselm's Abbey, a Benedictine monastery. These places constituted the major sites for my religious upbringing, and they strongly shaped it. Some years ago, my German cousins took me on a walk through their hometown of Glandorf. In the town center looms the Catholic church; its nearby cemetery includes the family plot. Not far outside of town is a shrine in the woods, dominated by the Stations of the Cross. It also has a small chapel open on one side. Inside is a wall painting depicting emigrants leaving the area and listing the places in the United States where many of them settled. This town, especially the shrine in the woods, evoked the traditional, rural Catholicism of my family's distant past.[1]

As my experience attests, people's sense of divinity is mediated through places. It is also evoked through texts, as suggested by the epigraphs to this book drawn from Anne Michaels's beautiful book *Fugitive Pieces* (1996). The same is true of other artistic forms. The title of a favorite movie of mine, *Being There* (the 1979 classic starring Peter Sellers), captures the two interrelated concerns of this book: "being," which for the ancient world consisted of God or deities perceived as the "ground" of reality for people; and "there," space and place conceptualized as specific physical areas. In a

1

definition amply illustrated by the present study, place "can be defined as a meaningful locality, produced by local practices, intersecting trajectories of movement and accumulated material assemblages; and it is maintained by stories, legends, and other forms of local knowledge."[2]

The first texts of Jewish and Christian traditions, the Hebrew Bible/ Old Testament, acknowledge place as a critical dimension in representing divinity. The very word for "place" (*māqôm*) may signal the divine dwelling (Hos 5:15; Mic 1:3; Isa 26:21; 1 Kgs 8:30//2 Chr 6:21). It is thought that Esth 4:14 refers to help coming "from another place," "perhaps as reverential periphrasis for Yahweh."[3] Other Jewish sources assume the critical importance of place. In a fifth-century BCE Aramaic papyrus from Elephantine in southern Egypt, Menachem ben Shallum swears "by the temple,"[4] the sort of function served otherwise by deities.[5] Jewish tradition captures the importance of place in using "the Place" (*hammāqôm*) as a divine title, in other words "the Omni-present."[6] Different languages use words for "place" to refer to holy places (Akkadian *ašru,* Ugaritic *'aṯr,* Phoenician *ʾrt,* and perhaps Aramaic **ʾrt).*[7] In late antiquity, words for "place" (Greek *topos,* Latin *locus*) could refer to the tombs of martyrs, which served as shrines for Christian devotion.[8] Modern commentators recognize the fundamental function that space plays in social reality. The *Annales* historian, Fernand Braudel, remarked in this vein: "let us not forget one last language, one last family of models, in fact: the necessary reduction of any social reality to the place in which it occurs."[9] Deities were fundamental to the social and political realities of the ancient world, and their places and spaces marked—and performed—their social and political significance.

Despite the importance of deities, place in relation to deities has rarely received a broad treatment in the scholarly discussion of divinity in the Bible.[10] In this book I analyze biblical and extra-biblical representations of deities in various spaces and places, as found in texts, iconography, and other material remains in what the subtitle calls the "biblical world." This "world" comprises modern-day Syria, Lebanon, Israel, Palestine/the "occupied territories," and Jordan (what is also sometimes called "the Levant"). The bulk of this work is an exploration of how representations of deities are related to a variety of physical spaces: homes and shrines (Part One), royal sanctuaries at Dan and Bethel (Part Two), and cities (Part Three). Such places are the homes of deities, especially in human form (anthropomorphism), and they serve the critically important purpose of divine-human communication. They provide a stage that allows deities to perform their roles with—and for—humans. In short, humans with their spaces typically give human (or anthropomorphic) features to deities, yet as we will see, these same places also identify deities as more than—and other than—humans.

The primary sources for this study consist of the Hebrew Bible/Old Testament and the Ugaritic texts, along with other West Semitic texts and relevant iconography and archaeological remains. It is often overlooked how much the Hebrew Bible partakes of the larger West Semitic cultural matrix that includes the Ugaritic texts and other extra-biblical texts from the region.[11] To be sure, the Ugaritic texts and the Hebrew Bible differ in a number of ways,[12] and Israel shows some distinctive features. However, it is common in scholarly comparisons to overstate how the Hebrew Bible or ancient Israel is different from nearby literatures and cultures. When it comes to the topic of this book, the similarities between the Ugaritic texts and the Hebrew Bible are extensive and quite profound despite the distinctive features on both sides. In general, the Ugaritic texts provide a literary and cultural backdrop for the biblical texts.

2. Between Ancient and Modern Theorizing

In this book I challenge some contemporary assumptions about how to approach ancient evidence. Many scholars take ancient sources as virtual blank slates to which they apply modern ideas and theories with little concern for the implicit theorizing embedded in them. I probe the ancient record not only for data, but also for the ideas and implicit theory within that record. At the same time, I draw occasionally on contemporary theorizing about space. Over the past several decades, space as a fundamental dimension of human experience has been given fresh perspective. Scholars have reflected on a place's materiality, such as topography, location, and physical resources; or on space produced by human practices of architecture, urban planning, or even urban life; or, on experienced space, lived through the images and symbols used for and about the space.[13] These interrelated types of human space have been elaborated in the works of the French Marxist sociologist Henri Lefebvre (1901–1991)[14] and the geographer Edward W. Soja (b. 1941). Soja in particular has used the terms "Firstspace" for physical space, "Secondspace" for perceived or conceptual space ("symbols, meanings, and narratives about space"), and "Thirdspace" for lived or experienced space (use of space, including "discourses about social practices, behaviors, and performances").[15] Despite some differences between Lefebvre and

Soja, their theoretical approach to space has become quite prominent in biblical studies.[16]

This approach broadly informs the perspective of this book. In it I address the Bible's "Secondspace" representations ("symbols, meanings, and narratives") through philological and historical study of texts, iconography, and material culture. I focus less on the structural materiality of divine spaces and places ("Firstspace")[17] or on the human practices that went into such places. Instead, I primarily address textual and artifactual expressions of the imagined activity conducted in such spaces and places. We do not know to what degree the literary evidence conveys religious experience ("Thirdspace").[18] Instead, it is "imagined space" that we often see in the ancient record. Thus, it seems fitting to understand our literary sources generally as representations of conceptual space ("Secondspace").[19]

The representations of divine spaces that the ancient Levantine writers imagined are partially descriptive in character. They are often prescriptive as well. They sometimes show how producers of artifacts thought people should understand deities. Both descriptive and prescriptive, texts and other objects come with the perspectives of their producers and sponsors. Thus, the ancient evidence does not simply constitute windows into the worldview of their ancient producers. They also represent efforts to engage and persuade the receivers of such artifacts about their representations of reality. Sometimes modern readers can tell how a source is prescriptive in its thrust; sometimes this level of information is presently unavailable. Sometimes texts name the social and political sectors explicitly behind their production; sometimes these can only be guessed at. The capability and power of gods and goddesses, a common concern of the texts and other artifacts, apparently related in a variety of ways to their producers' capability and power, whether desired or actual.

Throughout this work I am selective in my discussion of material culture related to deities and space. For example, I do not focus particularly on the layout of temples,[20] nor do I pursue in any depth a number of literary matters. For example, how does the genre of texts affect the representation of deities and their spaces? For now we may note that in literary texts deities are characters evoked in the third person, while in rituals they are participants invoked in the second person. In wisdom texts deities are third-person subjects of reflection often apart from place. By contrast, in prophecy deities are reportedly agents in places, and in prayer they are intended addressees in various spaces. Although issues of genre arise at various points in this study, they are not major subjects of this work. In sum, this work is not a general survey, but a series of interlocking probes that address foundational notions of deities and space.

3. A Word About Anthropomorphism

In this work I discuss spatial aspects of deities as manifested particularly in human form (anthropomorphism)[21] that they show in temples, shrines, and other spaces in the biblical world. Modeled on human spaces of home and palace, divine spaces of shrines and temples are literally in-formed by human form. As we will see in Part Two, deities assume other forms as well, notably animal form (theriomorphism). In these spaces deities and humans engage in communication. Communication between humans is the basic model for communication between humans and deities.[22] For this reason, deities are often attributed human characteristics.

Human images for deities generally derive from society or nature, the basics of human experience in antiquity. While social models for deities may seem obvious, the centrality of natural imagery may be less so. Mott T. Greene has observed:

> The "ancients," as we generically refer to everyone from the time of Plato back to *Homo erectus,* lived and worked outdoors, and did most of their thinking there as well. Because we have come indoors in the last hundred years, much that was obvious to earlier generations of scholars about ancient mythology is no longer obvious to us. That myths are to a large extent stories about nature has passed in the last few generations from something that "goes without saying" to something that "cannot be said."[23]

Greene's point applies to the biblical world, as we can see in the combination of human and natural images for Baal or Yahweh as warrior storm-gods.[24] In this complex of divine imagery, the rainy storm cloud moving eastward is identified as the god's chariotlike vehicle; its lightning is recognized as divine weaponry and its thunder as the god's mighty "voice" (see Ps 29; Ps 18 = 2 Sam 22:8–10). A corresponding combination of the human and the natural is seen in the westward movement of the stormy warrior-god. "The Lord of the East Wind" (to use Aloysius Fitzgerald's phrase) is manifest in the dry storm as it moves from the eastern desert, wielding divine destructive power and death (see Hos 13:14–15; Nah 1:2–8; Isa 19:1, 5–7; 50:2–3; Jer 51:34–37, 42–45).[25] In sum, the Bible assigns to Yahweh divine roles traditionally associated with both the west and east winds.

Various aspects of human life are also sources for divine anthropomorphism. Family metaphor, whether patriarchal[26] or matriarchal,[27] is central to biblical language for God. Family deities and in particular the personal god, venerated in the context of family religion, were central in Israelite conceptualizations of divinity.[28] The making of covenants and treaties involved members of different families, royal or otherwise; it also influenced Israelite notions of God's covenant(s) with Israel.[29]

Major forms of social and political leadership likewise informed representations of the divine. The monarchy played a central political role for representing the divine.[30] Royal identity is commonly tied to the divine warrior role noted above. A royal sensibility also informed the prophetic representation of God as head of the divine council (1 Kgs 22:19; Isa 6 and 40:1–8; Zech 4; see also Jer 23:18 and 22, and perhaps Ps 82).[31] Royal conceptualization likewise underlies temple ritual in which the divine king grants audiences to his human vassals delivering tribute and other gifts in the form of sacrifices.[32]

Perhaps less recognized is priestly representation of God.[33] The holiness of God is tied to the holiness of the priesthood in Lev 21:8, following restrictions on priestly contact with the dead in Lev 21:1–4 and priestly marriage in Lev 21:7–8. Even higher restrictions on contact with the dead and marriage are delineated in Lev 21:10–14 for the leader of the priesthood, namely "the priest, the one greater than his brothers on whose head the oil of anointing has been poured." These priestly restrictions seem to correlate with a priestly conceptualization of God as lacking sexual relations or death. Indeed, no priestly passage in the Pentateuch represents God with a body.[34] Finally, the realms of law and wisdom also served as vehicles for representing divinity in the Hebrew Bible.[35]

As this brief survey indicates, anthropomorphism plays a key role in representing divinity in the biblical record. Accordingly, one may ask how this anthropomorphism should be understood. This has been an immense subject in theological and philosophical studies for nearly two millennia,[36] and it is considered a central feature of religion more generally.[37] Discussions have often focused on anthropomorphism as a problem: to what degree, if any, is any anthropomorphism of God showing what God is really like, or is the anthropomorphic representation of divinity merely a matter of human projection? The thrust of the modern discussion (not to mention the philosophical views of Maimonides and Thomas Aquinas)[38] has tended in the second direction.

Yet in recent years, biblical anthropomorphism has received a fresh appreciation. For example, Esther J. Hamori rejects the philosophical "assumption that anthropomorphism constitutes a primitive or theologically unsophisticated perspective."[39] Instead, biblical anthropomorphism for Hamori is a sophisticated discourse: "The metaphorical nature of theophanic language functions to organize our view of God in a way that highlights certain characteristics and pushes others to the background. . . . The lens of metaphor does not replace reality: it demonstrates a particular aspect of reality . . . the theophanic expression does not reduce or replace other aspects of the divine nature, but rather exhibits something additional."[40] Hamori also suggests that anthropomorphic theophanies express God's freedom. She concludes, "We see, among other things, that even what we think we know about God we do not know."[41] Metaphor is central to Hamori's discussion of theophany. Both metaphor and theophany efface the distinction between what is materially real and what is immaterially imagined.[42] A good deal of recent work on metaphor stresses that what it expresses is real no less than what so-called literal language represents.[43] For some authors, metaphorical language often pervades common language that may be thought of as literal.[44] On this score, Hamori's approach to anthropomorphism is quite valuable.

Another way to approach the question of anthropomorphism is to ask: what does it do for people? In a basic sense, anthropomorphism is a form of analogy. Recent work in psychology and cognition has examined the role that analogy plays in how humans solve problems and make discoveries. According to David N. Perkins,[45] people vary in their capacities in using analogy. Some people devise not only more obvious analogy or what he calls "near analogy," which is quite common, but also what he labels "distant analogy." Perkins suggests that those who are able to deploy distant analogy are among the more creative minds: "Sifting their minds for models, problem solvers may remember pole lamps and construct the floor-to-ceiling garment rack by analogy."[46] Perkins cites Michael Ruse's proposal that "notions of causality, basic ideas about number, analogy making, and the notion that claims are verified by a convergence of evidence from various sources are all likely consequences of evolutionary processes, all very fundamental adaptive characteristics of mind with a genetic basis."[47]

Psychological studies going back to Jean Piaget[48] suggest the importance that anthropomorphism plays in children's analogical efforts to make sense of the nonhuman elements of the world: "for actions or thoughts to be understood, the unknown must be related to life as humans know it. In these terms, anthropomorphism is a psychological process attempting to deal with the unknown. In children it represents an effort to deal with a largely unknown world (i.e., a child gives human qualities to a favorite toy)."[49] Anthropomorphism helps children move from the known to the unknown. In a more recent study, the psychologists Justin L. Barrett and Rebekah A. Richert demonstrate the flexibility that children deploy in applying anthropomorphism to God.[50] According to their study, children sense that God is different from humans even as they use anthropomorphism to understand God. For adults as well as children, Pascal Boyer suggests, anthropomorphic representations help them draw inferences about reality that have "salience."[51] Anthropomorphism offers a way to bring order to perceptions and to provide "a more complex organization on the available stimuli."[52] "Salience," in Boyer's terms, also suggests the human recognition of difference behind the similarity: "Religious representations would probably not be acquired at all if their counter-intuitive aspects did not make them sufficiently salient to be an object of attention and cognitive investment."[53] In other words, anthropomorphism helps people not only to organize information, but also to provide insight into this information beyond its surface meaning.

Anthropomorphism is centrally focused on the body,[54] offering ways for people to process, categorize, and gain insight into nonhuman aspects of the world. Body terms in Biblical Hebrew serve to organize space.[55] External body terms apply to topography and architecture. For example, "face" (pānîm) is used for the front of a building as well as the surface of the earth and waters; "eye" ('ayin) denotes a spring (occasionally also for a surface); "mouth" (peh) can refer to the opening of a cave or ravine or the opening to a city; "head" (rō'š) can designate the top of a mountain; and "shoulder" (ketep) can signify the slope or side of a mountain or the side of a sacred building or space.[56] While languages vary in using body parts to refer to nonbodily realities, body parts commonly served as a means for mapping out space and other aspects of reality.[57] This point applies also to divine bodies and their spaces. The body served as a basic pattern recognition tool in organizing the world and for human intuitions and insights about various phenomena, including deities. Understood in human terms and yet also more than—and different from—humans, deities bear human features, including their bodies within human spaces and places. This fundamental matter of anthropomorphism is central to this book.

4. The Plan of This Book

This book consists of three parts, each with two chapters. Part One examines basic issues about deities in relation to their spaces. Chapter 1 addresses divine bodies in relation to space and place. It sketches out a typology of God's bodies according to location, which can often be correlated further with size or scale. Viewed in these terms, the Hebrew Bible represents not one but three sorts of divine bodies. Chapter 2 analyzes analogies that texts make between deities and their temples. The temples express the basic characteristics of what constitutes a deity, often in comparison or contrast to what human beings are. In other words, temple spaces show how deities are both anthropomorphic and "super-anthropomorphic."

Part Two explores anthropomorphism in relation to theriomorphism (animal form) used for deities. Chapter 3 first addresses how biblical and other West Semitic sources construct anthropomorphism through predications made of both humans and deities and through similes comparing deities and humans. A final section treats theriomorphism in association with anthropomorphism, showing how the two are often intertwined. Chapter 4 takes up a particularly important case of theriomorphism, namely the bull-calves at the royal cult sites of Dan and Bethel. Contrary to 1 Kings 12 that posits one image each at Dan and Bethel, a number of sources seem to reflect multiple images of the calf at Bethel, suggesting in turn different conceptualizations of the deities involved.

Part Three turns to deities in cities. Chapter 5 examines examples of divine names (DNs) plus geographical names (GNs), generally cities or towns. Each of the syntactical formations representing DN + GN presupposes an anthropomorphic model of the deity. The scholarly discussion of these predications has largely revolved around a model that understands each of these DNs + GNs as manifestations of the same DN. This chapter puts forward a more complex paradigm that further identifies a range of ways in which one DN + GN could affect the same DN in another GN. Chapter 6 addresses royal cities as ritual spaces for deities. As stages for the performance of divine anthropomorphism, cities are temples writ large. The city was a significant space of the gods, evident both from divine titles ("the gods of the city") and from city rituals. This chapter closes with a reevaluation of the female personifications of cities. As perhaps the ultimate anthropomorphism of space, the city personified embodies its people in relationship to its god. Finally, the Epilogue considers aspects of ancient theorizing about anthropomorphism and space in light of what the chapters have revealed about these topics.

With these preliminary matters in mind, we turn to the representations of divine space and anthropomorphism expressed by the three bodies of God.

PART 1

Spatial Representations of Divine Anthropomorphism

1 The Three Bodies of God in the Hebrew Bible

I. Introduction to God's Bodies

In recent years, many scholars have discussed the anthropomorphism of God's body in the Hebrew Bible.[1] Authors, myself included, have lumped together biblical references to God's body[2] or have focused on one aspect of these references.[3] To date, no general framework has been proposed for the biblical references to God's body. Before such a framework is suggested, it is important to acknowledge the contributions made by a number of scholars, most notably Esther J. Hamori, Benjamin Sommer, Andreas Wagner, and Anne K. Knafl.[4] In this chapter I sketch out a general typology of God's body according to location or setting, which can be correlated sometimes with differing sorts of physicality and size or scale.

The typology proposed here suggests that the Hebrew Bible represents not one but three types of divine bodies. The first involves a body human in scale and materiality and manifest on earth. The second entails a superhuman-sized body manifest on earth. While human in form, it is not physical like a fleshy, human body; instead, it is often luminous.[5] The third likewise partakes of bodily form while the nature of its physicality remains unclear.[6] Unlike the second body, it is located at or above the heavens. This is the type of body that continued into Judaism[7] and Christianity, and perhaps into early Islam as well.[8] After surveying these three bodies, I undertake an assessment concerning their background.[9]

Before beginning, it is important to offer a definition of the word "body," since it affects what is to be included in the discussion. In his important study *The Bodies of God and the World of Ancient Israel*, Benjamin

Sommer defines a body as "something located in a particular place at a particular time, whatever its shape or substance."[10] For Sommer, priestly *kābôd* (usually translated "glory" or "effulgence"), whether with reference to a body (as in Ezek 1) or not (as in priestly material in the Pentateuch), qualifies as a divine body. In theory, Sommer's definition might include all sorts of non-living objects not usually regarded as bodies. His definition seems broader than either the word's modern usage or the biblical sense of bodies as living organisms. According to the *Oxford English Dictionary*, a body is "the physical or material frame or structure of man or of any animal."[11] According to the *American Heritage Dictionary*, a body entails "the entire material structure and substance of an organism, especially of a human being or an animal."[12] More importantly, a definition without reference to the human body would not seem to account for the central role that it plays in biblical anthropomorphism in general and in biblical representations of God's body in particular. Viewed in these terms, priestly *kābôd* in priestly passages in the Pentateuch (as opposed to Ezek 1) would seem not to qualify as a divine body.[13] Nonetheless, priestly *kābôd* in the Pentateuch is important for the topic of God's bodies, and so I conclude this chapter with how it fits into the larger picture.

2. God's Natural "Human" Body in Genesis

In Genesis 2–3, Yahweh seems to have a body.[14] On the one hand, several details in Genesis 2, such as divine speaking (2:16, 18), making (2:4b; see also v. 7), and taking (2:15), do not require a concrete body. On the other hand, other details are suggestive of a body. Yahweh "breathed into his nostrils the breath of life," perhaps in the manner of mouth-to-mouth resuscitation (2:7).[15] Yahweh also plants a garden (2:8), a rather physical activity that humans do. Later there is "the sound of the Lord God moving about in the garden at the breezy time of the day" (3:8, NJPS). Here Yahweh sounds like a great king strolling in his royal garden,[16] and the description perhaps conjures up depictions of monarchs not uncommonly represented as taller than their royal subjects in ancient Near Eastern art.[17] This divine body would be on the scale of human bodies. At the same time, the sound of the deity moving about in the garden need not be a picture of walking but could denote a vague picture of divine movement (see *hlk* in the *Dt*-stem for the deity also in Deut 23:15; 2 Sam 7:6; Ps 68:21; and Prov 20:7).[18] This movement at "the breezy time of the day" (Gen 3:8) may resemble the evocative picture of God moving in the tops of the trees in 2 Sam 5:24. In this passage, the divine presence is to be recognized by the troops when they "hear the sound of marching in the tops of the balsam trees,"[19] in other words, when the wind moves through the tops of the trees. Similarly, the deity moving about in the breeze of the day might be like a wind. Thus Genesis 3 may evoke a divine body decidedly without flesh like humans. Genesis 2–3 may also represent the deity as the superhuman-sized host to humans in his palace and not as the guest in the home of humans, as we see more clearly with the next example.

If Genesis 2–3 is not entirely clear about the nature of the divine body, doubts should be dispelled by Genesis 18–19.[20] In Gen 18:2, "Yahweh" is one of the "three men standing near" Abraham. The other two are "the two angels," mentioned in 19:1 (cf. vv. 16 and 22).[21] This is one of the few passages in the Bible that refers to Yahweh as "man," according to Esther J. Hamori.[22] The fact that the three figures are called "men" (18:2; see also vv. 16, 22; 19:5, 10, 12, 16) suggests a bodily appearance on the part of God and "the two angels."[23] Abraham offers hospitality to them: "wash your feet and rest yourselves under the tree" (18:4); then he offers them food (v. 5). From this activity, the bodies of three men appear to be human in scale. This impression also fits the description in v. 8: "he stood by them under the tree while they ate."[24]

After their meal, the three figures ask Abraham: "Where is your wife Sarah?" (18:9). It might be thought that the question is rhetorical and that the three know where she is; perhaps they don't.[25] One figure, identified as Yahweh (vv. 13, 17, 20, 22, 26), converses twice with Abraham, first with Sarah present (vv. 9–15) and then without her (vv. 23–32); in between is a remarkable interlude with Yahweh speaking to himself (vv. 17–19, 20–21). Abraham then initiates conversation (v. 23), and Yahweh responds. The picture of Abraham and Yahweh here is nothing less than two men who walk and share in conversation. In short, this god, along with the two figures who accompany him, walks and talks, eats and drinks.

Genesis 19 offers a similar picture of the two figures, now identified as "two angels" (v. 2). They eat a meal prepared by Lot after he encounters them in Sodom (vv. 1–3). The next episode describes the townspeople gathering around Lot's house demanding that he surrender his two guests for their sexual use (vv. 4–11). Such a request suggests a fully human perception of the two divine figures. In this episode these two guests also "stretched out their hands and pulled Lot into the house with them, and shut the door" (19:10, NJPS). Thus the two "men" seem to be about the same scale as Lot, and they use their hands as any human might (see also v. 16). Verse 11, though, shows superhuman abilities on the part of these two figures, for "they struck with blinding light [*sanwērim*]" (NJPS) the people at the entrance of Lot's house. The phrase occurs only one other time in the Bible, in 2 Kgs 6:18, when the prophet Elisha is confronted with an Aramean army. Elisha prays to Yahweh to "strike this people with a blinding light," and Yahweh complies. The action suggests divine agency in Gen 19:11. It may also imply that the story of Genesis 18–19 in its current form was not written before the eighth century if the Hebrew noun for "blinding light" is an Akkadian loanword into Biblical Hebrew, as several scholars think.[26]

Genesis 19 offers one final clue about the two figures. In their speech to Lot in vv. 12–13, the two tell Lot about their mission: "we are about to destroy [*mašḥītim 'ănaḥnû*] this place" (v. 13, NJPS). The verb form used here is the same as the noun used for Philistine strike-forces (1 Sam 13:17 and 14:15).[27] So the two "men" in Genesis 19 seem to represent the military retinue of the warrior-god who later in the chapter rains down sulfur and fire (v. 24). This divine warrior may be regarded as the personal or family god[28] accompanied by his retinue. In sum, Genesis 18–19 presents not only Yahweh with a human body, but also his two divine companions.

Another divine being called "a man" is Jacob's opponent in Genesis 32 (see v. 24).[29] The story begins with Jacob sending gifts to his brother, Esau, whom he fears (vv. 3–8). He prays to God for deliverance (vv. 9–12) and sends more presents ahead to his brother (vv. 13–21). Jacob expresses the hope that the gifts will mollify Esau when "I shall see his face" (v. 20). After sending his family across the river Jabbok (punning on the name of Jacob) in vv. 22–23, Jacob is alone. Without any introduction, "a man wrestled with him" (v. 24). The struggle continues until the mysterious figure strikes Jacob's hip socket (v. 25). The two then converse (vv. 26–29). The unnamed figure asks to be let go, "for the day is breaking" (v. 26),[30] but why? The reason remains unclear. Jacob refuses the request without the figure's blessing (v. 26). After asking Jacob for his name and getting his answer (v. 27), the figure offers a name-change from Jacob to Israel.[31] Jacob in turn inquires about the name of the figure (v. 29), who in turn asks him why he requests that name. Without responding, the figure performs his final act: "and there he blessed him" (v. 29). At this point, the "man" inexplicably drops out of the narrative just as suddenly as he had entered it in v. 24.

Several elements about the story are unclear, in particular the nature of the mysterious figure. According to v. 30, Jacob recognizes him as *ʾĕlōhîm*. Some translations (NRSV, NABRE) render this word as "God," and many commentators follow this approach. Others (for example, NJPS) translate the word as "a divine being." The context of the wrestling match calls for a singular.[32] The word may be understood as "divine being" or "divinity," also in keeping with the mysterious nature of the encounter, and especially the problem mentioned by the figure himself: "Let me go, for the day is breaking" (v. 26).

It is difficult to know exactly what sort of figure the passage reflects. Some scholars take a cue from the parallel in the book of Hosea (12:4–5).[33] According to this passage, Jacob "strove [?] with a divine being [*ʾĕlōhîm*], he strove [?] against/with[34] an angel and prevailed."[35] The poetic parallelism of these two lines arguably serves to specify the divine being as an angel.[36] However, Genesis 32 does not mention an angel. Apart from the shared notion of a struggle with their shared idioms, the two contexts of Jacob's struggle may differ. Indeed, an angel might seem unlikely for Genesis 32, especially given the figure's wish to be released, "for the day is breaking" (32:26). In some cases, angels may meet humans during the day. For example, Judg 6:11–24 seems to take place at daytime, as v. 27 begins the next episode with "that night."

For many scholars,[37] Genesis 32 embeds an older tradition[38] about Jacob's struggling with some sort of divinity, whether a river demon[39] or a malevolent divinity at night,[40] a displeased deceased ancestor,[41] a personal or family god,[42] or the predawn phase of the sun.[43] Among these possibilities, a good candidate is the protagonist's personal god.[44] A blessing would be appropriate to a personal god even at night.[45] So would a conflict at night. The conflict represented between Yahweh and Moses in Exod 4:24 at a "night encampment" (so NJPS for *mālôn*) suggests that the personal god can both confront and bless. The combination of confrontation and blessing suits the identity of the personal god in this context. Whatever the precise identity of the mysterious figure, it is clear that the wrestling in Genesis 32 points to a physical, divine body.

The humanlike representations of God in Genesis are associated with famous personages of old. In these instances there is little human reaction noting something out of the ordinary about the divine body (unlike what we see in the following sections). The episodes may seem to suggest a literary progression, moving from a natural coexistence of the human and the divine (the Garden of Eden), to an interpersonal visit of the divine with the human (the Sodom and Gomorrah story), to a problematic interaction between the human and the divine (Jacob wrestling). Adam and Eve live in God's garden; Abraham walks and converses with God, and serves God a meal; and Jacob struggles with God, as befits his name. Such interactions with the divine in human form become less "normal." The fact that after Jacob there is no such interaction with God suggests that the experience of God's human body was seen to have occurred in the distant past, and only with the famous figures of that past. These bodily appearances take place in the book against a broad canvas of bodiless divine appearances marked by God's speech (Gen 4:6–7, 9–12; 6:13–21; 7:1–4; 9:1–11; 12:1–3; 13:14–17; 15:1, 4–5, 7–16; 17:1–16, 19–21, etc.), angelic appearances (e.g., Gen 16:7, 9; 21:7; 22:11, 15, etc.), and divine appearances in dream visions (Gen 28:10–15; cf. 31:11). Within this rich repertoire of divine manifestation, appearances in human form particularly stand out, and strikingly they are confined to Genesis. Indeed, the great figure Moses, who received the covenant law from God on Mount Sinai, has interactions with God that point to a different sort of divine body.

3. God's Superhuman "Liturgical" Body in Exodus and Isaiah

The second body of God is superhuman in scale. This divine body may be characterized as a "liturgical body," as it belongs to the constellation of themes associated with the deity's temple-palace located on the holy mountain.[46]

Two dramatic manifestations of God take place at Mount Sinai in the book of Exodus. The first instance, in Exod 24:1–11, is unclear about the scale of the divine body. In this passage, Moses, Aaron, and Aaron's two sons, Nadab and Abihu, along with seventy of Israel's elders, are summoned to worship at a distance; only Moses is to ascend the mountain (vv. 1–2). A covenant ceremony ensues:[47] the people agree to the covenant (v. 3); its words are written out (v. 4); an altar is built, with twelve stones set up for the twelve tribes (v. 4); and sacrifices are made (v. 5), with their blood marking the altar and the people (vv. 6–8). This section ends with Moses' declaration (v. 8): "See, the blood of the covenant that the Lord has made with you in accordance with all these words." Verses 9–11 return the narrative to Moses, Aaron, Nadab and Abihu, and the seventy of Israel's elders mentioned in v. 1. Rather than remaining at a distance as before (v. 2), they go up the mountain to formalize the covenant with a meal. There, according to v. 10, "they saw [*r'h] the God of Israel" (called "God" in v. 11). The popular fear about seeing (*r'h) God and dying as a result (Gen 16:13; 32:31; Judg 6:22–23; 13:22–23; Isa 6:5; cf. Deut 5:23–26)[48] comes into play in the next verse: "God did not lay his hand on the chief men of the people of Israel; also they beheld [*ḥzh] God, and they ate and drank." Here in v. 11 the problem of people seeing God is recognized, yet the leaders get to see God. Moreover, the verse reiterates the men's perception of God, though with another verbal root (*ḥzh), one perhaps denoting a visionary sort of experience expressed in the Psalms (cf. Pss 17:15; 27:4; 63:2, with both *r'h and *ḥzh). The use of the two verbal roots may signal that a literal perception of the divinity is not what was involved. The verb *ḥzh often denotes prophetic visions, and its use in Exod 24:11 may suggest this sort of experience for Moses, Aaron and his sons, and the other Israelite leaders.

Exod 24:10 offers a unique glimpse of God's body: "Under his feet there was something like a pavement of sapphire stone [lapis lazuli], like the very heaven for clearness." The feet are God's feet, and they are perceived by the human figures through what looks "like a pavement of sapphire stone" (see also the divine throne of "sapphire" in Ezek 1:26; 10:1).[49] Judging from descriptions elsewhere of the heavenly temple located on the mountain,[50] Brevard S. Childs surmised that Moses and the other leaders are looking up through the flooring of the temple.[51] The men may be viewing the deity (or at least the divine feet) in his throne room, but without being able to enter it. In short, the superhuman-sized God is enthroned in the palace on the mountain, with the divine feet perhaps resting on a divine footstool, as surmised by Friedhelm Hartenstein.[52] The giant footprints of the deity carved into the sanctuary floor at 'Ain Dara[53] might suggest a similar size for the divine feet in Exod 24:10 (cf. 2 Sam 22:10//Ps 18:9; Nah 1:3; cf. Zech 14:4).[54] By implication, the rest of the divine body that goes unmentioned in Exod 24:10 would also be superhuman in scale. The passage ends with the covenant meal on the mountain (Exod 24:11).[55] The context does not provide any other information about the divine body, and its size is not made explicit. A single body part, such as the feet, could suggest the image of a divine body while signaling its unknowability. Indeed, the passage may prescind from providing more details in order to evoke the mystery of a god beyond human perception.

Exodus 33–34 provides a more explicit witness to the superhuman-sized god. Yahweh tells Moses that he cannot see the divine face, but he can see Yahweh's back as Yahweh passes (33:22–23): "while my glory passes by I will put you in a cleft of the rock, and I will cover you with my hand until I have passed by; and I will take away my hand, and you shall see my back, but my face shall not be seen." The next chapter narrates Yahweh passing before Moses and pronouncing the divine name and attributes (34:6–7). Yahweh proposes to cover Moses in the cleft of the rock as the god passes by; this divine offer suggests a divine body large enough that the divine hand can cover Moses. A divine hand that can cover Moses suggests a hand that is the size of a human. By implication, the divine body is therefore huge (it might be imagined to be sixty-five to seventy feet, or twenty to twenty-one meters, tall).

The divine body in this scene is not as naturalistic as that in the Genesis stories. Yahweh is not walking as in Genesis 18 (v. 33). Instead, this god "passes by" Moses standing in the cleft of the rock of the mountain.[56] Furthermore, the divine body here does not seem to be physical like a human being. Instead, the picture seems to involve the divine glory sweeping by the mountainside.[57] Exodus 33–34, however, omits this information and instead focuses on the divine revelation to Moses, in particular the name of Yahweh and the divine attributes of mercy and justice (34:6–7). This omission may add to the overall impression that the experience is not regarded as a literal one, but one that accords with Moses' status as a super-prophet. Still, in the divine speech to Moses, the passage offers a glimpse of the superhuman body of the deity.

Isaiah 6 offers another example of God's superhuman-sized body.[58] The prophet lays out the scene before him: "I saw my Lord [*'ădōnāy*][59] sitting on a throne, high and lofty; and the hem of his robe filled the temple" (v. 1; cf. Amos 9:1). According to this verse, the prophet saw the deity in a fairly straightforward manner. (This may be because this human who can see the deity without such a problem is a prophet, which would further suggest that a literal physical body is not what is seen, but a liturgical, "envisioned" body.) What the prophet sees of the god is a seated body enthroned "high and lofty." The prophet seems to be having this experience in the Jerusalem temple (reflected also in the mention of the doorposts and the "House" in v. 4). So the throne where the divine body is seen may not be the divine throne in heaven (cf. 1 Kgs 22:19; Jer 23:18, 22). Instead, the divine throne in Isaiah's vision appears to involve the cherubim located in the Holy of Holies of the Jerusalem temple. In addition, the divine clothing in Isa 6:1 fills the temple.[60] Radiating from the divine body in the temple, the divine glory fills the earth (v. 3; cf. Num 14:21 and Jer 23:24). These details point to the superhuman size of the deity.

So does the context of the temple, as known from 1 Kgs 6:23–28.[61] According to this passage, the throne of God in the temple consists of two cherubs,[62] measuring "ten cubits" in height. With a cubit measuring a foot and a half (half a meter), the height of the two cherubs comes to fifteen feet (four and a half meters). The cherubs in the Holy of Holies are usually imagined to constitute the seat of the throne (although they also provide armrests in some depictions). The description evokes a "mental image"[63] of the seat of the deity, measuring about fifteen feet high.[64] It suggests that the seated god in Isaiah's vision is about ten times human size. This is also similar to the size of Yahweh in Exodus 33–34. Isaiah does not see a literal, human body for God, but a superhuman-sized body. It would seem that the divine body that both Moses and Isaiah experience is not physical like a human body; it appears to be a body of "glory" manifest on earth at the temple (cf. Ps 29:9).

4. God's Cosmic "Mystical" Body in Later Prophets

The third divine body is a heavenly or super-heavenly reality. Unlike God's human and superhuman bodies, it is not manifest on the earthly level. In view of its cosmic location and its association with named prophets that I note in the following discussion, it may be called God's "mystical" body.[65] I briefly note some allusions to this body before turning to its great exemplar in Ezekiel 1.

An allusion to the divine cosmic body is found in the question posed by the anonymous prophet of the exile in Isa 40:12: "Who has measured the waters with the hollow of his hand and gauged the heavens with a span?" The answer is God; this is the divine hand that is so large that it can take in the cosmic waters and the heavens.

The final chapter of the book of Isaiah contrasts the cosmic temple with the earthly temple (66:1):

Thus says Yahweh:
The heavens are my throne,

The earth is my footstool:
Where then is the house that you would build for me,
Where then would be my resting-place?

Here Yahweh is seated over the heavens and earth, in other words, the whole universe. This is the cosmic body of God, larger than the heavens.[66] Similarly, Ps 113:6 describes the enthroned God on high who "condescends to look about in heaven and on earth" (my translation; see also Deut 10:14 and 1 Kgs 8:27). These passages allude to a divine body that is cosmic in location and scale.

While the divine body is given a cosmic location in Ezekiel 1, its size is unclear. The prophet is said to see something of the divine body on a divine throne (vv. 26–27), after describing creatures with faces, wings, and legs (vv. 5–12).[67] The figures are also characterized in terms of fire and its effects, somewhat like the temple and the seraphim (*śrp, "to burn") presented in Isaiah 6.[68] In Ezek 1:4, the description entails a divine appearance, beginning with "a stormy wind,"[69] "a great cloud with brightness," and "a fire flashing forth continually, and in the middle of the fire, something like gleaming amber."

In some of its details, the representation of the divine in Ezekiel 1 compares with the prophetic vision in Isaiah 6, yet in other respects they differ considerably. In seven verses Isaiah describes what the prophet sees of the deity and the seraphs with their six wings, as well as their praise of God ("Holy, holy, holy") and the shaking of the temple (Isa 6:1–7). By contrast, Ezekiel 1 takes twenty-eight verses to describe three phenomena: (1) the four winged cherubim with four faces (vv. 4–14),[70] (2) "a wheel on earth besides the living creatures" beneath the dome of the world (vv. 15–25), and (3) "the appearance of the likeness of the glory of the Lord" on a throne above the dome of the world (vv. 26–28).

The second great difference involves the focus of each vision. Isaiah's is earthly with its temple location (6:1 and 4), while Ezekiel sees the heavens open, followed by visions of God (1:1). The description of Ezekiel's visions moves from the winged creatures on earth, up to the world's dome (sometimes called the "firmament"),[71] and farther up "to the appearance of the likeness of the glory of the Lord." Unlike the human and superhuman divine bodies on earth, this divine body is on top of the cosmos.

The third major difference between the two prophetic stories involves the nature of human perception. Where Isaiah sees the deity without qualification (6:1), what Ezekiel sees are not the divine persons or things in themselves. When it comes to the perceived phenomena, he sees their "appearance" (*mar'eh*, 1:5, 10, 16, 26, 28 [two times]).[72] The descriptions of what Ezekiel sees are also studded with "something like" (*kě-*, 1:5, 13, 16 [two times], 22, 26, 27 [three times]). Thus Ezekiel sees approximations of things, again not the things themselves.[73] Where Isaiah "saw" the deity (6:1), here Ezekiel's language shows three qualifications, not only "appearance" and "likeness," but also "glory," the older language for the divine appearance in the storm in Psalm 29 and elsewhere. In Ezekiel 1, fire serves to mark the divine at crucial junctures in the prophet's vision (1:4, 13 [three times], 27 [two times]).

Ezekiel's description of God's body in vv. 26–28 begins "something like a throne, in appearance like sapphire; and seated above the likeness of a throne was something that seemed like a human form." The "throne-looking" phenomenon appears "like sapphire," recalling the sapphire of the heavenly site in Exod 24:9–11 (discussed in the preceding section). Then there is "something that seemed like a human form." This is the divine body, but apart from its form, this divine body is not like a human body. According to v. 27, the part of this form above what appeared like the "loins"[74] gleams like amber, and it is "something that looked like fire" (see also Ezek 8:2). In restricting the explicit mention of bodily terms to "loins," the appearance of the cosmic divine body here is left vague. It is evidently intended to be difficult to understand.[75]

Several aspects of this description should be noted. First, despite the many qualifications and approximations of perception on the prophet's part, a human form with loins lies at the heart of this description of the divine appearance (v. 27). Second, this is also the only description in the Bible that explicitly locates this divine appearance above the firmament. Third, this is the only biblical description of divine travel on four creatures, each with four faces (v. 10), each with its own chariot wheel (v. 15),[76] each with eyes in the wheel rims (v. 18), and each wheel animated by "the spirit" (vv. 12, 20, and 21). Given the faces of the creatures in all four directions and the eyes in the wheel rims, the cosmic god can see all people on earth. Fourth, no precise sense is given for the size of this body. In its unusual description of the divine body, Ezekiel 1 is hinting that fundamentally, humans cannot grasp the reality of God.

The fiery God in the heavenly throne room would become a standard representation of the cosmic body. In another vision presented in Daniel 7, "the Ancient of Days" takes up his throne (v. 9a), described in the following terms: "His throne was fiery flames, and its wheels were burning fire" (v. 9b). This body is fiery in nature: "A stream of fire issued and flowed from his presence" (v. 10).[77] This basic depiction appears in roughly contemporary texts, such as 1 Enoch 14, as well as later texts, including 1 Enoch 46 and 71; 2 Enoch 20, 22, and 39; and the Apocalypse of Abraham 18–19.[78] Some of the biblical texts noted above would also be echoed in later literature.[79] One side of a Persian-period coin (ca. 400), marked with an inscription read variously as *yhd*, "Yehud" (the name for Judah at the time) or *yhw* (the name of the Yehudian god, Yahweh), depicts a bearded figure seated on a wheeled chariot and thought to represent the deity.[80] This image seems to reflect the third type of divine body. Whether in textual sources or in iconography, this divine body is envisioned as located in heaven (or even above it).

5. The Settings and Production of God's Three Bodies

At first glance, one might see a linear development in the three divine bodies: the human-looking body in the older, prose storytelling tradition of Genesis; the superhuman divine body of the eighth-century prophetic tradition, as seen in Isaiah and the prose traditions surrounding Moses; and the cosmic divine body of the sixth-century prophetic reflections in Third Isaiah and Ezekiel. The background of these divine bodies is more complex, however, and they do not represent a straight, linear development.[81] Instead, the first two bodies appear to be traditional, while the third represents a later innovation.

The settings for the three divine bodies differ considerably. The first, the natural "human" body of God, had its setting in the family,[82] to judge from the relevant comparative evidence. The hospitality scene in Genesis 18 has long been compared with a passage in the Ugaritic story of Aqhat, in which the craftsman-god Kothar receives hospitality from Danil and his wife, Danatay.[83] Both Danil and Abraham receive the god at their tent and serve him food and drink.[84] There are additional cases of multiple deities coming to the home of a human family: a collectivity of major deities comes to the palace of King Kirta, and the divine collective of goddesses known as the Kotharat enter the home of Danil and receive hospitality from Danil, much like Kothar.[85] The Kotharat eat and drink in the human home, like Kothar in Aqhat and Yahweh and the two other divine figures in Genesis 18.

The model of divine-human relations in these texts entails human hosts who welcome a god or a group of divinities into their homes and receive a gift:[86] a child for Abraham and Sarah; a child for Danil and his wife, Danatay; a bow for Danil; and a blessing for Kirta and his bride. The stories of Kirta and Aqhat as well as Genesis 18 and 32 also suggest that such home visits may have been an early Israelite tradition associated with the family or personal god. The first body of God was perhaps represented materially in the form of household "gods" or figurines, as known in Genesis 31 (called "gods" in vv. 30 and 32, but *tĕrāpîm* in vv. 19, 34, 35; see also 1 Sam 19:13, 16).[87] The literary evidence for figurines has been tied to material evidence by Othmar Keel and Christoph Uehlinger,[88] despite some problems.[89]

This model of God's human body survived with the angelic "messenger" (*mal'āk*), which could appear to family members (Judg 6 and 13). By comparison, Yahweh does not appear with a human body beyond the book of Genesis. This type of story about Yahweh appearing in the family context (especially to Abraham and Jacob) probably originated in traditional storytelling about the family or personal god and then developed further as stories assumed their written literary form as enshrined in the Bible. The scribal context perhaps provided an opportunity for further religious probing about the God of Israel (for example, the dialogue between Yahweh and Abraham in Gen 18:22–32). As a result, the stories with the first body of God developed into some of the most intriguing and most theologically dense pieces in the Bible. This may be the reason for what Esther Hamori has suggestively called the "anthropomorphic realism" in Genesis 18 and 32.[90]

The roots of the second divine body, the supersized body of God, are also traditional. They go back to ancient temples or shrines.[91] In Isaiah 6, the prophet sees God in the Jerusalem temple. The meeting of Moses and others with God in Exodus 24 and 33–34 likewise comes out of a temple worldview. The heavenly temple, located on top of the divine mountain in Exodus 24, echoes Baal's heavenly palace located on top of his mountain, Sapan, as known from the Ugaritic Baal Cycle.[92] This mountain is the site of Baal's enthronement and the place from which he issues his thunder, lightning, and rains (cf. Exodus 19 and 20). Baal's palace is built with lapis lazuli (cf. the "sapphire" in Exod 24:10).[93] The second divine body further presupposes the notion of the deity as king giving an audience to his human subjects in his temple-palace.[94] Where it is deities in the form of the first divine body who may bring a gift to their human hosts, it is humans who bring gifts (in the form of sacrifices) to the temples of deities. Where household figurines might represent the material representation of the first divine body, cultic images in anthropomorphic form constitute material representations of the second divine body in the temple. Moreover, the deity's size relative to the human audience suggests the asymmetry in the relationship, as does the deity's seated position signaling the overpowering presence of the divine king.[95]

The superhuman size is a critical feature of the second divine body, as seen for God in Exodus 24 and 33–34 and the massive throne of Baal in the Ugaritic Baal Cycle (*KTU* 1.6 I 56–65).[96] The superhuman size of Baal is also represented in the so-called Louvre Baal stele, a depiction of the god standing with weapons in either hand, along with a much smaller human figure.[97] The god is depicted more than three times the height of the human figure, which has been interpreted as the king. A temple excavated at 'Ain Dara in northern Syria likewise exhibits this idea of the supersized deity, with footprints of over three feet (one meter) carved into the temple flooring.[98] With the distance between the supersized footprints being about thirty feet (nine meters), the deity was imagined as being about sixty-five feet (close to twenty meters) tall.[99]

Another feature that largely distinguishes the second "liturgical body" is the importance of seeing the deity.[100] Seeing the deity does arise in cases of the first divine body,[101] but it is not as critical a feature in passages involving the second divine body. Moses and the other leaders in Exodus 24 see God, and the problem of seeing God is mentioned there. In Exodus 33, Moses desires to see God but cannot except for the divine back. Isaiah, by contrast, sees God according to Isa 6:1. The desire to see the deity is expressed also in a number of psalms, all associated with the temple, for example in Ps 11:7 ("the upright shall behold his face"; see also Pss 17:15; 27:4, 13; 42:2; 63:2). In short, this divine-human interaction in these texts, we might say, is a liturgical one. Seeing the deity is a critical dimension—and issue—with these cases of the supersized, "liturgical" body of God, in contrast to the "human" body of God, which is seen without any comment in Gen 18:1 and 19:1.

This contrasting situation with humans seeing God corresponds to the material forms of the first two bodies. The first divine body is fleshy like human bodies. The second body, by contrast, is not; it is luminous. Yet like the first body, it may leave an anthropomorphic impression, as illustrated by the footsteps carved into the 'Ain Dara temple. The supersized divine body is understood as having a material presence that can make a physical impact. To echo Morgan Meyer, the second body's lack of a conventional body is still an absence that can be "placed and traced." Meyer comments: "absence has a materiality and exists in—and has effects on—the spaces people inhabit and their daily practices . . . absence [is] not as a thing in itself but . . . something that exists through relations that give absence matter. Absence, in this view, is something performed, textured and materialized through relations and processes, and via objects. We therefore need to *trace* absence."[102] The steps preserved in the 'Ain Dara temple capture a traditional sense of the warrior-deity returning from battle and striding into the divine palace to take up the divine throne. What Tim Ingold says about human walking applies here to divine steps: "walking down a city street is an intrinsically social activity. Its sociality does not hover above the practice itself, in some ethereal realm of ideas and discourse, but is rather immanent in the way a person's movements—his or her step, gait, direction and pace—are continually responsive to the movements of others in the immediate environment."[103] In others words, the steps in the 'Ain Dara temple aim at showing off the deity. The warrior-deity strides (with one footprint followed by another), yet also pauses (the two footprints next to one another) for all to see. This largely immaterial and invisible presence creates the imagined materiality of the second divine body.

Unlike the first two bodies, the third body is not in the world. Instead, it seems to constitute a cosmic version of the second body. As with the second body, the third body sometimes entails the deity being seen. Perhaps in the spirit of Exod 33:23, postbiblical texts reflect on the problem of divine vision: "It was difficult to look at it" (1 Enoch 14:19; cf. "the face of the Lord is not to be talked about," in 2 Enoch 22:1 J).[104] However, there are also three significant differences with the third divine body. First, the third body appears on the cosmic level, unlike the first two bodies. Second, human sighting of this third body in Ezekiel 1 is considerably more problematic and qualified, compared with the second body, and several instances name a visionary (e.g., Ezekiel, Daniel, Enoch). Thus the visionary is drawn into a visual experience in the heavens. Third, while the first two bodies were traditional to the Levant from at least the Late Bronze Age, this does not appear to be the case with the third.

Drawing on Mesopotamian astronomical writings and iconography, Baruch Halpern[105] and Christoph Uehlinger and Suzanne Müller Trufaut[106] suggest that Mesopotamian ideas about the heavenly vault issued in a new and corresponding Israelite view of the cosmic "firmament." Uehlinger and Müller Trufaut have identified this vault in Neo-Assyrian seal impressions. On these seals, Mesopotamian genies (called *kusarikku*) support the heavenly firmament; above it is part of the anthropomorphic deity.[107] The main Akkadian term for firmament is *burūmû* (*burummû*): "when the gods in their assembly created the [. . .] and fashioned the firmament."[108] The gods who control this firmament are likewise cosmic in scope. Of the god Assur, "the creator of himself," it is said that his "figure was exalted in the Abyss . . . living in the [pur]e starlit heave[ns] [*bu-ru-ú-me*]."[109] Marduk is said to be the one "who holds the ends of the firmament."[110] There may be more to Akkadian *burūmû* (*burummû*) than "firmament": what the *Chicago Assyrian Dictionary* translates as "firmament" may conform somewhat to the tradition of the biblical concept. The *Online Etymological Dictionary of Akkadian* instead translates the word as "heaven, sky."[111] Wayne Horowitz understands the Akkadian word as "the level of the stars of the sky or the night sky in first millennium texts."[112] Mesopotamian texts from this period also identify multiple spheres as the homes of various gods.[113]

In Ezekiel 1, as in Genesis 1, a heavenly vault or dome (often translated "firmament") enclosed the earth and sky (Ezek 1:22, 23, 25, 26; Gen 1:6–8, 14–15, 17, 20). While the second divine body's abode is on top of the divine mountain (e.g., Exod 24:9–11), in Ezekiel 1 the enthronement of the third body was considerably higher, at or above the heavenly vault. Like the heavenly homes of the gods in these Mesopotamian texts, God's third body in Ezekiel 1 (and arguably implicit to God's location in Genesis 1 as well) is situated at the cosmic level of the firmament. The new cosmology in Ezekiel 1 locating God on the firmament represents a spatial adjustment of the older, traditional supersized divine body from its enthronement on the mountain, perhaps in response to the new Mesopotamian theory locating the god enthroned on the firmament. Halpern surmises that this "new idea arrived in Jerusalem" from Mesopotamia during the seventh-sixth centuries BCE. By contrast, Uehlinger and Müller Trufaut would locate this cultural exchange within Mesopotamia, given Judah's experience there in the sixth century.[114] This would fit with Ezekiel, who departed for Babylonia in 597 BCE. It would also comport with common scholarly dating for Genesis 1, likewise placed in the exile (though it could also reflect a later time).[115]

In either scenario, a new Mesopotamian idea of the universe developing during this period may have influenced the spatial location of God's body on top of the firmament and thus helped to develop the idea of God's cosmic or mystical body as found in Ezekiel 1 and presupposed in Genesis 1. Given the priestly background of both of these texts,[116] the setting for this cosmic body was evidently priestly. Perhaps the cosmic body was more specifically the creation of priestly scribalism, given the theories of professional scribal exchange posited by Halpern and by Uehlinger and Müller Trufaut. As a corollary, the representation of the cosmic "mystical" body corresponds broadly in time to the expressions of what has been called Israel's "monotheistic" worldview. In several works of the seventh-sixth centuries, including the priestly work of the Pentateuch (such as Genesis 1), Deuteronomy, Ezekiel, Jeremiah, and Second Isaiah, "monotheism"—or perhaps better, a "one-god" worldview—emerged in their understandings of divinity.[117] The "one-god" worldview comported with the third divine body.

This emergent religious expression had a number of effects. For example, it effaced an older, traditional form of cosmic bodies as manifest in the sun, moon, and stars. Ronald S. Hendel has observed, "Gods often simultaneously had anthropomorphic bodies and heavenly bodies."[118] As cases of traditional "cosmic bodies," Hendel points to heavenly bodies with various forms of identity and agency in the Hebrew Bible: the host of heaven standing before Yahweh in 1 Kgs 22:19; the morning stars identified as divine beings singing in Job 38:7; and the stars fighting from heaven in Judg 5:20. Hendel also notes Mesopotamian cases, for example, the god Sin simultaneously as the moon and as the moon-god.[119] As Erica Reiner notes, "the gods of the night . . . are stars and constellations of the night sky,"[120] as seen in astronomical omen literature (*Enuma Anu Enlil*). Francesca Rochberg explains that in this literature, "the heavenly bodies were thought of as gods—not manifestations of gods, but identical to and synonymous with gods."[121] At the same time, the deities and the heavenly bodies were conceptually distinguished: "the celestial bodies cannot themselves be one and the same with the gods their name-sakes."[122] Astral bodies were likewise identified conventionally with West Semitic deities.[123] Traditional cosmic bodies were materially represented in Levantine astral iconography.[124] While the new Mesopotamian cosmology incorporated the older conceptualization of astral bodies as divine bodies, the influence of Israel's monotheistic worldview, in tandem with the impact of the newer Mesopotamian cosmology, displaced the traditional notion of astral deities and their bodies. It was largely effaced and displaced by the cosmic body of God, as seen in Ezekiel 1, Daniel 7, 1 Enoch 14, and other texts noted above.

Other biblical traditions respond to the traditions of the divine body in different ways. By contrast to Ezekiel 1, in the priestly conception in the Pentateuch the divine *kābôd* lacks a body.[125] For example, Pentateuchal priestly tradition (P) locates God's *kābôd* in the tabernacle (Exod 40:34–35) along the lines of the second model, except that it is not a body.[126] Instead, it is the aura or effulgence of divine presence, without a body or body parts. This sense of divine presence goes back to the effulgence[127] sometimes associated with the divine body (as in Ezek 1), itself an echo of the chariot-cloud that the divine warrior rides (2 Sam 22:9–14//Ps 18:8–13; cf. Ps 29). Deuteronomy, as well as the books that it influenced, works out the question somewhat differently. This tradition locates God in heaven (4:36, 39; 26:15; cf. 1 Kgs 8:27, 30, 34, 36, 39, 43, 45, 49), while the divine name is apparently in the earthly temple (1 Kgs 8:16, 19, 20, 29, 44).[128] Elsewhere God speaks from a fire (Deut 5:4), sometimes said to be from heaven (Deut 4:36) and sometimes without a visible form (Deut 4:12, 15; see also v. 24).[129] In short, some of these sources (P and D) show a trend moving away from the idea of a divine body in any location, while others (Ezek 1, Second Isaiah, Dan 7, and 1 Enoch) were moving toward a transcendent, cosmic body.

The understanding of this third body would continue to develop. The influence of astronomical learning inspired the notion of multiple heavens during the Greco-Roman period, illustrated by Paul's reference to his ascending to "the third heaven" (2 Cor 12:2) or by the seven heavens said to be experienced by Enoch (2 Enoch 3–22).[130] Perhaps similar shifts in the understanding of the cosmos and God are under way today, thanks to new scientific discoveries about the universe dramatically unfolding in our own time. What the three bodies of God may hold for Christians and Jews today is likewise a moving target.[131]

The importance of the divine body lies further in the terrestrial expressions that temples give to deities. I turn now to this subject.

2 Like Deities, Like Temples (Like People)

Of the three types of divine bodies that I have surveyed, it is the second—the superhuman "liturgical" body—that dominates temple ritual. In this chapter, I look at the set of concepts shared by deities and temples. Temples convey characteristics of deities, and they do so in four specific ways.[1] First, deities *intersect* with humans at temples, expressing what deities may provide to humans and vice versa. Second, temples *recapitulate* the stories of deities, showing how they act for humans. Third, temples *participate* in the features of deities, conveying what deities are, often in contrast to humanity. Fourth and finally, deities and temples *correspond*, suggesting that they are analogous. These four modes of expression are not entirely separate from one another. Rather, they provide a kaleidoscopic sense of what temples express about deities.

1. Intersection: Blessing and Revelation

As noted in the preceding chapter, the operative paradigm informing temple practice features the divine king offering an audience to his human subjects who come to pay tribute in the form of sacrifices.[2] In this context, temples and shrines serve as spatial points of intersection between the deity who bestows blessing and the human community that in return offers sacrifices.

Various verbs reflect the idea of temples as divine property and architecture. The deity is credited with a sanctuary's foundation (**ysd*), its choice (**bḥr*) and establishment (**kwn* in the *D*-stem), sometimes metaphorically called "planting" (**nṭ'*). Deities build (**bny*) and raise (**rwm* in the *D*-stem) their temples, in which they subsequently dwell (*ytb/*yšb) and "tent" (*škn). As a result, they show divine attachment or "love" (*'hb) to their homes. Nouns for the temple express a parallelism between the heavenly palace of the god and his earthly dwelling. For example, house (byt) and palace (hkl) apply to both the god's cosmic palace and terrestrial temple. One mark of intersection between the two is the palace's window in the clouds, from which the storm-god is conceived as manifesting his power in lightning and thunder as well as his blessing in the rains. Accordingly, Baal's window in his house is called a "break in the clouds" (bdqt 'rpt), as well as an "opening" (hln) and a "window" ('urbt).³ His palace is thought to be located in the clouds that cover the top of his mountain, Mount Sapan (cf. ṣāpôn in Ps 48:2). Second Kings 7:2 and 19 show this motif for Yahweh: "Even if Yahweh were to make windows in the sky, could such a thing happen?" Solomon is promised a divine blessing of rain when he prays at the temple (1 Kgs 8:35–36). Malachi 3:10 correlates divinely given rains from the heavenly window with the humanly provided tithe to the temple (cf. Deut 28:12; Isa 24:18). The mythology of the cosmic window also informs the image of the "floodgates" in the flood story of Genesis (7:11 and 8:2).⁴

The palace of the god also lies behind the idea of Eden in Genesis 2–3. To unpack this idea, let's return to the window in Baal's palace. Before this palace is built, the goddess Athirat (biblical Asherah) expresses her hope for the construction of the god's palace and the resulting fertility (*'dn) on earth:

> So now may Baal fructify [*'dn] with his rain,
> May he enrich richly [*'dn] with watering in a downpour,
> May he give voice in the clouds,
> May he flash to the earth lightning bolts.⁵

This passage compares with the divine beneficence enjoyed by people in the temple (Ps 36:8): "They feast on the abundance of your house, and you give them drink with the river of your delights [*'dn]."⁶ The word "Eden" in Gen 2:15 (also from the word or root *'dn) suggests that it is a place of "delight, abundance, luxuriance."⁷ The Aramaic portion of a bilingual inscription calls the storm-god Hadad (a title of Baal in Ugaritic) the one "who makes all lands luxuriant" (m'dn mt kln). As Jonas C. Greenfield recognized,⁸ this understanding holds the key to the Ugaritic word 'dn in the passage from the Baal Cycle quoted above as well as the name of Eden in the Bible. Through his rains, the storm-god Baal provides, as it were,

"Eden" or "abundance, fertility, delight." This notion of the earth's fertility thanks to the god is reinforced later in the Baal Cycle. Thanks to Baal, El knows that "the heavens rain oil, and the wadis [*nḥlm*] run with honey."[9] This expression compares with *nahal* in the biblical phrase used with reference to the Jerusalem temple in Ps 36:8, "river of your delights" (*nahal 'ădānêkā*). The storm-god's temple is the focal point for the appearance of his rains and the fertility of the earth. In other words, it is the place of Edenic blessing and fertility.

The traditions behind the theme of Eden are ancient. According to P. Kyle McCarter, Eden as a sanctuary located in the Lebanon and Anti-Lebanon ranges was a particularly old tradition reflected not only in West Semitic sources such as the Ugaritic Baal Cycle and the Bible, but also in Mesopotamian and Egyptian royal texts concerned with the acquisition of cedars.[10] McCarter believes that behind these reports stands an old local Levantine sanctuary tradition (or to use his phrase, "a cultic reality").[11] This tradition is reflected also in the Old Babylonian version of the Gilgamesh story, which locates the mount of assembly in the cedar forest, specifically in Lebanon. In an old West Semitic tradition now embedded in the Gilgamesh story, the cedar mountain said to be located in Lebanon and Saria (biblical Sirion) is called "the abode of the gods,"[12] as well as "the secret dwelling of the Anunnaki."[13] This constellation of temple themes appears also in the Ugaritic Baal Cycle.[14] The wood for Baal's palace is obtained through a journey for cedars in Lebanon and brought to Baal's mountain where the palace is to be constructed.[15] Baal's heavenly palace consists of gold and precious stone (specifically, lapis lazuli, the stone associated with the heavenly palace in Exod 24:9–11).[16] In sum, the Baal Cycle, like Genesis 2–3, embodies traditional themes of the temple as royal garden-sanctuary.

For a Phoenician attestation of this tradition, McCarter points to Ezekiel 28. This passage assumes a Phoenician tradition of the divine garden located on the god's mountain graced with cedar, gold, and precious metals. Like their Mesopotamian and Egyptian counterparts, Phoenician rulers sent missions to the Lebanon for cedar.[17] Philo of Byblos also attests to the Phoenician tradition of the northern mountains as the home of the divine sanctuary. Philo comments on Mount Casios (= Mount Sapan), the Lebanon, the Anti-Lebanon, and Mount Brathy: "From these . . . were born Samemroumos, who is also called Hypersouranois."[18] Philo then informs readers that Hypersouranios settled Tyre. Samemroumos has long been connected with the expression "high heavens" (*rmm šmm*) used in a Sidonian inscription (Hypersouranios appearing to be a Greek translation).[19] Moshe Weinfeld notes that Samemroumos is a term for a temple and that the equivalent Hebrew word *rāmîm* refers to the Jerusalem temple (Ps 78:69).[20] Phoenician temple traditions appropriated the old notion of the sanctuary located in the northern mountains, and biblical tradition followed suit.

The site of Jerusalem inherited this long tradition. In this connection McCarter specifically notes "the House of the Forest of the Lebanon" in 1 Kgs 7:2. Following a long line of scholarship, McCarter also observes that Ps 48:2 represents a Jerusalemite appropriation of this thematic constellation in identifying the city as "the recesses of Saphon" (*yarkĕtê ṣāpôn*, "in the far north," NRSV), the root being the same as the name of Baal's mountain. Whether one regards the word more generically in its biblical meaning, "north," or the name Saphon itself (as preferred by many scholars), Ps 48:2 evokes an older West Semitic tradition of the special divine abode located in the Lebanon mountains.

Finally, the Baal Cycle connects the fertility issuing from the divine palace with the revelation of this reality. In the Baal Cycle, the message of divine revelation proceeds from "the midst of my mountain, divine Sapan, on the holy mount of my heritage, on the beautiful hill of my might."[21] This turning point in the Baal Cycle reveals the storm-god's impending revelation that is to take place at his temple-palace. The divine sanctuary as the site of revelation is also a biblical theme (Isa 2:3): "For instruction shall come forth from Zion" (cf. divine instruction in Pss 50 and 81).

2. Recapitulation: Divine Narrative of Cosmic Conquest and Enthronement in the Mythic Home

Temple architecture tells stories about deities. The Jerusalem temple communicates the story of Yahweh's victory over the sea, his acceptance of the people's offerings, his accession (or reaccession) to his throne in his house, and his blessing of the people.[22] The temple courtyard bore symbols conveying Yahweh's triumphant entry. Upon defeating the chaotic forces of nature represented by "the molten sea" (1 Kgs 7:20–26), the god of the Israelites accepts the sacrificial offerings placed on wheeled stands (1 Kgs 7:27–39). The deity enters the temple while bestowing blessings on the king and the people, as recorded on the columns flanking the temple entrance named Jachin and Boaz (1 Kgs 7:21–22). These names are plausibly construed as a blessing formula meaning, "May he [Yahweh] establish [the temple/king/people] in strength." This reading of the names compares well with the blessing expressed in Ps 29:11, "May Yahweh give strength to his people!" Inside, the god is enthroned on his cherubim throne (1 Kgs 6:23–28), as invoked in Ps 29:10. In short, the narrative of the god's entrance and enthronement marked by the temple symbols matches the narrative progression in biblical texts such as Psalm 29 and the heart of the Baal Cycle.

The story of the Jerusalem temple is, in a sense, also the story of the Garden of Eden. The temple entails not only simply fertility and abundance associated with the name of Eden, as noted in the preceding section; its decoration also evokes the beauty of Eden. Elizabeth Bloch-Smith notes, "Solomon's choice of palmette and cherubim motifs to adorn the walls and doors conveyed to Temple visitors that the Temple proper recreated or incorporated the garden of Eden, Yahweh's terrestrial residence."[23] In addition to these marks of the temple's Eden imagery, Bloch-Smith observes, "The molten sea perhaps symbolized secondarily the primordial waters issuing forth from Eden (Gen 3:10), and the twin pillars modeled the trees (of life and knowledge) planted in the garden."[24]

Scholars have highlighted the role of the garden imagery in the story of Genesis 2–3.[25] While Terje Stordalen notes the imagery of the temple *qua* garden in the Baal Cycle and Genesis 2–3, Lawrence E. Stager goes further in arguing that the goddess's tree was a seminal feature of the temple gardens.[26] Saul M. Olyan has also observed that *ḥawwâ* (Eve) may echo a title of the goddess, citing the divine titles "the Lady, the Living One, the Goddess" (*rbt ḥwt 'lt*, *KAI* 89.1).[27] In light of these observations, Genesis 2–4 may point to an ideology of the Jerusalem temple as the garden-home of the divine couple to which the king has access, perhaps after his "birth" (i.e., his coronation, for example in Ps 2:7).[28] Read in this way, features of the Genesis story emerge more clearly: the tree of knowledge echoes the asherah; the snake is suggestive of the goddess's emblem animal; the name of Eve (*ḥawwâ*) may echo a title of the goddess; and Eve's statement in Gen 4:1, "I have acquired/established a man with Yahweh" (*qānîtî 'îš 'et-yhwh*), might be explained by recourse to Asherah's title, "the establisher (or creatress) of the gods" (*qnyt 'ilm*).[29] This verse perhaps presupposed and even polemicized against an older royal myth (with the known cultural understandings added in square brackets): "And the male [i.e., the god El] knew [in 'sacred marriage'] Hawwat [the goddess], and she bore and she conceived . . . and she said: 'I have created [*qny] a man [i.e., the newly crowned human king] with DN [here said to be Yahweh, but formerly El, secondarily identified as Yahweh]."[30] All in all, these details in the Genesis narrative seem to reflect traditional ideas that the text's audience would have understood. Perhaps the story, as we have it, served as a rereading—or a correction—of these traditional motifs.

As the divine home of Yahweh on earth, the temple in Jerusalem carried a number of mythic associations. These evidently included deities who were subordinate to Yahweh (as seen in Ezek 8–10). Yet the picture of this divine home changed. Divine blessing and fertility would continue to be expressed by the temple rebuilt in the Persian period, as shown in Haggai 1 and Malachi 3. However, with other deities removed, the temple in the Persian period apparently expressed the viewpoint of priestly groups, arguably realigning various traditional notions into expressions of oneness: in other words, one deity, one temple, one people, one priesthood, one prophet, one teaching.[31] The reason for this development is apparent from shifts in Israelite discourse about holiness.

3. Participation: Power, Eternity, and Holiness

A temple may be expressive of a god's power. More specifically, a temple is thought to draw its power from its patron deity. This idea may be understood more fully by noting the parallel idea of a human king's power, which may come from or "participate in" the power of his patron god. Similarly, the power of the sanctuary site derives from the power of its deity.

This idea is communicated in several ways. Baal's mountain is the place of his "victory."[32] Similarly, Yahweh's strength is manifest in the tradition of Jerusalem's strength (Ps 46; cf. Isa 33:20–21). This deity's titles include terms of power and security, "refuge and strength" (Ps 46:1), and "refuge" (Pss 46:7, 11; 48:3). Shalom E. Holtz has highlighted the use of these terms for both God and the Jerusalem temple (for example, in Pss 27, 52, and 61).[33] Given the widespread nature of this discourse of power in biblical texts, this feature might be regarded as one of the more prominent predications made between deities and their temple-mountains. Just as the deity guarantees the security of the mountain, the mountain manifests the deity's power. To walk about the city and to see its ramparts is to perceive signs of the god's strength (Ps 48:12–14). The temple-city in turn is established by the deity "forever" (Ps 48:8), partaking of the deity's own eternity.[34]

A further expression of power involves holiness. Divinities in the Ugaritic texts are marked for holiness, as reflected by their general designation as "holy ones" (literally, "sons of holiness" or possibly "sons of the Holy One").[35] Phoenician refers to the deities as the "holy ones."[36] Israelite texts also mention the holy ones as a divine body or assembly led by Yahweh, their king. Psalm 89:5–7 is often cited in this regard, with its reference to "the assembly of the holy ones." Zechariah 14:5 assumes a similar notion: "And the Lord my God will come, and all the holy ones with him."[37] In turn, holiness was attached also to holy places. They are marked and demarcated for holiness. Indeed, the presence of divinity imparts holiness to those places. Not only the deities' dwellings, but also their mountains partake of their holiness. So Baal's mountain, Mount Sapan, is called both "holy" and "divine."[38] So, too, Yahweh's dwelling place is called "his holy mountain" (Ps 48:2) and "the holy dwelling place of the Most High" (Ps 46:5). In sum, temples participate in the deity's holiness.[39]

The words for "holy" and "holiness" bear further connotations. According to Karel van der Toorn, Akkadian *ellu* denotes not only holiness, but also cleanliness.[40] Here cleanliness entails not simply the absence of dirt, but also brilliance and luminosity (what in American English is evoked by the phrase "sparkling clean"). Similarly, the brickwork of Baal's palace on his mountain (consisting of gold and silver and even lapis lazuli) is called "pure," referring to its brilliance and luminosity.[41] The brickwork of the divine palace on God's holy mountain is likewise called "pure" or "brilliant" (Exod 24:10): "and they saw the god of Israel, and beneath his feet was like lapis brick-work, and like the very heaven with respect to purity [or brilliance]."[42] The brilliance of the stonework is a motif of the heavenly temple all the way down to the book of Revelation. Revelation 21 introduces three great themes known from the Baal Cycle (the victories over the sea and death, and the appearance of the heavenly palace, here understood as the heavenly Jerusalem) in vv. 1–4, and then it continues with its description of this heavenly palace in v. 11 (NABRE): "Its radiance was like that of a precious stone, like jasper, clear as crystal."[43] Holiness or purity is based analogically on the profane notion of cleanliness, both in its negative sense as free of dirt and in its positive connotation of brilliance.[44] Both are germane to the human experience of deities: divine appearances characteristically transpire in places regarded as clean from a cultic perspective, namely spaces ideally uncontaminated by human sin or impurity; and such theophanies are often marked by the brilliance of the deity's presence.

Divine holiness and its numinous character are well attested in the Bible and well beyond.[45] Divine holiness is associated with shaking, whether of places of theophany (*KTU* 1.4 VII; Ps 114) or of people who experience it (*KTU* 1.4 VII; Isa 6:4).[46] The divine "holy voice," whether belonging to Yahweh or Baal, signals a theophany, which may wreak destruction (Ps 29) or communicate revelation (as in Num 7:89); it induces flight and fear on the part of the god's enemies (*KTU* 1.4 VII 29–37).[47] Similarly, sanctuaries can be regarded as awe-inspiring like the deities who own and inhabit them.[48] It has been common for this experience of the holy to be understood in terms of awe and fear. In modern discussions of religion, this idea is customarily traced to the theologian Rudolf Otto, who characterized this confrontation with the divine as *mysterium tremendum et fascinosum*. Thorkild Jacobsen followed Otto in stressing the "wholly other" character of the numinous.[49] Yet because such experience is mediated by human experience and language, it is not by definition entirely "wholly other." Ancient texts identify the numinous in natural effects of a rainstorm or dream experience at night. In these experiences, the "other" partakes of the here and now. Moreover, as indicated above, divinity throughout the ancient Middle East is also experienced personally, and not entirely as "other." Indeed, anthropomorphism is a hallmark of the classic deities of the pantheon by comparison with divine monsters in many Mesopotamian and Syro-Palestinian myths of primordial conflict.[50] The view of ancient Middle Eastern religion (and consequently divinity) fostered by Otto's notion of *mysterium* captures one side of the perception of the divine. The *mysterium* was "other," yet it was also not "other," as underscored by van der Toorn. It is this combination that helps make it, to repeat Otto's expression, *tremendum et fascinosum*.[51]

The "this-worldly" quality of holiness is also a matter of power. As the historian of religion Stewart E. Guthrie has emphasized, the category of holiness is also a delimitation and expression of the power of those who maintain such spaces.[52] Guthrie stresses that in Israel holiness is attached to the elite and the monarch, a point that may apply as well to Ugarit. He comments how the radiance of the deity became associated with the power of the king: "Holiness here is ideology, and designed to serve a particular social system."[53] In his discussion of sacred order, another historian of religion, W. E. Paden, remarks in a similar vein: "Power and order are intertwined and mutually conditioning elements of religious world-building. Each is a premise of the other. The gods presuppose the very system that invests them with their status as gods, even though the world-order may itself be perceived as a creation of the gods."[54] Paden further comments: "The rites for honoring a religious leader or a king and those for honoring a god are often hard to distinguish."[55] Paden sees rites honoring a human figure as honoring a divine one as well. It may be said that myths arguably achieve the opposite effect: in honoring a deity explicitly, they thereby honor a king or priesthood implicitly. Accordingly, it may be thought that holiness appeared to ritual participants as a top-down phenomenon from gods to kings and priests to people. In contrast, it may be argued that the ritual practice informing these notions of holiness serves to focus the holiness of the whole people onto the experience of the divine in temples, mediated by priests and prophets and sponsored by kings. In other words, the holiness of a place expressed relationships of power and status in the form of a bottom-up human investment undergirding a praxis that was understood and marked as emanating from the divine top down.

As many scholars have noted,[56] holiness in ancient Israel developed a further nuance in the notion of "apartness." The origins of this particular connotation are unclear, but they might be traced to the development of priestly notions about separation of the holy from the profane, represented systematically, for example, in Genesis 1.[57] The Israelite priesthood's definition of divine holiness entailed a separation from death and sex. Indeed, the presentation of Yahweh generally as sexless and unrelated to the realm of death would appear to have been produced precisely by a priesthood whose central notion of Yahweh as holy would view this deity as fully removed from realms of impurity, specifically sex and death.[58] Several prohibitions governed the impurity of sexuality[59] and death (Num 19:11, 14–19; 31:19). Members of the priesthood were restricted in their selection of a spouse specifically because of the issue of holiness (Lev 21:7), and they were restricted also in their contact with the dead.[60] Unlike the other priests, the chief priest was even more restricted in not being permitted contact with any dead (Lev 21:11–12) and in being permitted for a wife only a woman who had not yet borne children (Lev 21:13–14). As the single human permitted to enter the divine sanctuary, the chief priest attempted to approach it in the greatest holiness humanly possible.[61] Within priestly sacred space, the deity was, in the words of Michael B. Hundley, "the most holy" and "the superlative element within that sphere."[62] Holier than the Holy of Holies, the deity came to epitomize the fullest possibility of sacredness and separation, avoiding sexuality and death. It may be that older mythologies involving divine death and sex did not survive in the biblical corpus.

(There is perhaps a hint of the theme of divine death in Hab 1:12: "you will not die.")[63] On this score, we may contrast mythologies of sex and death in Lucian of Samosata's *De Dea Syria* 53–54, even though the priesthood there is said to observe purity rules involving the deceased and food.[64] The loss of divine sex and death mythology in Judah may not have transpired only because the priesthood actively censored such views (although such a situation is theoretically possible). Instead, such mythologies did not cohere with the emergent priestly tradition's normative understanding of the divine (nor the Deuteronomic view of the divine), and so as part of an explanation for their absence from biblical literature, perhaps they fell into disuse in these traditions.[65]

Before priestly and Deuteronomistic writings, there was a wider fund of sexual physicality. El's sexual invitation to Athirat seems so conventional in the Baal Cycle temple narrative[66] that divine mating may have served as common material for temple stories. The royal cult as expressed in *KTU* 1.23 likewise assumes recollections of divine sexuality.[67] Divine sexuality may have been accorded a broad place in temple myth in West Semitic cultures. One source potentially reflecting divine sexuality are the Kuntillet 'Ajrud inscriptions that refer to "Yahweh . . . and his asherah."[68] Thanks to this epigraphic evidence (as well as to a thematically related inscription from Khirbet el-Qom), it is commonly argued that the goddess Asherah was worshipped in the Jerusalem temple, in the form of the symbol of the asherah.[69] While a pairing of this sort seems to be reflected in the blessing of El and "Breasts and Womb" (aka, Asherah) in Gen 49:25–26, a number of scholars,[70] myself included, dispute this understanding of the evidence. Instead, the asherah by the eighth century may have been viewed as something that, as the inscriptions say, is "his," namely a symbol of fertility and perhaps even female sexuality associated with Yahweh without referring to a goddess as such. On this point, Ziony Zevit asks: "What would it have meant to say that the goddess *belonged to* or was *possessed by* Yahweh?"[71] The putative association of the asherah with a goddess in passages such as 1 Kgs 15:13 and 2 Kgs 21:7 and 23:4, 6 may represent a polemic against a view associating Yahweh with the asherah symbol of sexuality and fertility.[72] This would explain the vast preponderance of biblical references to the symbol over and against the goddess, and it would also help to explain the references to the goddess in the later parts of 2 Kings. The debate about asherah/Asherah in the Late Iron II period may not have involved simply (or even primarily) a goddess in the temple. In sum, it might be argued that the imagery of divine sexuality was known for the temple in the Iron II period, only to be displaced or omitted from the ancient record subsequently.[73] Indeed, the priestly avoidance of sexuality noted above may suggest a competing view of the divinity as sexless.

4. Analogy: Size and Attractiveness

As we saw in Chapter 1, Baal and Yahweh are described with supersized bodies, with temples and temple accouterments as points of comparison.[74] In the Ugaritic Baal Cycle, Baal is the focus of expressions of superhuman strength and size. The magnificent size of Israel's god is implied by his cherubim throne located in the Holy of Holies. The same point applies to the temple courtyard's immense tank denoting God's victory over the cosmic waters. Ten cubits in diameter (ca. 17 feet or 5.3 meters), it is estimated to have held nearly 10,000 gallons (38,000 liters). Including the height of the wheels and the band that supported the basin, each stand ("laver") measured 4 cubits square (ca. 7 feet or 2.1 meters) and 7 cubits high (ca. 12 feet or 3.7 meters). The basin supported by each of the ten stands had a capacity of forty baths (ca. 243 gallons or 920 liters). The exaggerated size of the structures in the temple courtyard would suggest that they were not intended for human use, but belonged to the realm of the divine, as noted by Bloch-Smith.[75] These instances assume a sort of homology between the size of the deity and the size of the temple. Such a homology between the divinity and the temple functions to increase the identification of the two: the temple does not just house the deity; it also expresses characteristics of the deity.[76]

Ancient texts render divinity and temples also in terms of attraction. The well-known female personification of Jerusalem, the temple-city (e.g., Ezek 16 and 23; Lam 1), goes back to traditional notions of the attractiveness of the temple (or temple-mountain) that partakes of the god's attractiveness. Before noting the language of the temple's attractiveness, we may note how common it is for deities. In Ugaritic, Anat is characterized generally as "lovely," and Athtart is said to have "beauty" (followed by a description of their eyes being like lapis and alabaster).[77] The newborn gods of *KTU* 1.23 are called "the lovely gods."[78] The same gods are called "beautiful."[79] In general, "loveliness" is regarded as a standard feature of West Semitic divine appearance. The same terms apply analogically to other features of deities, for example, El's years.[80] Baal's "loveliness" is predicated of his capacity as a provider of water, understood as a quality of his voice.[81] Biblical examples for divine "loveliness" are rarer, but both Yahweh's name and Yahweh enjoy "attraction" (*n'm). Yahweh's name is n'ym (Ps 135:3), and Yahweh is said to have n'm that can be dispensed to humans who pray to the deity (Ps 90:17).

The temple-mountains of the gods also have n'm. As noted above, Baal's mountain is said to have "holiness" (qdš) and "victory" (tl'iyt), but it also has attractiveness (n'm).[82] The first two features are regarded as derivative of the god. Just as Baal is the god of victory, victory is associated with his mountain; similarly, Baal's mountain is regarded as holy because it is associated with the god. Thus, it follows that the mountain is regarded as having attractiveness (n'm) because it partakes of the god's n'm. To be sure, a given mountain might have been selected because of its own natural attractiveness (for example, Sapan as Baal's mountain because it is high and cloud-covered). Nonetheless, just as other features of the mountain derive from the god, so the feature of attractiveness seems to as well. The materials associated with the temples in Ugaritic myth and biblical narrative, namely cedar, gold, and silver in both Baal's house and Solomon's temple, evoke luxury and aesthetics. Similarly, the heavenly palace of Baal, like that of Yahweh, involves brickwork of lapis lazuli.[83] In sum, the mountain participates in the god's n'm, and his n'm is manifest on his mountain.

By the same token, n'm is associated with the house of Yahweh or at least the god's presence in the house in Ps 27:4.[84] The two can be difficult to distinguish. Psalm 16:11 discusses n'm in connection with the deity, apparently in a sanctuary context, perhaps by a priest.[85] Moreover, Zion, the holy mountain of Yahweh, is called ypy, "beautiful," in a number of phrases: "beautiful [yĕpēh] of height, joy of all the earth" (Ps 48:2); and "perfect [*kll] of beauty [yōpî]" (Ps 50:2). The personification of Jerusalem as a woman in Ezekiel 16 apparently relates to the notion of the place's beauty, since *ypy in vv. 13–14 (cf. Song of Songs 4:7) is used with *kll, just as it is in Ps 50:2. Finally, the divine dwelling in Jerusalem (Ps 84:1) is called yĕdîdôt ("lovely," NJPS), as well as an object of yearning (Ps 84:2). In short, the vocabulary of attraction for the temple-mountain includes language of desire.[86]

This survey suggests a range of traditions inherited by the Jerusalem temple to convey its royal divine power and Edenic beauty. Aesthetic language served as a powerful force for distinguishing Jerusalem and perhaps capital cities more generally. The language of aesthetics was not only lavished on Jerusalem because the city was lavished with public works, in particular palace and temple (other cities received such works). Such aesthetic language is common to the ancient Near Eastern genres of temple hymns and temple narratives sponsored by local kings. In other words, the vocabulary of aesthetics is a discourse of royal power. By lining the discourse of power with the vocabulary of attraction, it is made beautiful and thereby even more powerful. The attractiveness of deity and temple involves a reciprocal social and political power, and perhaps even seduction.

6. Afterthoughts on the Divine and Human

Temples focus public attention on deities, more specifically on the connections between human celebration and problems on one hand, and the perceptions of divine presence and aid on the other hand. Out of the various sorts of relations discussed in this chapter, five divine characteristics associated also with temples in West Semitic culture stand out: strength and size, fertility and beauty, holiness, immortality, and knowledge. These correlate to the general features of deities.[87] Thus temple spaces fill out the

Table 1. Correlations between the human condition and deities and temples

Human problems	Human contradictions	Divinity	Temple
Powerlessness	Limited human power, but experience of suffering and evil people	Strength, size	Strength, size
Lack of prosperity infertility	Experience of divine presence and divine absence	Sexuality/love, beauty	Channel of blessing, beauty
Unholiness	Knowledge and experience of self as both wrong (sinning) and whole (holy)	Holiness	Intersection, transition
Mortality	Limited time, but intuiting eternity	Eternity	Duration
Ignorance	Limited knowledge of the world/God, but experience of disorder and unintelligibility	Wisdom and knowledge	Source of divine revelation

biography of the deity beyond the physical divine body, as we saw in Chapter 1. In general, West Semitic texts and iconography may represent deities with superhuman strength and size; they are embodied and gendered; they are holy and immortal; and they have knowledge or wisdom. In these respects, deities are like humans, or perhaps better, humans are like deities but not nearly so. As humans and deities partake of several of the same characteristics, humans have them in a discernibly inferior mode.[88] Anthropomorphism captures many of the ways in which deities and humans are alike, yet it also shows deities exceeding human capacities. By definition, there is a fundamental correlation between deities and humans, but there is no less an asymmetry between them. In short, anthropomorphism provides a measure not only of deities, but also of humans.

The same categories apply to temples as well as to deities and humans. Table 1 lists features of the human condition that correlate with divinities and temples, as understood in the ancient Levant. Temples indicate both where deities are and what and how they are. Bringing deities and people into contact with one another, temples express a variety of relationships between them. The crucial term here is the word "like." It is the fulcrum-point between similarity and difference, between connection and disjunction. The mediating power of sacred places and spaces captures and expresses the relations between people and their deities. Even as deities could seem like humans, deities were also understood to be well beyond them. The anthropomorphism of deities was complicated by a further expression of divine form, namely theriomorphism—the subject of the next two chapters.

PART 2

Anthropomorphism and Theriomorphism in Cultic Space

3 The Construction of Anthropomorphism and Theriomorphism

In the preceding two chapters, I noted how both deities and temples show considerable anthropomorphism, a phenomenon that I discussed in the Introduction. It remains to be understood how ancient texts create this anthropomorphism. In this chapter I begin by addressing the underlying ways anthropomorphism is constructed. One way involves the attribution of physical actions and emotions of human beings to deities. A second way entails similes comparing deities and humans.[1] Here I survey statements made of deities and humans as well as similes comparing them in order to see how deities are given human form. In addition, I examine deities represented in animal form, or theriomorphism.[2] Anthropomorphism and theriomorphism might seem very different, yet their representations are often intertwined, as I note in the final section of this chapter.

1. Statements Human and Divine

Statements made of both humans and deities may be divided into two categories: identical predications and similar predications. Some actions and states are attributed to deities and humans in identical terms. In the Ugaritic texts, these include physical actions: raising the eyes to see,[3] raising the eyes and seeing the approach of a deity,[4] raising the voice and speaking,[5] movement into one's house or palace,[6] and applying cosmetics and washing.[7] Deities may have the same emotional responses as humans, such as fear.[8] The reception of bad news is met with the same bodily response of fear.[9] Deities, like humans, lament over and bury deceased family members.[10] Humans and deities alike may break into a smile and laugh.[11] Both rejoice.[12] Gods, like humans, may even have a revelatory dream vision.[13] Sometimes gods do not know,[14] like their human counterparts.[15] Like the "form" of human bodies,[16] a Ugaritic deity may have a "form."[17] As a final example of an identical predication for both humans and deities, there is one notable nondivine, nonhuman term. The god El is called "Bull" (as in his title, "Bull El my Father"). A human is called "Bull" in a Ugaritic administrative text: "The sons of PN: three heads [*b'lm*], and their master/father [*'adn*][18] Bull and his four daughters."[19] This representation of the "bull" may inform the representation of the biblical God with horns (Num 23:22 and 24:8).[20] This particular usage suggests that predications may be made involving the divine, the human, and the animalistic all at the same time.

From identical predications we may turn to general predications about deities acting and being like humans. Ugaritic deities show activities and states attributed generally to humans. In the story of Aqhat, Danil gives food and drink to the gods[21] and to the Kotharat goddesses;[22] they eat and drink. In Aqhat, Baal approaches and makes a request of El to bless Aqhat, who does so.[23] According to the list of filial duties in Aqhat, both Baal and El have a house.[24] The Kotharat enter and exit Danil's home.[25] The god Kothar is said to walk; he brings a bow and arrows.[26] These are all activities predicated of humans, and these are also generally evident for God in the Bible. Despite some biblical expressions emphasizing the difference between God and humanity (Num 23:19; 1 Sam 15:29; Hos 11:9; cf. Ps 50:21), metaphor for the biblical God includes a remarkable range of physical anthropomorphisms. God has a bodily "form" (Num 12:8; Ps 17:15; cf. Job 4:16).[27] God sees (Jer 23:24; 30:6; Ezek 8:12; 16:6, 8; Ps 33:13; Job 28:27), God eats (Gen 18:8), and God sleeps (Ps 44:23). God sits (Gen 18:8), and God stands (Gen 18:2). God has a washbasin (Pss 60:8; 108:9); God bathes others (Ezek 16:9). God wears clothing (Isa 6:1), splattered with blood (Isa 63:1–3). God converses with people (Gen 18:23–33; Exod 33:12–23).

Ugaritic deities also have emotional lives. Athirat can rejoice.[28] Baal sometimes hates,[29] and at other times he has compassion.[30] Additionally, he is said to enjoy love and passion.[31] Anat may show the most complex emotional life of any deity: she desires,[32] and her heart is "for Baal" with maternal emotion.[33] The goddess also experiences joy.[34] Her laughter seems to be scornful when she responds to Aqhat,[35] but her receiving the news that Baal has obtained El's permission for building a palace is received with the laughter of happiness.[36] El laughs with pleasure when Athirat arrives,[37] and he laughs upon learning about the abilities of the creatures about to be born.[38] Kothar laughs when Baal accedes to his earlier advice to install a window in the palace.[39] The biblical God likewise shows cognition and emotional states. God laments with weeping (Isa 16:9; Jer 48:32; cf. Jer 9:9),[40] and God buries the dead (Deut 34:6). God laughs (Pss 2:4; 37:13; 59:8) and God rejoices (Ps 104:31). God acknowledges that God had thought that the other gods were real (Ps 82:6),[41] and God also expresses the possibility of divine fear in the face of other deities (Isa 41:23).

Ugaritic deities were said to experience life-cycle events much as humans do. They are born,[42] and more generally deities are called "sons of El."[43] Gods take spouses, and they produce offspring.[44] They manifest activities or states typical of humans, such as eating and drinking; and only most occasionally they die.[45] However, the death of a god in the Ugaritic texts is a rarity; the death of other gods is also rarely acknowledged in the Bible (Ps 82:6–7).[46] While explicitly marked sexual features or activity for the biblical God are generally lacking, traces of divine sexuality may be noted (e.g., God parallel with a divine figure called "Breasts and Womb" in Gen 49:25, as noted in the preceding chapter). Echoes of divinely inspired conception and birth may be heard in Eve's claim of acquiring a child with God (Gen 4:1, as also noted in Chapter 2) and in personified Wisdom's birth ("Before the hills I was born" in Prov 8:25, NJPS). God in the Bible has some familial relations with other gods.[47] Deuteronomy 32:8–9 (in 4QDeut[j] and the LXX) presuppose the notion of a divine family, in which Yahweh is one of seventy divine sons. These familial relations are hardly drawn out in the Hebrew Bible in the manner seen in the Ugaritic corpus. Indeed, the biblical god lacks divine death and sexuality. As noted in the preceding chapter, this lack seems to correlate with biblical restrictions on contact with the dead and sexual activity on the part of the priesthood.[48]

The Ugaritic texts present some gender-marked roles for deities, for example, Athirat's domestic chores.[49] Of importance for this discussion of anthropomorphism are goddesses hunting, the opposite of what is considered for human females.[50] In contrast to Anat and Astarte hunting, human females are expected not to hunt, as shown by Aqhat's question posed to Anat, "now do womenfolk hunt?" (or, perhaps as a sarcastic claim, "now womenfolk hunt!").[51] However these words are to be understood, it seems that when it comes to hunting and warfare, human women were thought generally to contrast with these goddesses. In this case anthropomorphism works in inverse terms rather than parallel terms; deities may be like humans, but occasionally they function opposite to the human situation.

Again, these cases also point to an important issue for comparisons with biblical material: domestic chores for deities are unknown in the Bible, and hunting for the god generally seems to drop out of the biblical picture for what may be complex cultural reasons.[52] As this case suggests, diachronic, cultural developments may be factors for the comparison of biblical and extra-biblical material.

The overall impression in the Ugaritic literary texts is of a general and broad anthropomorphism. At the same time, with the possible exception of Anat, Ugaritic anthropomorphism does not seem particularly deep in its representation of emotional or psychological states. This is not surprising, given the fact that psychological depth in Ugaritic myths and epics is likewise lacking for humans, again with the possible exception of a female, namely Pughat reacting in the face of her brother's demise. The same may be said for the older Hebrew poetry (twelfth to ninth centuries) most closely dated to the Ugaritic corpus. This traditional Hebrew poetry also lacks psychological depth.

Anthropomorphism also has limits. Overall, when it comes to the Ugaritic texts, different deities are known for typical sorts of behaviors and states. While they vary by context, they show some relative consistency. In other words, Anat and Astarte may be expected to hunt, but it would not be expected that they die. Similarly, El may be expected to drink but not to sacrifice himself or to commit suicide. Humans experience many things that deities generally do not experience. Deities may cause certain things, but those things, such as illness, do not generally happen to them as they do to humans. There is slippage between human and divine natures. While humans are often much like deities, deities are often more than humans, and in some arenas they are not so analogous to humans. There remains a basic asymmetry between deities and humans. Thus anthropomorphism not only suggests how deities and humans are like one another, but it may also point up how humans are not like deities—in short what humans are not, but might wish to be.

The anthropomorphisms that I have noted are not identical in Ugaritic and biblical texts. Nevertheless, the range of anthropomorphism in both is rich and substantial. Labeling anthropomorphism in Ugaritic texts as myth but in the Bible as metaphor, as has been done,[53] constitutes a serious effort to come to grips with the biblical refashioning of mythic imagery. At the same time, it may be asked whether this putative contrast overreads the overall difference between extra-biblical myth and biblical material. It perhaps does not appreciate sufficiently the depth of mythic imagery in the Bible, not to mention biblical myth, as it appears in Genesis 1–3 and arguably elsewhere (I would include apocalyptic texts in this discussion).[54] Furthermore, the alleged contrast between metaphor and myth is inherently problematic since metaphors and similes appear in myth. Myth itself may be understood as a narrative form that construes reality in extended metaphorical terms and that also embeds specific metaphors. (With these two metaphorical levels entailed by myth, it might be said that myth is "meta-metaphorical.") If myths may be understood as narrative metaphorical discourses about the constructions of reality, it seems that they also vary considerably as to the nature of their underlying metaphor.[55]

Finally, genre seems to affect anthropomorphic discourse. For example, anthropomorphism in Ugaritic and biblical prayer often focuses less on concrete body parts and more on these parts to express divine agency in the world.[56] Moreover, anthropomorphism in biblical prayer manifests many of the same sorts of body parts for Yahweh as Ugaritic literature does for several of its deities. As discussed in Chapter 1, the Bible also suggests a divine body. In both Ugaritic literature and the Bible, anthropomorphism for deities exhibits a spectrum, ranging from concrete expressions of bodies and body parts, such as the bodily form; to body parts exercised for a function, such as hands and arms for fighting, eyes for seeing, and ears for hearing; and to body parts as abstractions, such as a "hand" for power.[57]

2. Similes Comparing Humans and Deities

Simile, namely the comparison of one thing to another with the word "like" (*k-* or *km*),[58] is not commonly included in discussions of anthropomorphism. An obvious reason why is that similes are made between all kinds of parts of reality. For example, humans—like deities—are said to be like (*k-*) animals: "a cow calls to her calf, soldiers cry for their mothers, likewise the Udumians groan."[59] The image in the initial line applies also to Anat.[60] These similes hardly indicate that people are animals, only that they may be analogous to them in some manner. Accordingly, it might be thought that similes are not very useful for a discussion of theriomorphism and anthropomorphism. At the same time, similes sometimes constitute a powerful means for expressing similarity between deities and humans despite their differences. As we will see, similes contribute to understanding anthropomorphism. Before saying more about how, we look at some examples.

One type of simile entails comparisons of a deity with humans. These are relatively rare. One striking case involves El's highly anthropomorphic drunkenness, "like those who go down to the underworld" (in English we might say that El is "dead-drunk").[61] Here the deity is shown behaving in a less than ideal manner. Such comparisons signal a less than ideal situation about the deity involved. Deities are also occasionally the subject of similes related to animals ("like a kid in my mouth")[62] or vegetation ("like a dried olive").[63] When deities are compared with humans, animals, or vegetation, they are shown at their worst.

A second sort of simile concerns a number of comparisons of human traits and divine attributes (what we may call "theomorphism"). For example, human kingship is "like" (k-//k-) a god's: "does Kirta desire kingship like El's, domini[on] like the Father of Humanity's?"[64] Superlative human beauty is "like" (k-//km) the beauty of goddesses: "whose loveliness is like the loveliness of Anat, [whose bea]uty is like the beauty of Astarte."[65] Superlative human wisdom is also "like" (k-//k-) a god's wisdom: "El has heard your word—so i[t]'s like El's! You are wise like Bull the Kindly."[66] In these examples, similes comparing humans with deities express a superlative quality about humans. When humans are compared with deities, humans are shown at their best.

These types of simile contribute to the larger sense of how anthropomorphism of deities works. The first type suggests the potentially lesser, human qualities of deities. The second sort reflects the superlative traits of deities that may sometimes apply to humans; in other words, what humans might aspire to. These sorts of similes are forms of analogy between deities and humans. As noted in the Introduction, recent work in cognition and psychology has suggested that analogy provides models for solving problems and making discoveries, in short for probing reality. To my mind, this point applies to similes involving divinities. Similes provide a form of exploration of divine nature beyond predications and intersection. These similes constitute a sort of discourse that shows or assumes anthropomorphism, yet they do so with a different—and flexible—linguistic structure.

I now turn to a particularly dramatic case of extended simile (marked by k-), as well as metaphor:[67]

[Baal's enthronement/mountain]
Baal sits (enthroned) like the sitting of a mountain,
Haddu . . . like the (cosmic) ocean,

In the midst of his mountain, divine Sapan,
In [the midst of?] the mount of victory,
[Voice/weaponry]
Seven lightnings . . .
Eight storehouses of thunder (?).
A tree-bolt of lightning. [. .] .
[Head/precipitation]
His head is adorned (?) with Dewy
Between his eyes
. . . at his base,
. . . the horn[s] . . . on him (?),
His head with a downpour from the heavens
. . . the god, there is watering,
[Mouth/fertility]
His mouth is like two clouds of (?) . . .
[(his) lips] are like wine of two-cruets.
[Heart/?]
his heart is . . .

The precise force of each analogy with *k-* is not entirely clear, especially in the broken lines.[68] Whatever the precise understanding, it is apparent that the text begins with the notion of Baal's enthronement on his mountain as comparable to a mountain and an ocean. The text then correlates, largely by *k-* particles, Baal's physical self with various features of his precipitation at his mountain. It begins with his lightning and thunder (cf. Ps 29). His head and eyes are associated with precipitation, perhaps in the form of personified Dew, as known from the Baal Cycle.[69] Baal's mouth seems to be compared with two clouds, with his lips (?) perhaps providing wine of two cruets. The final analogue seems to be made of Baal's heart, but the passage breaks off without providing further information. The analogies suggest a superhuman scale, which for deities is hardly uncommon. What is uncommon is the correlation of Baal's superhuman, anthropomorphic self with the superhuman scale of his mountain, combined with features associated with his storm theophany.

The many cases of *k-* here may be contrasted with a biblical passage highly marked by *k-* particles, namely Ezekiel 1 (see vv. 26 [two times], 27 [three times], 28; note also vv. 7, 13, 14, 16, 22, 24).[70] Even as Ezekiel 1 strives for difference or distance between divinity and humanity with the *k-* particles, along with the repetition of likeness (*dĕmût*) and appearance (*mar'eh*) in vv. 26–28, the passage still shows "the tradition of *human* appearance," as James Barr has called it.[71] Ronald S. Hendel has insightfully called this sort of representation "transcendent anthropomorphism."[72] In *KTU* 1.101 the figure of Baal is not simply human in form and scale. This Baal is superhuman in scale, yet in a mode made particularly majestic like the mountain that visibly looms to the north of Ugarit. At the same time, it seems to make the person of Baal immanent in his natural manifestations. This sitting of the god is at his earthly mountain, and in this respect this passage altogether differs from Ezekiel 1. Baal's anthropomorphism is intensified and further correlated with the natural. Yahweh's anthropomorphism in Ezekiel 1 is qualified and made quite deliberately problematic; moreover, it is transcendent by comparison.

3. Anthropomorphism, Theriomorphism, Physiomorphism

The relationship between anthropomorphic and theriomorphic representations is complex.[73] On one level, theriomorphism construes deities in ways unlike humans. Deities are represented in animal form, which distinguishes them from humans. For example, Anat flies,[74] and she has wings[75] and horns.[76] Baal copulates with a heifer.[77] Baal may be represented here in a bovine form, perhaps as a young bull (see the reference also to his horns).[78] These cases suggest that specific animals emblemize deities. The use of "attribute animals"[79] seems to be a broad facet of ancient Near Eastern deities. Ugaritic narratives about Anat and Baal present these deities acting in theriomorphic modes within a world with deities who are otherwise anthropomorphic. In Ugaritic stories, a theriomorphic representation of deities seems to be a metaphorical or episodic depiction within a larger anthropomorphic narration. In these cases, the theriomorphic appears to mark a specific act or perspective within an otherwise anthropomorphic plot. Thus, the theriomorphic is not generally posed in opposition to the anthropomorphic. Instead, the theriomorphic may offer a distinctive image in combination with the anthropomorphic.

In addition to narrative representations of theriomorphism, animal titles and metaphors are not uncommon. Above I noted the title of El, "Bull," in its combination with other appellations for this god.[80] Athtar twice is seemingly referenced as a lion,[81] and Athtart is called a lion and a panther in a hymnic context:[82]

The name of 'Athtart let my voice sing,
May I praise the name of the lion.
O name, may you be victorious over . . .
May you/she shut the jaw of El's attackers.
A great panther is 'Athtart,
A great panther that pounces.[83]

This sort of theriomorphism, as well as what it conveys about the deity's potential for help, is known from the Hebrew Bible.[84] Theriomorphic language is applied to Yahweh in a hymnic mode, whether it involves having horns "like a wild ox" (Num 23:22; 24:8)[85] or attributed wings (especially in Psalms, e.g., Pss 17:8; 36:7; 57:1; 61:4; 63:7; and 91:4).[86] Yahweh's horns recall El's title, "Bull," perhaps not entirely surprising in light of the other El language in the context of the poems in Numbers 23–24.[87] Similarly, there is the title "Ba'lu-of-the-wing,"[88] thought to be a manifestation of Baal as a winged deity.[89] There is also considerable bovine iconography, thought to be representative of a number of gods (El, Baal, Yahweh).[90] That these theriomorphic forms were themselves thought to represent deities is illustrated by a thirteenth-century relief from Alaca Höyük showing human petitioners standing before a bovine on a throne or pedestal.[91]

Literary imagery may combine human and animal language for the divine. Andrea L. Weiss has drawn attention to Jer 25:30, with its combination of animal metaphor ("Yahweh roars from on high") and human simile ("He utters shouts like the grape-treaders," NJPS).[92] Both images involve loud noise, yet together they build a more complex picture: the first expresses threatening aggression toward the nations and the second God's pleasure or celebration in taking action against them. They generate a "metaphorical story" with different details about what they share in common, in this case the divine subject and the verbal action of roaring.

Iconographic evidence also combines human and animal traits in a number of ways.[93] Sometimes a single figure may combine the anthropomorphic and the theriomorphic. A stele from Iron II Bethsaida and two steles from the Hauran area show bulls with horns and bovine ears, standing with a sword on their waists.[94] The image in each of these representations combines theriomorphic traits (the bovine horns, face, and ears) with anthropomorphic characteristics (the standing figure and the sword).[95] The bull figure with human traits on the Bethsaida stele in particular seems to be arranged for worship on a platform, which signals a god.[96] Its location in the city gate further marks the public importance of this piece as "performance iconography" that all passersby would meet and engage. In these cases, two different sorts of representation on steles, the anthropomorphic and the theriomorphic, are combined into a single divine figure that would be experienced by the public.

Other iconographic representations show anthropomorphic and theriomorphic figures together. Examples of deities in human form standing on quadrupeds have been long known in ancient Syria and Anatolia,[97] but there is also evidence from ancient Israel.[98] For example, two Iron I scarab seals from Tell Fara show winged human forms standing on top of quadrupeds.[99] The quadruped has been considered a pedestal for the standing god,[100] but this explanation does not address why the platform is represented with a quadruped. Information from Tell Dan may offer a possible answer. The biblical tradition about Dan and Bethel suggests that the bull-calf is the national god in theriomorphic form (see 1 Kgs 12:28; cf. Exod 32:4, 8), a point long noted by commentators.[101] Moreover, iconography on a plaque found at Dan shows a winged human-looking figure standing on a bull.[102] I examine this evidence in detail in Chapter 4, but for now it may be suggested that the biblical and iconographic representations show the same deity understood in three different modalities: sometimes in human form alone, at other times in theriomorphic form alone, and at yet other times as a human form standing on top of a theriomorphic form. In other words, the anthropomorphic figures standing on bovines may represent a human-looking deity standing on an animal not only serving as his throne or platform, but also as his representation. In these cases, the human standing on the quadruped may be a double representation of the god.[103]

Before turning to the theriomorphic representations of Dan and Bethel in the next chapter, I note one last type of divine depiction. Deities may have specific natural properties (what Marjo C. A. Korpel calls "physiomorphic descriptions").[104] For example, in the Baal Cycle the sun goddess is said to burn,[105] yet in the same text she also plays her anthropomorphic role in service to El.[106] Baal, too, can move with his entourage, which consists of meteorological elements (clouds, wind, lightning bolts, rain), figures with names connected with precipitation (Pidray, Daughter of Light; and Tallay, Daughter of Rain), and seven boys//eight attendants, apparently corresponding to seven winds.[107] In these cases, the natural and anthropomorphic signal that deities are not simply figures of nature or of fertility. They have a twin reality entailing human and nonhuman dimensions. Natural images for deities that are neither anthropomorphic nor theriomorphic suggest a wider sense of deities beyond either of these categories. Perhaps physiomorphic representations offer yet further dimensions of deities not expressed by either anthropomorphic or theriomorphic depictions. Together these various divine forms offer a kaleidoscopic view of the deity. Deuteronomy 32 is a parade example, combining the physiomorphic ("rock," in vv. 4, 15, 18, 30, 31; cf. v. 37) with the anthropomorphic (v. 6; cf. vv. 10, 29) and the theriomorphic (v. 11).[108] Might this combination of divine forms constitute an ancient means for conjuring up not only divine incomparability,[109] but also divine ineffability?

As these instances illustrate, multiple images juxtaposing the anthropomorphic, theriomorphic, or physiomorphic point to a complex view of deities. At first glance, the anthropomorphic seems to suggest how deities are like humans, yet as we saw earlier, anthropomorphic imagery is also used to show how different deities and humans are. The theriomorphic and physiomorphic also appear to mark how deities are unlike humans. The combination of the human and the animal may offer more than two separate images for deities. The theriomorphic and anthropomorphic together serve as two ways for looking at a deity at the same time. The deity is similar to both and yet more than both; the deity is also different from either one. Here the examples imply a theorizing about deities. In being both human and animal in some sense, deities were imagined as both connected to concrete human experience and exercising an identity in the natural world distinct from human experience. This was not simply an abstract matter; it was made concrete in the cult. I now turn to what is perhaps the best-known case of theriomorphism in biblical cult, the calves at Dan and Bethel.

4 The Calf Images at Dan and Bethel

Their Number and Symbolism

This chapter moves from a general consideration of theriomorphism to the specific case of the bull-calf iconography of Yahweh at Dan and Bethel. Given the range of primary evidence, the cult of Yahweh at Dan and Bethel, and its bull-calf iconography, is not simply a major question, but a constellation of data sets and interconnected issues.[1] I first address the available information about the number of calves involved in Jeroboam I's cult. Then I examine bull and calf symbolism in the iconographic record, in an effort to clarify the calf icons at Dan and Bethel.

1. Biblical and Extra-biblical Texts

According to 1 Kgs 12:28–29, Jeroboam I established one bovine icon each at Dan[2] and Bethel,[3] located at opposite ends of his kingdom: "He set one in Bethel and one he put in Dan."[4] It is thought that Jeroboam I used a single calf image at each of the two sanctuaries in order to develop a northern, national identity. The old association of the calves with the exodus served to express national identity: freedom from Egypt became the model for the northern kingdom's liberation from Jerusalemite monarchy.[5] As scholars have long noted, the association of the calf symbol with the exodus is evident from the nearly identical wordings in 1 Kgs 12:28 and in the "Golden Calf" story in Exod 32:4 and 8. First Samuel 4:8 has likewise been cited in support of the association of the exodus with the formulary of the calves (see also Hos 13:4).[6] A single calf icon for each of the sites of Dan and Bethel may have been the case.

Many commentators focus only on the singular references to calves and overlook the plural ones.[7] The main textual evidence for a plurality of calf icons at Bethel derives from MT 1 Kgs 12:32 and Papyrus Amherst 63. In addition to these two texts, I will examine 1 Kgs 12:28 in the LXX, and finally a most difficult passage, Hos 10:5–6. These texts ostensibly refer to the cult of Bethel, and all involve a plurality of calves; they also entail significant textual difficulties, which I will unpack. The following examination of texts does not build toward a single counterconclusion regarding the plurality of calves at Bethel. Instead, the texts offer what might be called different snapshots of Bethel's calf cult, taken at different times and angles.[8] The witnesses date considerably after Jeroboam's establishment of the calves and were preserved largely by outside critics of various sorts.

First Kings 12:32 relates the date of the inauguration of Jeroboam I's cult at Bethel. It is also said to be "like the festival [ḥāg] that was in Judah" (NJPS: "in imitation of the festival in Judah"). As commentators have long noted, the date formula recalls Solomon's inauguration of his temple in the fall (1 Kgs 8:2). The text then relates that Jeroboam ascended the altar. The crucial section for the discussion involves the next clause in the MT for v. 32: "thus he made in Bethel to sacrifice to the calves that he had made" (kēn 'āśâ bĕbêt-'el lĕzabbēaḥ lā'ăgālîm 'ăšer-'āśâ; cf. LXX 3 Reigns: "and he went up onto the altar that he had made in Bethel to sacrifice to the calves that he had made") (NETS; kai anebē epi to thusiastērion ho epoiēsen en Baithēl tou thuein tais damalesin hais epoiēsen). Many commentators regard "thus he made in Bethel" (kēn 'āśâ bĕbêt-'ēl) as an intrusion. Setting this clause aside, James Montgomery and Henry Snyder Gehman as well as Wesley Toews would instead read, "to offer to the calves that he had made" ('el lĕzabbēaḥ lā'ăgālîm 'ăšer-'āśâ) as the continuation of the preceding clause, "he went up onto the altar" (wayya'al 'al-hammizbēaḥ).[9] This would clean up the sentence, but the reason for the intrusion remains insufficiently explained.

Julio Trebolle Barrera offers a different solution. He brackets as an addition the words in vv. 32–33: "to sacrifice [lĕzabbēaḥ] to the calves that he had made, and he placed in Bethel [bĕbêt-'ēl] ..."[10] Trebolle Barrera comments: "In my opinion this repetition accomplishes an editorial function, making possible the insertion of the enclosed text (of priestly or levitical origin).... Deleting such editorial links may smooth the present text, but prevents any understanding of its historical growth."[11] In this reconstruction, a redactor inserted the material and presumably read the Hebrew text of 1 Kgs 12:32 as it stands. Clearly, a redactor and later communities could read the sentence in this way, and there are commentators who accept the present form of the MT.[12]

Support for the secondary character of vv. 32–33 comes from three considerations. First, the verb *bd'* ("he had devised") in v. 33 may be late, with its only other use in Neh 6:8, and in both cases with negative connotation.[13] Second, the *waw*-consecutive form *wĕheʿĕmid* ("and he stationed") in v. 32 may seem out of place in a context of what is usually taken to be a straightforward series of past events. Although every instance of *waw*-consecutive perfects in the books of Kings need not be regarded as a secondary addition, W. Boyd Barrick makes a good case for this form as late.[14] C. F. Burney had already noted the "awkwardness" of the verbal form, and Montgomery and Gehman characterized it as "dialectical or late syntax."[15] The form here would be consistent with a late hand. Third, the compositional history of 1 Kgs 12:32–33 likewise points to late compositional activity within the verses. More specifically, as Trebolle Barrera observes, the two verses function together as a *Wiederaufnahme* or redactional bridge with 1 Kgs 13:33–34.[16] These considerations suggest that the tradition about the plural calves at Bethel in 1 Kgs 12:32 is late. It is notable that this verse shows no mention of Dan.

The question is why a late editor would add such information, given the information about a single calf at Bethel in 1 Kgs 12:29. This verse is clear about the arithmetic of calves: Bethel has one and Dan has one. In contrast, according to 1 Kgs 12:32–33 (with its threefold mention of Bethel), Bethel by itself contains multiple calves, *ʿăgālim*. Even if 1 Kgs 12:32b is late, it suggests a plural number of calves at Bethel, unless this is simply polemical, as Rainer Albertz argues.[17] Yet for a putative polemic, the presentation in 1 Kgs 12:32 is rather muted. Instead, both 12:28 and 12:32 may yet be communicating differing historical information despite their larger polemical context.

Papyrus Amherst 63, a difficult text with a long history, adds a significant witness to the issue.[18] This largely poetic work includes the liturgy of the New Year's festival of an Aramaic-speaking community in Upper Egypt, as well as a story about Assurbanipal and his brother, Shamash-shum-ukin.[19] It is thought to have been written at the beginning of the third century BCE. The original homeland of this community, called *rš* and *'rš* in the texts, has been identified by Richard C. Steiner as the land between Babylonia and Elam, called Rashu and Arashu by the Assyrians. Other Mesopotamian references in the text comport with this hypothesis. It is also evident that before proceeding to Egypt, this community had moved from Mesopotamia to the environs of Bethel, which is also mentioned in the text.[20]

Steiner emphasizes the importance of columns XI and XII for the Israelite cult at Bethel. He notes Israelite divine names (Adonay seven times and Yaho one time). Perhaps the best-known passage from this papyrus is the Israelite prayer of column XI, lines 11–19, which parallels Psalm 20. Steiner also notes features in this text that recall the cult at Bethel. Psalm 20:1–6a represents a survival of this prayer via the Jerusalemite cult, while virtually the same prayer in Papyrus Amherst 63, column XI, lines 11–17, seems to have been absorbed and recontextualized in a non-Israelite usage.[21] In his words, "this prayer is a descendent of one used in Jeroboam's temple in Bethel."[22] The features pointing in this direction for Steiner are (1) the phrase "Yaho, our bull" (XI, line 17), (2) the divine title "lord of Bethel" (XI, line 18; cf. VIII, line 13), and (3) immediately before the prayer, the expression "a city full of ivory houses" (XI, line 9, which he compares to Amos 3:14–15). In connection with the title "Yaho, our bull," Steiner also notes the expressions in column V, line 12: "let them kiss [your] bull[s], let them desire your calves." Steiner closes his observations with a comparison with 2 Chr 13:8, 10, 12. Abijah's condemnation of Jeroboam and his calf cult in this passage may echo the prayer of Jeroboam's Bethel cult.

If Steiner's reconstruction of the historical context is correct, columns XI–XII presuppose the continuity of the cult of Bethel after the fall of the northern kingdom. Second Kings 17:28, in its polemic against the north, mentions a priest settling in Bethel following the fall of the north, and Bethel is a particular object of attack by Josiah in 2 Kgs 23:4, 15–19.[23] Bethel, as well as Ai, is included among the postexilic returnees from Babylonia (Ezra 2:28//Neh 7:32), suggesting (if historically accurate) the place's continuity down through the fall of the southern kingdom, perhaps not so surprising given its proximity to Jerusalem (approximately ten and a half miles, or seventeen kilometers, north). This would also explain the special attention that this site receives in 1 Kings 13 and 2 Kings 23.

Three details for Steiner link columns XI and XII to Jeroboam's cult at Bethel. None is without controversy, and I review these in order. The first detail from the prayer is the mention of Bethel in line 18: r.byt.r^m. Although the reading of the Demotic seems to be mostly agreed upon, it is disputed whether the line involves a reference to the god of Bethel[24] or the god Bethel.[25] The god is mentioned elsewhere in the text, more clearly where it is marked by the god determinative.[26] However, it needs to be noted that the reference to Bethel here lacks the god determinative, which is used in lines 11, 12, 14, 15, 17, and 18.

The second detail involves what both S. P. Vleeming and Steiner read as *yhwt.r.n.*[m].[27] In their older edition, Charles Nims and Richard Steiner had read *yh*[g] (DN *yh* plus determinative for "god") and the final letters as *.r.n.*[m] = *'ln*, hence "YH, our god."[28] Steiner has since noted that Nims had missed the letter before *r*.[29] Vleeming read *t.r.n;* J. W. Wesselius took this to be the end of a word following *yhw* (hence *yhwtrn*) and rendered it as a hafel imperfect third masculine singular of **ytr*, plus the first common plural verbal suffix, "may he cause us to be left."[30] Steiner accepts the reading, yet rendered the word as a noun plus suffix, "our bull." His interpretation has the advantage of providing parallel structure and a relatively straightforward syntax with the rest of the line. By the same token, the reading is hardly free of difficulties, which Steiner is very clear about; he informs me that the Demotic sign for the letter *t* is also ambiguous, as it could be read also as *dalet* or *tet*.[31] Despite the help his reading would add to the overall discussion, caution is in order, and not too much weight can be placed on the information provided by the reading and the interpretation based upon it. In its defense, Steiner's approach comports with what is otherwise known of Jeroboam's cult.

The third detail relevant to the topic concerns column V, lines 12–22, in particular line 12. Professor Steiner has most kindly provided me with his transliteration of the unpublished line in question, and he has most generously granted me permission to cite it here:

> let them kiss [your] bull[s] (*y.s.k.*[m] *t.r[yk]*[m] > *yšq(w) tr[yk]*)
> let them desire your calves (*yhm.tw*[32] *'.kryk.*[m] > *yḥmdw 'glyk*)

The lines contain several pieces of important information. First, they establish the bovine as the cultic representation of the deity. Second, they express the representation in the plural and not in the singular. Third, an act of "kissing" is referenced as the body language expressive of cultic devotion. This passage is not linked explicitly to the cult of Bethel (nor is it contextually tied to columns XI–XII where the other details about the Bethel cult appear, according to Steiner). Perhaps, then, caution is in order here in linking it to claims for Bethel as the cult site where this passage is to be situated. By the same token, it should be noted that in Koenen's critiques locating other details of Bethel as the locus for columns XI–XII of Papyrus Amherst 63, he does no more than note this passage in passing in a footnote,[33] and he does not otherwise explain the concentration of references in this passage to Adonay and Yaho (if read correctly). Thus, one may remain inclined toward Steiner's thesis despite the points that remain arguable.

Within the two lines, the plural form for the second noun is unreconstructed, while the first noun's plural marker falls in the reconstruction. On the assumption that the first is correct, it provides a new witness to the plural number of male bovines at Bethel. In view of this evidence, the information in 1 Kgs 12:32 is to be taken more seriously. These witnesses should not be reduced to emendation or harmonization to singular forms, fueled by the apparently contrary evidence of 1 Kgs 12:29; Exod 32:4, 8; and Neh 9:18. Instead, if the plural referent is taken seriously, a rethinking of the cultic situation on the ground at Bethel may be required. While these two lines of Papyrus Amherst 63 add important information, they also raise further questions. For Steiner, "bulls" (*tr)[34] and "calves" (*ʿgl) in the two lines seem to stand in synonymous parallelism, as in Ps 106:19–20[35] where they serve as alternative designations for a single bovine. Elsewhere there is an apparent "generation gap" between such bovines.[36] In view of Daniel Fleming's point that these two ages of male bovines should refer to two different generations of gods,[37] there appears to be some religious development with the two presented together. To judge from the parallelism, by this point in Bethel's cult there is no expression of two gods, only a single divine warrior-king.

The cultic practice of kissing calves is not new information, as Hos 13:2 seems to attest to it. While this verse does not mention Bethel specifically, it would seem to include Bethel within the scope of its polemic. First Kings 19:18 likewise refers to the cultic practice of kissing the cultic symbol of the deity: "every knee that has not knelt to the baal/Baal and every mouth that has not kissed him/it." This verse suggests that cultic kissing belongs to a larger devotional act of obeisance. As discussed by Mayer Gruber, this complex of body language enjoys a considerable number of parallel terms in Akkadian (*šēp/šēpe DN našāqu/nuššuqu*), used for cultic devotion to the icons of deities.[38] These expressions, for Gruber, compare with Hos 13:2 and 1 Kgs 19:18.[39] First Kings 19:18 in particular seems to imagine the cultic act involved as kissing the feet.[40]

This passage involves a unique witness to bovine iconography at Bethel. The MT to this verse reads the feminine plural *'eglōt,* while the LXX witnesses to the masculine singular, *moschō.* The MT appears authentic, in part simply because it runs against the grain of what is otherwise known. By comparison, the LXX masculine singular form looks like an effort to harmonize the verse with the masculine singular form attested elsewhere (as discussed above). Note that the feminine form in Hos 10:5 contrasts with the masculine plural form in 1 Kgs 12:32. Working with the assumption that the feminine plural noun *'eglōt* in Hos 10:5 constitutes some sort of historical information, the question is what it would represent. I will return to this question after I consider a few iconographic analogues.

2. Bull and Calf Symbolism in Iconographic Analogues

We have seen that textual witnesses point to both singular and plural images at Bethel. The variation in number may hinge on the cultic setting lying behind these witnesses. Many valuable iconographic parallels have been adduced for the cult of Jeroboam.[41] These tend to focus on a single bovine representation, which does not represent the deity according to some commentators.[42] Among the many examples from outside of Israel is the striking case of the bovine represented on a relief from Alaca Höyük. In this case, the king is shown worshipping Teshub in the form of a bull.[43] Examples within Israel include a deity astride a bovine (two cases from Samaria and a third from Lachish on scaraboids)[44] and bull-calf terracottas (three from Bethel and five from Samaria).[45] Often drawn into this discussion is the bovine figurine from the so-called Bull Site[46] and the quadruped depicted in the top tier of a tenth-century cult stand from Tel Taanach.[47]

The figure of a bull or ox depicted on fragments of an engraved bronze plaque (measuring 3.5 by 3 inches, or 9 by 7.6 centimeters) discovered at Tel Dan is particularly relevant, given that it was discovered at one of the two sites favored by Jeroboam I.[48] According to the excavator, Avraham Biran, the lower section of the plaque shows the figure of a bull or ox. On the left is a figure with outstretched arms and hands. On top of the animal is a figure whose left hand is extended, Biran says "as if in blessing," while the right hand "seems to be holding a round object." Spreading wings appear to extend from the central figure, whose body seems to be "enwrapped in a rectangular frame." In view of the evident worshipper, Biran seems correct in seeing worship depicted here. In other words, this is a cultic scene. The scene is presented in side-view: the viewer stands to the left of the scene and sees it sideways. This convention does not stop the scene from including two sets of wings. However, what the rectangular frame represents may not have been as easy to render. Given the worship scene, what may be here is a throne for the deity. Broadly speaking, it is true, as Biran says, that the winged goddess is better attested than a winged god in this period; he suggested Ishtar.[49] Anat may also come to mind, given her capacity to fly, as attested in the Ugaritic texts.[50] The object held by the figure may be a mirror, which would also suggest a female figure.[51]

Christoph Uehlinger rejects Ishtar as a candidate: "this goddess never stands on a bull in 1st-millennium Assyrian, Syrian, or Urartian iconography; rather, a male deity is represented."[52] In view of the "Aramaic context at Dan," he suggests, this deity has every chance of being Hadad."[53] There is some Levantine evidence of wings for gods, for example, the Ugaritic title "Baʿlu-of-the-wing."[54] Othmar Keel and Uehlinger comment: "Youthfulness and a pair of wings were characteristics of Baal already during the late Bronze Age."[55] They note some Iron Age IIB examples of the winged god in Israel, "a youthful god with four wings," which they take to be Baal or "one of the mediating entities" that served what they call "the 'Lord of Heaven.'"[56] According to Philo of Byblos (PE 1.10.36), Kronos had "four wings" (*ptera tessara*).[57] Yahweh likewise is presented as having wings, some reflecting a sanctuary context (Pss 17:8; 36:7; 57:1; 61:4; 63:7; 91:4; cf. Ruth 2:12).[58] Jonathan Greer concludes that the winged deity motif combined with the bovine imagery "may point more toward association with a male deity, perhaps even Yahweh."[59] The deity depicted on the Dan plaque may be Yahweh with protecting wings in a sanctuary context. Finally, there is the matter of the bull. It would appear from this plaque that the cult at Dan involved one bull. Given that this plaque was discovered at one of two cult sites developed specifically by Jeroboam, it was probably related to his cult somehow. If the overall approach to the plaque and its ninth-century date as claimed by Biran are correct, it might visually reference the royal cult of Yahweh established by Jeroboam I.

There is also some evidence combining plural bovines with the singular. For example, Neo-Assyrian material attests to both the bull that carries the image of Adad (as on the stone relief from Hadatu) and "the pedestal (under) the bulls of the gateway of the temple of Adad."[60] Another analogue is provided by a second-millennium assemblage of twin bulls accompanying the storm-god described in an inscription of Sin-iddinam of Larsa. In the construction of a "throne of glory" for the storm-god, Ishkur, the king is presented as adding a "wild bull" (*rīmu*) on either side of this throne: "He set below, on the right and the left two great wild bulls butt[ing] at the enemies of the king."[61] This horn imagery in Israel perhaps informs the phrase "the horn of my help," applied to Yahweh in the military context of 2 Sam 22:3//Ps 18:2.[62] This divine attribute may lie also behind Zedekiah's symbolic act and message in 1 Kgs 22:11. Speaking before a royal court held in Samaria, Zedekiah makes iron horns and says: "Thus says Yahweh: 'With these you shall gore Aram even to their complete destruction.'" In context, the prophecy presupposes that these horns belong to "you," namely the king; by the same token, the power for this human victory derives from the prophet's divine patron and the dynasty's national god.[63] The military force of the bull-calf iconography in particular is likewise evident from the military context that Exodus 32 evokes (compare also the military setting of the formulary in 1 Sam 4:8).[64]

If one were to take the multiple grammatical forms for bovines at Bethel seriously and reconsider them in light of the forms of bovine iconography, they would suggest a complex tradition of calf iconography at Bethel. The masculine singular referent in 1 Kgs 12:28–29 (and possibly in the suffixed forms in MT Hos 10:5b–6 as well as the antecedent noun in the LXX to the same verse) points to a single icon, perhaps in a cult niche. Perhaps this form of bovine iconography at Bethel was the one housed in what Amos 7:13 calls "the king's sanctuary." The singular suffixes in Hos 10:5b–6 could also reflect such a cultic reality. This passage seems to refer to a singular dominant icon, thought to have a certain *kābôd*, not an atypical marker of divinity. If, as many commentators prefer, *'eglôt* in Hos 10:5 were to be emended to **'ēgel* or the like, then it too would be a witness to this icon. However, the emendation has little basis.

As for the masculine plural referents in 1 Kgs 12:32 and Papyrus Amherst 63, these passages might be explained by proposing a further iconography at Bethel involving an anthropomorphic figurine astride two bull-calves. Heuristically, this approach might be supported by the witnesses of the stela of Jupiter Heliopolitanus and the inscription of Sîn-iddinam of Larsa noted above. In general, while widely disparate in time and space, these data imply the setting of a temple. In short, this iconographic complex would present the god in anthropomorphic form and his two bull-calf emblems. The two differing iconographic representations might suggest a cultic renovation or rearrangement at some point at Bethel that somehow included the bull-calf as a cultic symbol as well as an elaborate throne consisting of one or two bovines.[65] It might imply a response in the northern cult to the double-cherub throne of Yahweh in the Jerusalem temple. Both the double cherubim and the single cherub were traditional in the south, as suggested by the single cherub in 2 Sam 22:11//Ps 18:10 as opposed to the double cherubim in 1 Kgs 6:23–28; 8:6–7. Given the relatively late witness to the plurality of calves, the time of Jeroboam II might be the period best suited in terms of northern prosperity. Indeed, the name of Jeroboam II evoked that of the north's "founder" by the same name, and the state of the royal cult during the time of Jeroboam II may have followed suit.

Although the extant evidence for the plural representation at Bethel postdates the single calf of Jeroboam I, both may have been traditional forms for presenting the emblem-animal of the patron warrior-god. The calves are not simply a pedestal; they are part of the representation associated with the deity, called "gods" (ʾĕlōhîm) in 1 Kgs 12:28. Under this form of collective plurality, this may be the ʾĕlōhîm thought to bring the Israelites from the land of Egypt. This proclamation may be located within the ritual context that celebrated the divine victory over Egypt. The military terms suggest ritual played out in a religious context that celebrates this victory (perhaps in anticipation of future victory; see Ps 20 in the discussion above). Accordingly, Jeroboam I's cult arguably entailed a temple ritual celebrating military victory and homage paid to the divine victor in the act of kissing the bovine icon.

Finally, there is the matter of the feminine plural referent in Hos 10:5. Working with the assumption that this form represents some sort of historical information, the question is what the feminine plural form of ʿeglôt would refer to. One might rule out a reference here to either form of the iconographic complex discussed above for the masculine forms. Instead, some other sort of plural form of bovine icon may be entertained for this feminine form, ʿeglôt. As one possibility, they may refer to votives in the form of the icon purchased by pilgrims. As an alternative, it is tempting to think in terms of masks. The notion of a bull emblem is known in PE 1.10.31: "Astarte placed upon her own head a bull's head as an emblem of kingship" (hē de Astartē epethēken tē idia kephalē basileias parasēmon kephalēn taurou).[66] Elizabeth Bloch-Smith has connected this passage with the practice of cultic masks used in conjunction with offerings at Kition:

On the Kition temple floor near the offering table lay 15 skulls of young bulls and a cow, cleaned from the back for use as masks, as described by Lucian. Similar cleaned masks come from Cypriot Enkomi's 12th c. temple of the "Horned God" near the altar and the 11th c. temple of the "Ingot God.". . . The practice is attested by 7–6th c. (Archaic period) terracotta models of humans donning bull masks from the Cypriot coastal sites of Kourion and Aya Irini. According to the ancient sources, both supplicants (Lucian) and individuals representing regnant Astarte (Philo of Byblos) wore animal masks.[67]

Phoenician, Israelite, and Judean masks are also attested.[68] Might some ritual involving masks lie behind the use of 'eglôt? As a third alternative, there are bovine figurines in the form of "wild bull" (rīmu) intended for the goddesses Ishtar and Ishara.[69] So might the 'eglôt be votives for a goddess associated with the bovine head? Unfortunately, we have more questions than answers for MT Hos 10:5.

In closing, the masculine singular bull-calf, the masculine plural bovines, and the feminine plural bovines evoke a multifaceted cultic reality that combined the anthropomorphic with the theriomorphic. Both the anthropomorphic form and the emblem-animal(s) may have been the gods who, for Jeroboam's cult, brought up Israel from the land of Egypt. Such royal sites as Dan and Bethel point to cities as bearers of divine identity, the subject of the next two chapters.

PART 3

Gods of Cities, Cities of Gods

5 Gods and Their City Sites

1. The Grammar of Divine Manifestation

For more than a century, scholars of West Semitic religion have understood major deities as having manifestations at different earthly locations. On the afternoon of 10 December 1891, in one of his Burnett lectures delivered at Aberdeen University, William Robertson Smith expressed this view: "I think we can see that when the same god came to be worshipped simultaneously at many sanctuaries and was held to be present at them all, a distinct step was taken towards a larger conception of the divine nature than that which is involved in the worship of the Baal of a single sanctuary."[1] This approach coexisted in Robertson Smith's work with the view of deities as originally local or tribal, a view that was quite prominent in the nineteenth century. John Day, the editor of Robertson Smith's lectures, noted this tendency in his work: "Robertson Smith's emphasis on the local character of the deity has tended to recede since the discovery of the Ugaritic texts, which reveal West Semitic gods such as El and Baal to have been universal deities of cosmic power. But it seems to me that there was a local aspect to them that has been overshadowed in more recent scholarship."[2] This model of major deities manifest in different local cult sites has been a significant idea for many scholars.[3]

In the 1980s, this scholarly understanding received a decidedly grammatical grounding. John A. Emerton comments on divine names: "their appearance in the construct state may indicate a particular manifestation of a deity in distinction from other manifestations of the same deity."[4] Following the classification of divine name (DN) plus geographical name (GN) proposed by Michael L. Barré,[5] P. Kyle McCarter discussed several examples.[6] McCarter understands DN in immediate syntactical relation to GN as "local forms or manifestations of the national god."[7] He adds: this "type [of name is] well attested in non-Israelite divine names. These names take the form DN of GN, where DN is the name of the national god or another major deity and GN is the name of the locality where DN was worshipped. The resulting combination, a construct chain meaning 'DN of GN,' identifies a local manifestation of the deity, that is, DN as worshipped in GN."[8] McCarter also includes DN "in" (*b*-) GN[9] and DN "dwelling in" (*yšb b-*//*škn b-*) GN,[10] as well as some examples of *b'l* ("lord") + GN.[11] Thus four grammatical constructions involving DN + GN were identified.

This topic has been taken up more recently. Benjamin D. Sommer has addressed the implications of deities in various locations.[12] Jeremy Hutton has focused on "Yahweh of Teman" (*yhwh t[y]mn*) and "Yahweh of Samaria" (*yhwh šmrn*) as competing manifestations of Yahweh at Kuntillet 'Ajrud.[13] Spencer L. Allen has asked whether or not a given DN at different locales is to be regarded as the same deity or multiple deities; for Allen, the different Ishtars and Baals are different deities, while the different Yahwehs are not.[14] Finally, Martin Leuenberger has suggested that a basic component of the Jerusalem temple theology was the divine presence in a city, reflected in the title "the god of Jerusalem."[15] In other words, a fundamental relationship between temple and city would inform DNs + GNs.

Before I discuss these views, the following list provides examples for the four grammatical constructions involving DN + GN mostly from the West Semitic record, as noted in the work of Barré, McCarter, and Allen.[16] To the first category are added some examples of a related construction, DN *ḏ*- GN; under the different categories some similar expressions are compared. Although some Mesopotamian instances are mentioned below, these cases,[17] as well as Hittite and Luwian instances, generally lie beyond the scope of this discussion.[18] Finally, the following list is not comprehensive; instead, it is intended to be representative.

I.   Divine Name of Geographical Name (DN of GN)
a.   *Hebrew*
   • *yhwh tmn/tymn* (the Kuntillet 'Ajrud inscriptions, Pithos B; and plaster inscription),[19] "Yahweh of Teman"; cf. *yhwh htmn* (the Kuntillet 'Ajrud inscriptions, pithos inscription),[20] "Yahweh of the Teman"
   • *yhwh šmrn* (the Kuntillet 'Ajrud inscriptions, Pithos A),[21] "Yahweh of Samaria"

Cf. *'ašmat šōmĕrôn* (Amos 8:14), "guilt of Samaria," as polemical word-play for **ašrat šōmĕrôn*, "Asherah of Samaria"?[22]

Cf. *'ĕlāh yĕrûšĕlem* (Ezra 7:19), "God of Jerusalem"

Cf. *'ĕlōhê yĕrûšāla(y)im* (2 Chr 32:19; Khirbet el-Qom inscription),[23] "the god of Jerusalem"

b. *Ugaritic*

- *'aṯrt ṣrm* (*KTU* 1.14 IV 35, 38), "Athirat of Tyre"[24]
- *b'l ṣpn* (*KTU* 1.105.5, 1.148.27, etc.; see below), "Baal of Ṣapan"[25]
- *b'l 'ugrt* (*KTU* 1.105.2, 1.148.27//RS 92.2004.7, ᵈX ḪUR.SAG *ḫa-zi*, etc.; see below), "Baal of Ugarit"
- *b'l ḫlb* (*KTU* 1.109.16, 1.130.11, 1.134.7, 1.148.26//RS 92.2004.6, ᵈX *ḫal-bi*; 4.728.1–2), "Baal of Aleppo" (?)[26]
- *mlk 'ṯtrt* (*KTU* 4.790.17), "Mlk of 'ṯtrt"[27]
- *'nt ṣpn* (*KTU* 1.46.17; 1.109.13–14, 17, 36; 1.130.13), "Anat of Ṣapan"
- *'ṯtrt ḫr* (*KTU* 1.43.1,[28] 1.112.13), "'Athtart of Hurri"[29]
- *ršp bbt* (*KTU* 1.105.25, 1.175.3), "Resheph of Bbt"[30]
- *ršp gn* (*KTU* 1.165.3, 4.219.3), "Resheph of Gn"[31]

c. *Akkadian*[32]

Hana

- ᵈ*dagan ša ḫurri*,[33] "Dagan of Hurri"

Mari

- *dagan ša mari* (Mari letters),[34] "Dagan of Mari"
- *dagan ša terqa* (Mari letters),[35] "Dagan of Terqa"
- *dagan ša tutt[ul]* (Mari letters),[36] "Dagan of Tutt[ul]"
- *dagan ša subatim* (Mari letters),[37] "Dagan of Subatim"
- *dagan ša uraḫ* (Mari letters),[38] "Dagan of Urah"

Emar

- ᵈIM *ša ki-na-i* (Emar 446.107–8),[39] "Storm-god of Canaan"

Ugarit

- ᵈU ᵈḪUR.SAG *ḫa-zi* (RS 26.142.19),[40] "Storm-god (Baal) of Mount Hazi"
- ⁱˡ*ištar ḫur-ri* (RS 16.273.9;[41] RS 18.01.3, 6),[42] "Ishtar of Hurri (?)"

Ashur

- ᵈ*ištar ša* ᵘʳᵘ*Ninua* (Vassal Treaties of Esarhaddon, column i, lines 20, 30),[43] "Ishtar of Nineveh" (NA)

- ^d*ištar ša* ^{uru}*Arbela* (Vassal Treaties of Esarhaddon, column i, lines 20, 30),[44] "Ishtar of Arbela" (NA)

Cf. *bēlet ša* ^{uru}*gubla*, "lady of Byblos" (EA 68:4, 73:4, 74:2–3, 75:3, 76:3–4, 77:8–9, 78:3, 79:3–4, 85:4, etc.)

d. *Aramaic*
- *hdd skn* (Tell Fekheriyah),[45] "Hadad of Sikan"[46]

e. *Phoenician/Punic*
- *'štrt ḥr*,[47] "'Ashtart of Hurri" (?)
- *'štrt kt* (*KAI* 37 A.5),[48] "'Ashtart of Kition"
- *'štrt pp* (*RES* 921.3–4),[49] "'Ashtart of Paphos"[50]
- *'štrt 'rk* (*CIS* I 135.1, 140.1),[51] "'Ashtart of Eryx"
- *'štrny* (*CIS* 5975),[52] "'Ashtart of Nineveh" (?)

Cf. DN **ḏ-* GN[53]

f. *Biblical Hebrew*
- *yhwh zû sînay* (Judg 5:5), "Yahweh, the One of Sinai"
- *'ĕlōhîm zû sînay* (Ps 68:8), "God, the One of Sinai" (cf. v. 18)[54]

g. *Epigraphic South Arabian*
- *'ttr ḏdbn* (Sabaean inscriptions from Maḥram Bilqîs [Mârib]),[55] #559.16, #561.15–16, #564.27, etc.), "'Athtar Him of Ḏabân" (a sanctuary)[56]

2. DN *b*-GN or DN GN-*h* (with the preposition *b*-,[57] or the locative suffix *-h*)

a. *Hebrew*
- *yhwh bĕṣiyyôn* (Ps 99:2), "(great is) Yahweh-in-Zion" (cf. Lam 2:6; Ps 132:13; see also Jer 8:19)
- *'ĕlōhîm bĕṣiyyôn* (Pss 65:1; 84:7), "God-in-Zion"
- *yhwh bĕḥebrôn* (2 Sam 15:7), "Yahweh-in-Hebron"
- *dāgôn bĕ'ašdôd* (1 Sam 5:5), "Dagon-in-Ashdod"

b. *Ugaritic*
- *mlk b'ttrt* (*KTU* 1.107.42), "Mlk in 'ttrt"
- *dgn ttlh* (*KTU* 1.100.15), "Dagan at Tuttul"
- *'nt w 'ttrt 'inbbh* (*KTU* 1.100.20), "'Anat and 'Athtart at Inbb"
- *yrḫ lrgth* (*KTU* 1.100.26), "Yariḫ at Lrgt"
- *ršp bbth* (*KTU* 1.100.31), "Rashpu at Bbt"
- *ẓẓ wkmt ḥryth* (*KTU* 1.100.36), "Ẓẓ w-Kmth at Ḥry"

- *mlk 'ttrth* (*KTU* 1.100.41), "Mlk at 'ttrt"
- *ktr wḫss kptrh* (*KTU* 1.100.46), "Kothar wa-Hasis at Kaphtor"
- *'ttrt mrh* (*KTU* 1.100.78),[58] "'Athtart at Mari"

c. *Ebla*
- ᵈ*adam-tum in 'à-da-ni-du*ᵏⁱ,[59] "Adamtum at Adanidu"

d. *Phoenician/Punic*
- *lrbt l'štrt wltnt blbnn* (*KAI* 81.1), "to the Ladies, to 'Ashtart and to Tannit in Lebanon"[60]
- *štrt blpš* (Lapethos 6),[61] "'Ashtart in Lapethos"
- *štrt bgw* (*KAI* 17.2),[62] "'Ashtart in Gw"
- *b'l ḥmn b'ltbrš* (Hr. Medeine N 1, line 1),[63] "Baal Ḥmn in Althiburus"

e. *Ammonite*
- *št<rt> bṣdn* (Ammonite seal),[64] "'Ashta<rt> in Sidon"

f. *Moabite*
- *kmš bqrḥh* (*KAI* 181.3),[65] "Kemosh in Qarho"
- *kmš bqryt* (*KAI* 181.13),[66] "Kemosh in Qiriot"

3. DN *yšb*/*škn* (participle) (sometimes with *b-*) GN

a. *Hebrew*
- *yhwh yōšēb ṣiyyôn* (Ps 9:11), "Yahweh dwelling/enthroned of Zion" (cf. Ps 2:4)
- *yhwh šōkēn bĕṣiyyôn* (Joel 4:21; see also Pss 123:1; 135:21; Isa 8:18; Joel 4:17, 21), "Yahweh settled in Zion"[67]
- *šōkĕnî sĕneh* (Deut 33:16), "Settler of Sinai" (?)[68]

b. *Ugaritic*
- *rp'u mlk 'lm* . . . *'il ytb b'ttrt* (*KTU* 1.108.1–2), "Rapiu Eternal Mlk . . . the god dwells/is enthroned in 'ttrt"[69]

c. *Aramaic*
- *hdd yšb skn* (Tell Fekheriyeh),[70] "Hadad dwelling of Sikkan"
- *yhw 'lh' škn yb* (Elephantine),[71] "Yahu the god settled of Yeb" (cf. Ezra 7:15, "the God of Israel whose dwelling is in Jerusalem")

d. *Akkadian*
- DN *a-šib-ti* ᵘʳᵘIšin,[72] "Gula, who resides in Isin" (MB)
- "May Mullissu, who resides in Nineveh [*a-ši-bat* ᵘʳᵘNINA.KI], tie a flaming sword at your side . . . [May] Ishtar, who dwells in Arbela

[*a-ši-bat* ᵘʳᵘ*arba-ìl*], [no]t show you mercy and compassion" (Succession Treaty of Esarhaddon, column vi, 457–60; NA)[73]

- "May Mullissu, who resides in Nineveh, tie a flaming sword at your side" (NA)[74]
- "Ishtar, who dwells in Arbela [*a-ši-bat arbail*], delivered . . ." (NA)[75]
- "Adad dwelling at Sikan" (NA)[76]

4. DN *b'l/b'lt* in construct to GN ("lord/lady of GN")[77]

a. *Ugaritic*
- *b'l ḫkpt* (*KTU* 1.17 V 20, 30), "lord of Memphis" (referring to Kothar)

b. *Akkadian*[78]
- *addi bēl kallassu* (Mari letter of Nur-Sin to Zimri-Lim),[79] "Adad, lord of Kallassu" (OB)
- *addi bēl ḫalab* (Mari letter of Nur-Sin to Zimri-Lim),[80] "Adad, lord of Aleppo" (OB)
- ᵈIM *bēl* ḪUR.SAG *ḫazi* (RS 20.24),[81] "Storm-god, lord of Mount Hazi" (Baal; MB)
- ᵈ*iškur* EN *i-mar* (Emar 373.132, 378.25),[82] "Storm-god, lord of Emar"
- *bēlet arbail*,[83] "Lady of Arbela" (Ishtar; NA)
- ᵈ*ištar bēlet* ᵘʳᵘ*Ninua*,[84] "Ishtar, lady of Nineveh" (NA)

Cf. "queen (*šarrat*) of Ekron"[85] (Succession Treaty of Esarhaddon from Tell Tayinat, column vi, line 47; Ptgyh [?];[86] NA)

c. *Phoenician/Punic*[87]
- *mlqrt b'l ṣr* (*KAI* 47.1), "Melqart, lord of Tyre"
- *b'l kty* (Kition D 37), "baal/Baal of Kition"
- *b'lt ṣr* (*KAI* 5.2), "lady of Tyre"
- *b'lt gbl* (*KAI* 7.3–4, 5; 10.2, 3, 3–4, 7, 8 [two times], 10, 15), "lady of Byblos"

d. *Epigraphic South Arabian*
- *b'l bn'* (CIH 427/2, etc.),[88] "lord of Bana'" (title of Athtar)
- *'ttr wnsrm b'ly bn'* (Ryckmans 196/2),[89] "Athtar and Nasr, lords of Bana'"
- *b'lt bry* (CIH 294/2),[90] "lady of Bary" (title of *šms*)

Each of these four types of DN + GN applies also to humans. The first, DN of GN,[91] is analogous to PN of GN used for people (*KTU* 4.147.12;

4.352.4; 4.384.1).[92] These semantics locating a person of a place compare also with "David of Hebron" (2 Sam 4:8). This may not be a title but shows the association of this king in a specific locale.[93] In the second type, DN in GN, the deity's location is known to be in or at places; it is likewise used for people in Ugaritic lists (e.g., PN b-GN,[94] in *KTU* 4.124.2; 4.244.12, 13, 23, 24; 4.379.7, 8; 4.408.4; 4.643.11–19, 25–26; 4.748.11).[95] The association of a person in a place is made for the royal figures "David in Hebron" (2 Sam 3:22) and "Absalom in Hebron" (2 Sam 15:10).[96] While these also need not be titles as such, they likewise illustrate the association of these royal figures with particular places.

The third type, DN *ytb* b-GN,[97] may denote residence for deities, as seen in related expressions: "the mountain that God desired for his dwelling (*yšb*)"//"indeed, (where) Yahweh resides (*škn*) forever" (Ps 68:16); and "Jerusalem your established dwelling-place (*yšb*)" (Ben Sira 36:18).[98] It applies as well to people (PN son of PN, *d ytb* b-GN, in *KTU* 4.382.23–34; Gen 4:16; 13:12, 18; 14:7, 12, etc.)[99] and to the enthronement of kings (e.g., Josh 12:2; 2 Sam 11:1; 1 Kgs 15:18).[100] The verb-preposition combination *škn* b- is likewise used for dwelling in a place (e.g., Gen 14:13; 26:2; 35:22; Judg 5:17; Jer 25:24; 48:28; 49:16//Obad 3; Mic 4:10; cf. Gen 9:27; Judg 8:11; Isa 34:11, 17). The fourth type using "lord" (*b'l*) or "lady" (*b'lt*) denotes land ownership or dominion over a place. The usage denotes property ownership in several corpora: "the lords of the city" (EA 102:22 and 138:49),[101] "the lords of Shechem" (Judg 9:2, 3, 6, 18, 20, 23, 24, 26, 39, 46, 47, 51),[102] and "lords (citizens, inhabitants) of Yb" in the Elephantine papyri.[103] This usage also appears in Ugaritic, in *KTU* 4.360.2, 5, 7, and 11.[104] *B'l/b'lt* serves as a royal title as well. For example, *KTU* 2.81.3 mentions "the lord of all of the land of Egypt," and the considerable titulary of King Niqmaddu of Ugarit includes *b'l trmn*.[105] The texts EA 19:19, 26:1, and 28:7 refer to Teje as "the lady of Egypt."[106]

The relationship of a deity to the same place may be designated by more than one of these four categories. Yahweh in Hebrew texts, *Mlk* in the Ugaritic corpus, and Ishtar in Akkadian sources are all related to the same locale by different geographical constructions. As seen above, the parallel Aramaic and Akkadian texts in the Tell Fekheriyeh bilingual inscription employ different formulations for the storm-god in the same locale. Finally, a single text may deploy multiple idioms for the deity's location. For example, Psalm 84 uses DN in GN in v. 7, while it refers in v. 1 to the same place as "your dwelling."[107]

2. "Fragmentations" of Divinity, Multiple Deities, Focalizations of Divinity, or Expressions of Divine Power?

McCarter offers an important observation about divine manifestations: "at the time of the Israelite monarchy, therefore, the various local manifestations of Yahweh were often quite distinct in the manner of their conceptualization and worship. . . . There was a tendency . . . for the local Yahwehs to become semi-independent, almost as if they were distinct deities."[108] At the same time, he regards these as "local forms" of the deity.[109] McCarter seems to take a "both-and" approach to DNs + GNs: it is "as if" they are distinct deities, yet they are also forms of the same deity. Herbert B. Huffmon remarks somewhat similarly: "we frequently find aspects or epithets of particular deities becoming separate entities with separate cults, as also happens in the case of deities who become differentiated by reference to different localities or cult centres (e.g., Baal-zaphon and Ishtar of Nineveh as separate deities)."[110]

With respect to Ishtar, Tzvi Abusch comments: "a number of possibly separate goddesses appear under the name of Ishtar of a particular place (e.g., Ishtar of Nineveh)."[111] Following in this vein, Spencer L. Allen claims that attestations of Baal and Ishtar with different geographical names constitute different deities, while the manifestations of Yahweh do not.[112] Finally, Benjamin D. Sommer views references to deities in different locations as various "avatars," which he also describes in terms of "fluidity" and "fragmentation."[113] Sommer claims that West Semitic sources represent the same deity as being in multiple places at the same time.[114] He further suggests that a deity has a body in heaven while the same deity is manifest on earth.[115]

It is true, as Sommer would suggest, that a deity in a text such as Psalm 20 could be operative on both heavenly and earthly levels,[116] but this does not mean that the same deity was thought of as having two different bodies as such. In fact, no text shows the deity with two different bodies. Instead, in several biblical passages, the same god shows the same body coming down from heaven and being manifest. For example, "he [Yahweh] bent [literally, extended] heaven and descended, thick cloud beneath his feet" (Ps 18:9//2 Sam 22:10). Similarly, in the Ugaritic Baal Cycle, Baal of Sapan (conventionally called Baal Sapan) is in his heavenly palace and this same Baal appears on earth.[117] The text does not seem to represent these heavenly and earthly manifestations of Baal Sapan as multiple bodies. Sommer does acknowledge divine locomotion,[118] but he suggests that divine descent is an "avatar" of Yahweh.[119] Although it is true that an audience and author would understand that God in various passages is hardly limited to this one representation, no single text describes two divine bodies or the same deity in two locations simultaneously.[120] In other words, no single biblical or Ugaritic text represents a deity's bodily "fragmentation" in the form of two or more divine bodies.

If the Hebrew Bible does not provide a clear representation of what Sommer calls "fragmentation," how would an ancient Near Eastern text represent it? Unlike the biblical or Ugaritic material, texts elsewhere in the ancient Near East do show explicit recognition of a single deity manifest in multiple forms at the same time. Let us look at a number of possible examples. First, texts about Ishtar offer some cases for our consideration. A hymn of Assurbanipal to the Ishtars of Nineveh and of Arbela, named as "the Lady of Nineveh" and "the Lady of Arbela," refers to them as "my goddesses."[121] This usage might be used to support Sommer's notion of "fragmentation," while for Allen it serves as evidence for his view that for the producers of such texts, various manifestations with the name of the same deity could be regarded as different deities. At the same time, it is to be observed that in a letter to the same king, Mullissu and "the Lady of Arbela" are referenced in the plural in lines 3–7, but then the letter shifts to the singular.[122] Martti Nissinen comments: "The goddesses, referred to in plural thus far, now merge together and speak as one divine person."[123] Thus one text seems to show the same goddess name plus GNs as multiple goddesses, and the other appears to reference the two Ishtars as one deity. The question is whether or not there is sufficient evidence with Ishtar for "fragmentation" (in Sommer's terms) or multiplicity or "splintering" of deities (as Allen claims).

Second, a Hittite ritual in a prayer addressed to the goddess Ishtar evokes her various manifestations not only in the cult centers of Hatti and in cities of Syria, but also at Nineveh (named at the very top of the list) and at Assur. The mention of the goddess at many different sites in this text offers a case study for "fragmentation" (as Sommer calls it):

§4 [. . .] He says as follows " . . . O Ishtar [. . .] I will keep [. . .]ing and for you . . . [If you are in Nineveh] then come from Niniveh. (But?) if you are [in] R[imushi, then come from Rimushi]. If you are in Dunta, then come from Du[nta]. §5 (O Ishtar, [if you are] in [Mittanni], then come from Mittanni. [If you are in . . . , then come from . . . If you are in Dunippa then [come from] Duni[ppa, if you are in Ugarit] then com[e] from Ugarit . . . §6 If (you are) in the rivers and streams [then come from there]. If for the cowherd and shepherds [you . . .] and (you are) among them, then come away. If (you are) among [the . . .], if you are with the Sun Goddess of the Earth and the Primor[dial Gods], then come from those. §7 Come away from these countries. For the king, the queen (and) the princes bring life, health, streng[th], longevity, contentment (?), obedience (and) vigor, (and) to the land of Hatti growth of crops (lit., grain), vines, cattle, sheep (and) humans.[124]

At first glance, Ishtar's potential manifestations in different places might reflect an indigenous notion of "fragmentation" in Sommer's terms.[125] The passage expresses the goddess's geographical extent, which serves to magnify her power.[126] It is notable that she is not represented as being at these different places all at the same time; on the contrary. So it may be concluded that in this case she is not represented as explicitly "fragmented."

Third, more explicit evidence for "fragmentation" can be found in two ritual texts from Kizzuwatna involving "the Deity of the Night":

Thus (says) My Sun, Mursili, Great King, son of Suppiluliuma, Great King, Hero: When my forefather, Tuthaliya, Great King, split the Deity of the Night from the temple of the Deity of the Night in Kizzuwatna and worshipped her separately in a temple in Samuha.[127]

. . . he speaks thus before the deity: "Honoured deity! Preserve your being, but divide your divinity! Come to that new house, too, and take yourself the honoured place! And when you make your way, then take yourself only to that place!"[128]

Here the divinity of this god is viewed as potentially divisible in order to establish divine presence for a "new house," that is, a new sanctuary for the deity. The rituals implicitly recognize the power of the deity in a prior-standing sanctuary place, and the power of the deity is extended to a new sanctuary site. The evidence seems to point to "fragmentation" (in Sommer's terms), but not to multiple gods (so Allen).

In the West Semitic evidence, no such representation of "fragmentation" is attested. Instead, a biblical text such as the hymn of Psalm 29 suggests continuity between the heavenly deity and his terrestrial manifestation. When the deity is manifest in an earthly locality, such a representation offers a terrestrial focalization on the deity. As for Allen's claims of multiple deities for Ishtar, perhaps this multiplicity is at least in part a matter of the rhetoric reflecting the perceived importance of the extension of the Neo-Assyrian empire itself. This, to be sure, does not "explain away" Ashurbanipal's expression of "goddesses" for "the Lady of Nineveh" and "the Lady of Arbela," but it may suggest a political context for what may be a relatively exceptional expression. By contrast, an analogous political context is not operative in the West Semitic milieu. In the case of Baal of Sapan and Baal of Ugarit, these would not appear to have been recognized as different gods as Allen suggests. Instead, Baal of Ugarit is seen as related to Baal Sapan, as I now document in detail.

3. Baal of Sapan and Baal of Ugarit at Ugarit

In the traditional model, DNs + GNs represent different manifestations of the same deity. However, there is considerably more to the story of Baal of Sapan and Baal of Ugarit. Sommer rightly notes: "Baal of the city Ugarit is Baal of the heavenly mountain Ṣaphon, but Baal of Ṣaphon is much more than Baal of Ugarit."[129] This statement is strongly supported by the evidence that I now examine by genre.

Ritual Texts: The "Ritual Baal Sapan"

While the Ugaritic ritual texts show a significant place for Baal of Ugarit, Baal of Sapan, as well as Mount Sapan, often represents a more important presence,[130] even in those rituals conducted in the temple of Baal of Ugarit. I begin with *KTU* 1.41 and 1.87, two versions of a fall ritual text, beginning with a cutting of grapes for the first day of the month, followed by a longer series of rituals running from the thirteenth day of the month through the twenty-first.[131] The primary rituals are a series of offerings, including two sequences of offerings for Baal of Sapan, Mount Sapan itself, and then Baal of Ugarit (lines 33–35 and 41–42). The two sequences suggest the importance of Baal Sapan relative to Baal of Ugarit, in terms of both their order and the mention of Sapan itself as a recipient of offering.[132] The second of these two sequences is preceded by an instruction (line 41) whose meaning is unclear.[133] Whichever the correct understanding of the verb in 1.41.41 is (the verb is missing in the corresponding line in 1.87.44), Baal's altar is the site where the sequence of offerings is made for Baal of Sapan, Sapan, and Baal of Ugarit. Baal in this text does not appear as the overarching category of divinity for Baal of Sapan and Baal of Ugarit.[134]

KTU 1.105 details offerings made "in the temple of Baal of Ugarit" (line 6'). Offerings are made some days later to Baal (line 17').[135] Five days later offerings are made "in the sacrificial pit of Sapan" (line 21'). These offerings are made to a number of deities, including Baal (line 24') and Sapan itself (line 24'). What is remarkable here is not only the offering made to Sapan as a divinely recognized entity, but also that Sapan has its own cultic site, perhaps in the temple of Baal of Ugarit. Where in the temple this is located exactly is unclear, but Dennis Pardee has noted the text's earlier reference to the temple of Baal of Ugarit.[136] Thus this pit seems not to be at Sapan, but appears to lie within the vicinity or environs of the temple of Baal of Ugarit.[137] If so, the cultic reality of Sapan itself and not simply the Baal of Sapan is identified within the local temple of Baal of Ugarit.

KTU 1.109 details a series of offerings in a month.[138] It includes "a feast of Baal of Sapan" (line 5), if correctly reconstructed. The offerings for the feast include Baal of Sapan (line 9) and Sapan itself (line 10). The ritual names "the temple of Baal of Ugarit" (line 11), with offerings made to Baal (line 13), Anat of Sapan (lines 13–14), Baal of Ugarit and Baal of Aleppo (line 16) and Anat of Sapan (line 17), and then again to Baal (twice, in lines 20 and 22) and Anat (line 22) as well as other deities. Further offerings are to be made to Baal of Sapan (lines 32–33), Sapan (line 34), Baal of Ugarit (twice, lines 34, 35–36), and Anat of Sapan (line 36). It would appear that the overall rubric of these offerings is Baal of Sapan. Sapan is further conspicuous not only for the offerings made to the mountain, but also for its use to designate Anat in this context. Baal of Ugarit is hardly lacking, occurring three times; still the referencing of Baal in terms of Ugarit is secondary, relative to the eight references to Sapan alone and in combination with Baal and Anat. As in the preceding text, Baal is largely named in terms of various places, which in this text include Aleppo. The site of offering is evidently the temple of Baal of Ugarit. In short, while Baal of Ugarit has a cultic reality in his temple in Ugarit, in this ritual text Mount Sapan and the deities, both Baal and Anat, named by Sapan, have a more dominant cultic reality in this temple.[139]

KTU 1.112 details a series of royal rituals that include offerings to Baal of Sapan (lines 22–23), followed by Baal of Ugarit (line 23). It is unclear how much importance is to be attached in this case to the order of Baal of Sapan before Baal of Ugarit. It may be that this text is expressive, though in a more muted manner, of the importance of Baal of Sapan relative to Baal of Ugarit. The coupling of the two together is notable.

KTU 1.119[140] begins with a series of rituals in the temple of Baal of Ugarit (lines 3, 9–10). The offerings made include a cow for "the Baal-deities" (line 6), a bull for the mdgt[141] of Baal of Ugarit (line 12), a neck for Baal (line 15), and then later a ram for Baal of Ugarit in the temple (lines 21'–22'). The text then gives instructions about the prayer to be given to Baal along with the offerings vowed if Baal will drive the enemy from "our gate . . . our walls" (lines 26'–35'). In this case, Baal of Ugarit is the only Baal in view. Note that in this text this Baal is responsible for the city's defense.

KTU 1.130[142] lists ritual offerings, including one to Baal of Sapan (lines 2 [?], 7), then two sets of offerings to Baal of Sapan and to Sapan (lines 7–8, 9–10). Baal is later mentioned in line 16 as a recipient, as is Baal of Ugarit (line 23) and Baal of Aleppo (line 24) and later Anat of Sapan (line 26). Sapan is clearly central in this ritual.

In all these ritual texts, Baal of Sapan occurs more often than Baal of Ugarit. Only KTU 1.119 is devoted specifically to Baal of Ugarit, and this may stem from the text's express concern for the city's safety from enemies. Where Baal of Sapan and Baal of Ugarit occur together, Baal of Sapan is typically listed first.[143] On the whole, the cultic reality of Sapan is recognized strongly within the Ugaritic ritual texts, even within the temple of Baal of Ugarit. In a sense, Baal of Sapan lends cultic power to Baal of Ugarit. It is the mountain outside the city that empowers the city itself. The ritual perception of the city and its patron god derives from the mountain outside the city and less from the city.

This perception was shared not only by the city's elite, but also by an elite Egyptian. A stela found in the temple of Baal in Ugarit depicts a figure standing with upraised hands before the god, and its inscription reads: "To Seth of Sapuna in favor of the royal scribe and keeper of the house of silver, Mami (or Maimi)."[144] In this case, a foreigner recognized the ritual reality of Baal of Sapan within the temple of Baal of Ugarit. Finally, the Akkadian texts from Ugarit refer to Baal as the "lord of Mount Hazi."[145] One legal text offers a rare glimpse into the social reality of the temple of Baal on Sapan: "the temple of Ba'al of Mount [Ḥazi] and [its pri]ests (?) shall not have claims against Kar-Kusuḥ."[146]

Deity Lists: The "Scribal Baal Sapan"

Dennis Pardee presents a deity list in three examplars consisting of two Ugaritic texts, *KTU* 1.47 and 1.118, plus an Akkadian text, RS 20.24, along with the listing of deities reflected in a ritual text, *KTU* 1.148.1–9.[147] As noted by Pardee,[148] the list begins alternatively with "the gods of Sapan" (*KTU* 1.47.1) and "the offerings of Sapan" (1.148.1); the other two texts lack the heading. Sapan is the way that this listing is marked in its heading.

The lists then give the following order of deities: Ilib, El, Dagan, and Baal of Sapan, followed by *b'lm*/^dIM (six times). Sapan itself appears later, as does *'il t'dr b'l*. Particularly difficult is the series of *b'lm* in the Ugaritic listings. It is parallel in the Akkadian list with ^dIM with numbers following (lines 5–10). In this listing, Baal of Ugarit never appears, nor does a generic Baal (without any further specification). In commenting on the figure of Baal here, Gregorio del Olmo Lete assumes that this Baal is "the great protector god of Ugarit (*b'l ugrt*). . . . His personality is defined by the attribute *spn*, with which are identified all the other possible epithets of circumstance and place, his epiphanies, mentioned in the texts (*b'l ugrt, ḫlb . . .*)."[149] In this formulation, del Olmo Lete is expressing the classic theory of the god's manifestations at different locales. However correct this formulation may be, it does not note sufficiently that Baal of Ugarit as such is absent from this text. In other words, Baal Sapan—not Baal of Ugarit and not even Baal in general (without GN)—is the rubric used by the scribal tradition of this text to represent Baal.[150] Whatever Baal may mean in this context, it is subsumed under Baal of Sapan. As Pardee notes, this text's headings suggest "the function of Mount Sapun in the cultural and geographical ideology of the Ugaritians."[151] Indeed, it is notable that all the gods are characterized in this setting in terms of Sapan.

Another deity listing occurs in two exemplars, one in Akkadian (RS 92.2004) and one in the second part of a Ugaritic ritual text (1.148.23–44).[152] Following *'il'ib*, "Earth and Heaven," El, and the Kotharat, the text lists *b'l ḫlb*[153] and then Baal of Sapan. The text lists Sapan itself and *b'lm* four times toward the end of the list. Again, Baal of Ugarit is not mentioned.[154] In sum, Baal of Sapan and Sapan itself are present in these two deity listings; Baal of Ugarit is not. This difference is evident also in the letters, to which I now turn.

Letters and Treaty Texts: The "International Baal Sapan"

That the Baal Sapan stands for the god of the city-state can be seen also in Ugaritic letters (*KTU* 2.23.19, 2.42.6, 2.44.10).[155] In one letter, *KTU* 2.23, Richard J. Clifford suggests that Baal of Sapan, by virtue of being in loose parallelism to "before Amun and before the gods of Egypt" in lines 21–22, is being represented as "the national god of the city of Ugarit, just as Amon seems to be the chief god of the Egyptian pantheon, at least for the reigning Pharaoh."[156] This view is suggested also by the initial position of Baal Sapan[157] in *KTU* 2.42.6–9 before all the other divine figures.[158] *KTU* 2.44, a third letter with Baal Sapan, is quite broken. It is evident that this letter is addressed by the king of Byblos to the king of Ugarit (lines 1–3). Both Baal of Byblos and Baal of Sapan are mentioned in the body of the letter (lines 8 and 10, respectively). These two gods are evidently the national gods of the parties. Perhaps just as importantly, in this context it is the king of Byblos who shows this recognition. In other words, the status of Baal Sapan as Ugarit's national god and not Baal of Ugarit is known internationally.

In contrast to these letters, Baal of Ugarit so far appears in no Ugaritic letter (none in *KTU*), and only once in an Akkadian letter. The apparent exception concerns specifically a request for help to make an image for the temple of Baal of Ugarit.[159] This reference to Baal of Ugarit in the letters (RS 88.2158.15'–16') is once again "the cultic Baal of Ugarit," which is not broadly attested. There is a similar distribution in treaty texts. Baal or Adad of Ugarit is not invoked in treaty texts; rather, it is Adad of Mount Hazi,[160] as it is also in royal decrees of gifts[161] and in the incantation *KTU* 1.100.9. In short, Baal Sapan, and not Baal of Ugarit, seems to be the "political Baal" for Ugarit in letters and treaty texts.

Literary Texts: The "Literary Baal Sapan"

The literary texts do not focus on the city or its Baal, but on Mount Sapan and its Baal. In the Ugaritic Baal Cycle, Sapan is the central major site.[162] It is the center of divine conflict and victory as well as divine manifestation, with the rains finally appearing from the window in Baal's palace. Moreover, Sapan is called '*il*, "divine," or "god" (*KTU* 1.3 III 29 and 1.3 IV 20).[163] By contrast, there is no reference to Ugarit or to Baal of Ugarit in the poem; the city itself does not formally exist in the poetic text, only in the two surviving prose colophons (*KTU* 1.4 VIII 49; 1.6 VI 57). The colophon reveals the royal-priestly patronage, which to judge from the poetic narrative looks upon Mount Sapan as a cipher for the city. Yet the city lies outside the narrative. Indeed, it is striking that the city plays no role in any of the mythology found at Ugarit. There is not even an allusion to Ugarit's divine establishment to compare with the founding narratives of other major places such as Mari: "ever since the gods created the city of Mari in primordial days."[164]

The point is not that the city of Ugarit is unimportant. On the contrary, in the Baal Cycle, Mount Sapan serves as the literary mirror for the city and its patron god. The mountain is the divine site for Ugarit's religious and political reality. The identity of Baal of Ugarit, the god of the city, is informed by the Baal who dwells on the highest mountain in the land, Mount Sapan. This observation extends to the narrative poetry beyond the Baal Cycle. Ugarit never appears in the other literary texts; in contrast, Mount Sapan does (*KTU* 1.10 III 30; 1.16 I 7; 1.16 II 45). *KTU* 1.16 I 7 is perhaps the most indicative passage about Sapan outside of the Baal Cycle. When it seems that the king is about to die, the passage relates:

> For you, father, the mountain of Baal weeps,
> Sapan, the holy bastion,
> Nan(n)i, the mighty bastion.
> The bastion with its wide crests.[165]

Here Baal's mountain is personified as a mourner for the king. The mountain and its relationship to the god is also the subject of a sustained religious reflection (*KTU* 1.101). The text (on its obverse)[166] introduces Baal enthroned on his mountain, with his body then compared with features of the mountain as well as his theophanic storm at that mountain.[167] The homology between the god and his mountain with its theophany further conveys the power of his enthronement and meteorological weaponry in lines 1–4. As an element of this homology, the mountain itself is called "divine" or "god" (*'il*) in line 2 (see also *KTU* 1.3 III 29, IV 19).[168] In any case, the mountain is identified with the national god.[169]

The religious understanding of Baal of Ugarit and his temple in Ugarit is premised not simply on the identification of Baal of Ugarit with Baal of Sapan or on the idea of the two as local manifestations of the same god. Instead, Baal in the Ugaritic texts is mostly understood as Baal of Sapan, and Baal of Ugarit is his local manifestation at Ugarit. As we will see below, several references to Baal Sapan at sites outside of Ugarit are to be understood in texts from Ras Shamra as expressions of the territorial extent of this Baal's dominion.[170] In the textual representations available, Baal of Ugarit apparently derives his cultic and political power in considerable measure from Baal of Sapan. This Baal from outside the city informs the identity of the god of the city and land of Ugarit.

This relationship between the two Baals may be due to an old prestige associated with Baal Sapan and his cult at the mountain. His cult on Sapan might also be older than Baal of Ugarit's. Hazi appears as a theophoric element already at Ebla, which is suggestive of a cultic tradition for the mountain by the end of the third millennium.[171] It is thought that a representation of Baal Sapan is preserved on a Syrian seal found in Egypt dating to the eighteenth century.[172] It is not known how old Baal of Ugarit is, but the Syrian seal, if correctly understood to be of Baal Sapan, may suggest an old tradition that would predate the heyday of the cult of Baal of Ugarit as known from the Ugaritic texts. In both space and time, Baal of Sapan seems to have served to magnify Baal of Ugarit.

In view of the Ugaritic evidence, Baal Sapan and Baal of Ugarit do not constitute independent deities. To be sure, other cases of *b'l* + GN may reflect other gods, as Allen argues (following a long line of scholarship noted above), but it is not clear that it is so in this example, and it may not be with some of the others. Indeed, when a single corpus represents a DN (where the DN really is a name and not an ambiguous term such as *b'l*) with two or more GNs, it seems that the DN is still that DN. This, it seems to me, was the basic reality that the ancient producers of texts at Ugarit would have recognized about these Baal names.

4. International Baals of Other Locales

As we have seen, Baal Sapan dominates Baal of Ugarit, even at Ugarit, and in turn Baal of Ugarit—or at least Ugarit—draws prestige and cultic power from Baal Sapan. This particular case may constitute one model for understanding one deity represented in multiple locales. In other instances the influence may be weaker, but still significant. The same DN of different GNs may stand in competition or their power relationship is under negotiation. The issue may not concern only power and competition between sites; other factors may be involved. At this point, I explore additional cases, beginning with Baal Sapan and Sapan at other sites.

Baal Sapan Abroad

The elevation of Baal Sapan at Ugarit extended to the international transferal of his cult. While Baal of Ugarit is unknown outside of Ugarit, Baal Sapan by contrast was a recognized god in Egypt during the Late Bronze Age.[173] He came to be recognized also in nearby Tyre,[174] in Tahpanes in Egypt (*KAI* 50:2–3), and at Marseille in France (*KAI* 69:1).[175] His name is also known in Papyrus Amherst 63: "May Baal from Zephon bless you," "and from Zephon may Horus help us," and "Baal from Ze῾ph῾on."[176] Classical sources come to translate his name as Zeus Kasios, and they recall his conflict with Typhon on that mountain.

Of the attested examples, one of the more interesting comes from a curse in a treaty of Esarhaddon, a king of Tyre, with Baal. The curses begin with Mesopotamian deities and then turn to West Semitic deities, invoking Baal Sapan after Baal Shamem and Baal Malage: "May Baal-shamem, Baal-malage and Baal Sapan raise an evil wind against your ships."[177] From the perspective of Tyre, this curse begins with the home god of Tyre, Baal Shamem; moves to Baal Malage; and then invokes the famous Baal Sapan to the north. Given the relative obscurity of Baal Malage,[178] it is difficult to determine the force of all three Baals here.[179] However, according to Michael L. Barré, "the very fact that this particular curse, to 'raise an evil wind,' is attached to all three indicates that the characteristic function of each has to do with the sea and/or storm."[180] In other words, the mention of all three Baals would evoke their destructive power at sea (cf. Jonah 1:4; cf. Ps 29:3 and 1 Kgs 18:44). Thus the curse may represent a Tyrian perspective on the extent of the Baals' power with respect to the sea and storms. It does so by mentioning first Baal Shamem, the Baal of the home, coastal site of Tyre (*KAI* 4:3);[181] then Baal Malage, perhaps a Baal associated with the sea; and finally the famous Baal Sapan of the northern coastal site. Whatever the precise situation with Baal Malage, Baal Sapan adds to the force of the curse associated with the Baal Shamem of Tyre.

Like these ancient texts showing the transferal of Baal Sapan to other lands, Psalm 48 calls "Mount Zion" "the summit of Saphon"[182] (v. 2, following NJPS; cf. "the far north" in NRSV).[183] This "city of our God" (v. 1) is also the holy mountain (v. 1) where the deity makes himself known (v. 3). Where Sapan evokes the thematic complex of the holy mountain as the site of theophany for the royal audience of Ugarit, Psalm 48 attributes this complex to "the city of our God," named as Zion (vv. 2, 11, 12), in other words, Jerusalem. Just as Sapan influences the site of Ugarit, so this psalm shows the extension of this influence to Jerusalem. Here the cult of the national god's home in Jerusalem evokes the cult site of Sapan. On one hand, this psalm shows a cross-cultural recognition of the old prestige of Sapan. On the other hand, this textual expression also arrogates this prestige to the national god of Jerusalem. It may represent an extension of the national god of Jerusalem, even as it shows the traditional prestige of Mount Sapan. This "translation" of places also moved in the other direction, from Zion to Sapan. Psalm 20 requests blessing by Yahweh, "and from Zion may he sustain you"(v. 2). This passage was translated into Aramaic in Papyrus Amherst 63, with the line corresponding to Ps 20:2 reading, "and from Zephon may Horus sustain us."[184] While in the case of Ps 48:2 the Zion tradition arrogates to its national god the tradition of Saphon, the Aramaic translation of Ps 20:2 renders the God of Zion in terms of the tradition of Saphon.[185]

The Lebanon and Its Deities in Phoenicia and Beyond

The Lebanon receives considerable recognition in sources beyond the Lebanon.[186] Its celebration in *Gilgamesh* is well known,[187] in particular its reputation as "the dwelling place of the gods, the throne dais of the goddesses"(SB, tablet V, line 6).[188] This reference suggests an old religious tradition of Lebanon as the mountain of the divine council. The Lebanon is also known in the Ugaritic texts.[189] It occurs specifically as a religious center in a ritual text (*KTU* 1.148.43),[190] where the gods of Lebanon[191] are to be the recipients of offering. This sounds like an echo of the tradition in *Gilgamesh*, where the deities have a known site of meeting in the Lebanon mountains. In this respect, the tradition at Ugarit with its reference to the "gods of Lebanon" is somewhat similar to "the gods of Sapan" as noted above. Both reflect a tradition of the mountain as the seat of the deities.

This religious tradition of the Lebanon is evident in sources outside of the Lebanon.[192] Baal of Lebanon is attested in a Phoenician inscription from Cyprus dated to the third quarter of the eighth century (*KAI* 31).[193] The tradition of this god may also inform the hymn in Papyrus Amherst 63 (column XI, lines 1–2): "From the Lebanon, O Lord, from the Resh, you beat (?) the earth, you stretch the heavens."[194] Like Baal of Sapan, Baal of Lebanon appears transformed into the name of a giant in Philo of Byblos (PE 1.10.9). The goddess known as Tnt is named as *tnt blbnn*, "Tannit-in-Lebanon," in an inscription from Carthage (*KAI* 81:1).[195] She is better known without the geographical specification in other Carthaginian inscriptions (e.g., *KAI* 78:2, 79:1, 85:1, 86:1, 87:12, 88:1). The title used in *KAI* 81:1 seems to evoke the prestige of her manifestation and cult in Lebanon. Yet this instance involves more than simply the prestige of the homeland, as this purpose would have been satisfied by a reference to Tnt in Tyre or Sidon (cf. *št<rt> bṣd(?)n*, "Asht<art>-in-Sidon").[196]

The prestige of the Lebanon may also be seen in the geographical location of imagery in Psalm 29. As long recognized, for example, by H. L. Ginsberg,[197] the topography represented in this text points to mountain ranges of Lebanon as the source of the imagery: "the voice (thunder) of Yahweh smashes the cedars of Lebanon. . . . He makes Lebanon dance like a calf, and Sirion, like the young of the wild ox" (Ps 29:5b–6). Accordingly, the imagery of the psalm here may go back to Baal of Lebanon. This reconstruction does not necessarily conflict with the notion that it may share Baal storm-god mythology with sites to the north, as expressed by Dennis Pardee: "Beyond the simple appropriation of one or two individual characteristics of Baal to Yahweh, however, Psalm 29 seems to reflect a familiarity with a significant portion of the Baal story as we know it from the Ugaritic texts."[198] Yet, given the geographical reference to the Lebanon and Sirion, this imagery would be most fitting for Baal of Lebanon and not for Baal of Ugarit or Baal Sapan to the north or to any Baal to the south in monarchic Israel.[199] How the mythologies of these various Baals are related is largely unknown. The mythology of Baal Lebanon may have shared a great deal with Baal Sapan's traditional lore, or the story of Baal Sapan may have exercised some influence on the mythology of Baal Lebanon. In any case, the Baal in the background of Psalm 29 may be Baal Lebanon.

Baal of Tyre and Carmel

First Kings 18 may reflect the influence of Baal of Tyre extending to the border area demarcated at Mount Carmel (v. 19)[200] and farther into the northern kingdom of Israel. According to the biblical narrative, the altar at Carmel had belonged to Yahweh but seems to have fallen into disrepair (v. 30). The political-religious conflict does not involve simply Baal versus Yahweh, but Baal of Tyre perhaps looming over the less threatening and older cult places of Baal in Israel (see v. 18)[201] and thus coming into conflict with the national god Yahweh (see vv. 31–32). This conflict is signaled by the temple of Baal in Samaria established under the aegis of the Omride dynasty (2 Kgs 10:21–27, cf. 11:18). If so, the story of 1 Kings 18 may constitute the spread of a politically potent form of Baal of Tyre, understood to be the same deity as Baal elsewhere in northern Israel and thus more threatening to the status of the god established as the national god of the northern kingdom with his own local manifestations.

5. Yahweh of Various Locales

Yahweh of Teman and Yahweh of Samaria at Kuntillet ʿAjrud

The multiplicity of Yahweh's sites has long been recognized. McCarter mentions Yahweh as the god with an ancient center in the southern desert and new centers in the land as well as at older Canaanite shrines where another god was previously honored.[202] These shrines show various relationships. The model of the older, more prestigious sanctuary site or mountain relative to the more recent royal center may underlie Yahweh of different locales in the Kuntillet ʿAjrud inscriptions. As McCarter observes, "Yahweh of Samaria" in the Kuntillet ʿAjrud inscriptions suggests a cultic tradition in the capital of the northern kingdom, whereas "Yahweh of (the) Teman" evokes the old, cultic tradition of the southern mountain region (Hab 3:3; cf. Amos 1:12). McCarter comments: "'Yahweh of Teman,' therefore, must be Yahweh as he was worshiped in the region of Teman. This does not exclude the possibility, however, that there was a particular shrine where the Temanite Yahweh's cult was located." He adds: "The cult of the Temanite Yahweh . . . may have preserved archaic liturgical forms and religious concepts, while that of the Samarian Yahweh . . . reflected the contemporary liturgy and theology of the national god." On the basis of McCarter's discussion, it would seem that northern interest in the Temanite Yahweh as represented in the Kuntillet ʿAjrud inscriptions reflects an acknowledgment of the older tradition relative to the new capital of Samaria.

Jeremy Hutton makes further observations about the two manifestations of Yahweh of GN attested at Kuntillet ʿAjrud. He suggests that the two expressions may constitute competing manifestations of this god.[203] With Yahweh of Teman attested on the plaster inscriptions and Yahweh of Samaria appearing only once and on a piece of pottery, Hutton proposes that Yahweh of Teman is not only the considerably better attested manifestation, but was "officially sanctioned." He also notes: "The proximity of the veneration of these two divine manifestations, as preserved in the epi-graphic record, suggests the following thesis: the boundaries defining sa-cred space were fluid. These boundaries could be permeated by other mani-festations of the same deity to whom the shrine was dedicated, even if they were in 'competition' with the 'host' manifestation."[204]

Southern Yahweh Sites in Habakkuk 3

Habakkuk 3 offers one of the most celebrated theophanies in biblical literature.[205] It does not take place on the mountain as such, but as the de-ity marches from the mountain, here called Teman and Paran (Hab 3:3).[206] This theophanic appearance is aimed against enemies (3:3–4), with the en-emies explicitly named as Yamm and Rivers (3:8). In this divine appear-ance, the god's rains fructify the earth and the enemies shake (3:6). The rain resulting from this theophany is evident in v. 10.[207]

A notable feature of this poem, as well as the book as a whole, is that in contrast to Yahweh's location in Teman and Paran, the speaker's location goes unnamed.[208] The book contains no explicit references to Jerusalem or Zion or even Judah, only to the land, city, and people (Hab 2:8 and 17). At the same time, Jerusalem appears to be the implicit point of standing for the prophet, as suggested by the reference to the king in 3:13 ("your anointed"). Accordingly, a contrast between explicit and implicit locations seems to inform the book. The older tradition of the southern mountain in Habakkuk 3 looms over Jerusalem, perhaps so much so that it goes without mention. The dynamic of Yahweh's cult sites here seems somewhat analo-gous to the temple of Baal of Ugarit in Ugarit and the mountain of Baal Sapan: just as Yahweh of Teman and Yahweh of Paran loom over the un-named Yahweh of Jerusalem in Habakkuk 3, the mountain to the north of Ugarit overshadows the city of Ugarit in the Ugaritic texts. By comparison, Habakkuk goes further, omitting the name of Jerusalem entirely.

Yahweh of Hebron in 2 Samuel 15

Another interesting case of Yahweh plus GN involves "Yahweh-in-Hebron" in 2 Sam 15:7–8. According to this passage, Absalom tells his fa-ther, King David, that he wishes to go to the old family seat in Hebron in order to pay a vow to "Yahweh-in-Hebron": "Let me go that I may repay my vow that I vowed to Yahweh in Hebron, for your servant vowed a vow while living in Geshur in Aram: 'If Yahweh ever returns me to Jerusalem, then I will serve Yahweh.'" Paul Dion compares this vow with one preserved on an Ammonite seal:[209] "(Regarding) Abinadab who has vowed to 'Ashta<rt> in Sidon, may she bless him."[210] Beyond a vow made to DN in GN, this inscription shares a significant similarity with 2 Samuel 15. This Ammonite seal suggests a geographical distance between Abinadab who made the vow and the goddess to whom the vow was made. An analogous geographical distance is operative with Absalom's vow as well. In the case of the inscription, the vow concerns an Ammonite who made a vow not just to any Phoenician goddess, but to the major Phoenician goddess of Sidon. This compares with the vow made by King Kirta to "Athirat of Tyre."[211] Kirta offers his vow to this goddess on his way to his siege of 'Udum but later fails to pay the vow. As a result, the goddess remembers the unpaid vow. The next clear scene presents Kirta as ill and near death, apparently because of the goddess. Like Absalom and Abinadab, Kirta is not at the site of the deity to whom he made his vow.

McCarter suggests that "Yahweh-in-Hebron" in 2 Sam 15:7 is comparable to the cult tradition of Jerusalem, more specifically "Yahweh-in-Zion" (Ps 99:2).[212] He does not pursue the political sensibility to this contrast, which is evident from the story's larger context. Charles Conroy rightly notes "the striking contrast between the pious tone of Absalom's request . . . and his real intentions known already to the reader (vv. 1–6)."[213] The expression "Yahweh-in-Hebron" in 2 Sam 15:7 recalls "David in Hebron" and "David of/at Hebron" in 2 Sam 3:22 and 4:8, respectively. In 2 Sam 2:1–4, Hebron is the city to which Yahweh tells David to go following the death of Saul and Jonathan. David is said to reign in Hebron at this point. According to 2 Sam 2:11 and 5:5, David reigned over Judah in Hebron for the seven and a half years before reigning "in the City of David" in Jerusalem. In 2 Sam 5:1 and 3, all the tribes of Israel came to David in Hebron. The political linkage between David and Yahweh in Hebron is evident from 2 Sam 5:3: "King David made a covenant with them in Hebron before Yahweh."

In light of this political situation, Absalom's speech in 2 Sam 15:7–8 may be evoking a cult of Yahweh traditionally associated with his family in Hebron[214] over and against David's more recently established cult of Yahweh in Jerusalem. In 2 Sam 15:10 the reign of Absalom as king in Hebron is announced. Here David's son is called "Absalom in Hebron," itself an echo of—and a contrast to—"David in Hebron" in 2 Sam 3:22 (cf. "David of/at Hebron" in 4:8). Now in 2 Sam 15:14, David is in Jerusalem. Echoing Absalom's vow, David takes his own vow (v. 25; see also v. 29 with the explicit reference to Jerusalem): "If I find favor with Yahweh, he will bring me back and let me see it and its abode." Here David is referring to the cult of Yahweh in Jerusalem. Second Samuel 15 seems to be acknowledging a political contrast between Hebron and Jerusalem for the family of David, and more specifically the Yahweh in Hebron invoked by Absalom versus the Yahweh in Jerusalem who is now the god for David. The chapter witnesses to the prestige of the older "Yahweh-in-Hebron" for David's family over and against the newer Yahweh cult in Jerusalem.[215] Given this political setting, Absalom's vow has political nuances. His vow made to "Yahweh-in-Hebron" concerns his return to Jerusalem; it sounds ominous. The wording of the vow moves from Yahweh in Hebron to Yahweh bringing Absalom to Jerusalem, retracing David's own political path. Viewed in this light, Absalom's words announce to the audience—and perhaps unbeknownst to David—the son's political machinations to displace his father.

The cases presented in this section suggest a range of religious relationships between Yahweh in his various locales. In some instances, a traditional sanctuary may be invoked in connection with a new political center. An old site may retain its prestige, without competing with the new one, which seems only to appropriate the prestige of the older one. The old site may lend prestige to the new site of the god—and thus serves to empower it. The evocation of the old site in connection with the new one steeps the innovation of the new cult in the tradition of the old one.

Sometimes the sites of Yahweh stand in a competitive relationship. As Hutton has insightfully surmised, the architecture of Kuntillet ʿAjrud appears literally inscribed with the old tradition of Teman, and it is further acknowledged in the portable inscriptions marked on pots. By contrast, the considerably later tradition of Yahweh of Samaria is restricted to inscriptions of pottery. This "newer" Yahweh perhaps serves to mark a minority voice in addition to the older, established tradition of Yahweh of Teman. This old Yahweh of Teman also seems to stand behind the poem of Habakkuk 3. In this poetic case, the evocation of the old Yahweh from Teman plays into an exaltation of the Judean royal establishment (Hab 3:12). No less important, there is no reference in the poem to the Judean king's own cult site center in Jerusalem. Instead, the Teman tradition is a glorious one associated with high antiquity that could be used without any particular need to defend or exalt—much less even mention—the Judean cult of Yahweh in Jerusalem. The mention of Teman and Paran serves to glorify the Judean king and his divine patron. Old memory is useful here, binding the present circumstances to the glorious Yahweh of old; it poses no competition or threat.

In 2 Samuel 15, the two cult sites of Yahweh of Hebron and Jerusalem serve to dramatize the competition between royal father and son. The son seems to appeal to the old, traditional site just as the father seeks to establish the new site. David makes no effort to draw on the traditions of Hebron as such (this site becomes lost to Israelite historiography following these stories). David, in effect, works for the supersession of Jerusalem over Hebron. Indeed, the latter was largely consigned to oblivion. Absalom's vow plays to the old cult tradition, but it is on the losing side of history. Religious and political competition may inform any number of DNs + GNs listed above, but the backdrop of such rivalries was perhaps lost to history.

6. The Responses of Deuteronomy and Priestly Works

The matter of Yahweh's cult sites represents a central question in the book of Deuteronomy. The requirement that Yahweh will have only one site according to Deuteronomy 12[216] seems to constitute a response to the plurality of this god's sites, as acknowledged not only in the earlier sources noted above, but also occasionally in other traditions, as I note below. Deuteronomy 12 states its opposition to such sites by associating them with non-Israelite practice ("all the places where the nations whom you are about to dispossess served their gods," v. 2). In short, all sites are taboo, except for "the place that Yahweh your God will choose out of all your tribes as his habitation to put his name there" (v. 5; cf. Exod 20:24 [20:21, MT]). This one place is the chapter's leitmotif (vv. 5, 11, 14, 21, 26; cf. v. 13),[217] yet it goes unnamed. Where place-names are central to the divine manifestations discussed above in this chapter, in Deuteronomy 12 the situation is the opposite. Deuteronomy 12 mentions that Yahweh may be properly served at one site, which is left unnamed. It is not clear that the text is referring to a specific site. Indeed, the lack of a place-name in the formulation may reflect the historical situation in which the site could change.[218] In not naming a site, the text may be implicitly referring to shifts in major cult sites. If so, then Deuteronomy 12 is a religious—and perhaps political—manifesto for ongoing supersessionism of cult sites.

This understanding conforms to Israelite cultic history. Several older sites, in both the north and the south, may have been replaced and displaced by newer monarchically sponsored sites. As a result, a number of older cult sites, such as Nebo,[219] Tabor,[220] and Hermon,[221] and perhaps some later ones, such as Gerizim,[222] were remembered vestigially. As we saw, displacement seems at work with Teman and Hebron likewise being replaced by Jerusalem. Other biblical texts show the issue of cultic supersessionism by Jerusalem. Psalm 68 recognizes the divine choice of an old, cultic mountain (see vv. 15–16)[223] superseded by Jerusalem (v. 29). Psalm 78 likewise acknowledges this theme in relation to Jerusalem with its replacement of the old northern site of Shiloh. In the face of the potential competition among sites, Deuteronomy 12 calls for a single site. This chapter does not name a particular place, yet in outlasting other sites Jerusalem became the ideological beneficiary of the chapter's religious manifesto.[224]

The other passage in Deuteronomy often invoked in the discussion of DNs + GNs is "the Shema" in Deut 6:4: "Hear, O Israel: Yahweh (is) our God, Yahweh (is) one." Some scholars propose that Yahweh as "one" (*'eḥād*) in this verse represented a rejection of multiple cult sites, namely Yahweh in his manifestations at various locales.[225] By contrast, other scholars note that the concern of "the Shema" in context is Israel's exclusive devotion to Yahweh,[226] as expressed in the NRSV translation, "The Lord is our God, the Lord alone."[227] The context of Deut 6:4 (with v. 5 and following verses) does not refer to cult sites or divine manifestations of Yahweh, but to single-minded devotion to the deity. Viewed in this light, Yahweh as "one" (*'eḥād*) would mean that the deity enjoys singular status. It would not be an allusion to the issue of Yahweh's multiple cult sites.

Deuteronomy 6:4 stands at a considerable textual and thematic distance from Deuteronomy 12, with its concern for a single site of Yahweh. If context is any indicator,[228] then Deut 6:4 did not develop originally as a response to the specific question of Yahweh's multiple cult sites. Instead, the prescription of a single cult site in Deuteronomy 12 might have been understood as a realization of the program of oneness expressed by "the Shema." In other words, Deuteronomy 12 evidently applies "oneness" when it came to the issue of the god's cultic manifestation, namely that it should take place at only the one place of divine choosing.

Ideological support for a single sanctuary is manifest in other biblical literature. The book of Leviticus generally refers to the "sanctuary" in the singular.[229] However, the plural, "my sanctuaries," also appears in the book (21:23; cf. 26:31), apparently reflecting the reality of multiple sites (so also Ps 74:8). A priestly analogue for the overarching Deuteronomic program of "oneness" is glimpsed in the vision of restoration in Ezekiel 37: the one sanctuary in 37:28–29 is espoused at the conclusion of the program of a single kingdom with a single king and ruler (vv. 21–23) who will follow all the divine laws (v. 24). The book of Ezekiel elsewhere denounces the practice of multiple sanctuaries (e.g., "eat upon the mountains," in 18:6, 11, 15).

7. The Song of Songs: When Two Become One

The ideology of Jerusalem as the one and only cultic site continued in the postexilic period. Jerusalem as the home of the one divine sanctuary is assumed by the books of Chronicles (2 Chr 30:8; 36:17).[230] It also seems to inform other postexilic works (such as Isa 62:7; 65:17–25; Zech 2:8–9, 16; 8:15; Ezra 7:19; Dan 9:17–20), despite the fact that multiple sites would arise in the postexilic context. This issue may also inform the Song of Songs. There is little doubt that the book offers wonderful poetry celebrating potent sexual love, as modern commentators agree. At the same time, this book may involve more. David M. Carr wisely asks, "Might it be possible . . . to read the Song on multiple levels, *both* as a song of passion between humans *and* as something more?"[231] Carr suggests that the book entails a "*cross-over*" of expression between the human-human level and the divine-human level.[232] That "more" may be spiritual as Carr suggests; it may also entail more concrete realities.

The book's spiritual dimension seems to be conveyed in geographical terms.[233] The "geography of love" in the Song of Songs allusively conjures up a picture of the female protagonist as the embodiment of Israel. The images of her bodily beauty are intensely geographical. She is compared with the old northern and southern capitals of Tirzah and Jerusalem (6:4). Geographical images of her beauty imaginatively evoke locales across Israel, including En-gedi (1:14), the Sharon (2:1), Gilead (4:1, 6:5), perhaps Carmel (7:6), and probably Baal-Hamon (8:11). Regions beyond also feature in Israel's political and cultic imagination and memory: Lebanon, Amana, Senir, and Hermon (4:8; see Lebanon in 4:9, 11, 15; cf. Pss 29:5–6; 42:6; 89:12; Deut 3:9, 2 Kgs 5:12); and Heshbon, Bath-Rabbim, Lebanon, and Damascus (Song 7:4; cf. Num 21:25; 2 Kgs 5:12). Some of these sites, certainly Lebanon and Hermon, would hold cultic resonance for ancient Israel. By means of the images of beauty evoked by reference to these locales, the woman is the female embodiment of the lovely land, especially the verdant and beautiful north.[234]

The woman's story in the Song of Songs includes the invitation by her lover that she come from Lebanon, Amana, Senir, and Hermon in the far north (4:8). Some of these locales held cultic associations for Israel. Antici-pating meeting her male lover (perhaps in a dream), the female protagonist pursues him in the city (3:2–3), just before one of the references to "the daughters of Jerusalem" (3:5), evoking Jerusalem as the couple's meeting place. Her title, "the Shulammite" (6:13), may pun on the name of Jerusalem and is evocative of the woman in—and as—Jerusalem. The "daughters of Jerusalem" invoked throughout the Song of Songs (1:5; 2:7; 3:5, 10; 5:8, 16; 8:4; "daughters of Zion" in 3:11) likewise evoke Jerusalem with its satellite towns, since elsewhere the "daughters of Judah" are the satellite towns of Jerusalem following the references to Zion in Pss 48:11 and 97:8 (see also Neh 3:12).[235]

These daughters are told to look at King Solomon on his wedding day (3:11). The male lover seems to be a king (1:4; 7:5), at first glance perhaps Solomon himself (cf. 1:5; 3:7–11; 8:11–12; cf. 1:1). Yet the understanding of the king in the book might not remain at the level of a human figure in its later, postmonarchic context, reflected in the apparent loanwords from Per-sian ("orchard, garden," *pardēs*, in 4:13) and Greek ("palanquin," *'appiryôn*, in 3:9).[236] The Song of Songs in its accumulated form, while expressive of hu-man love, perhaps functioned as the story of Israel that paralleled—and was inspired by—other images of female Jerusalem (e.g., 2 Kgs 19:21//Isa 37:22; Lam 1; Ezek 16 and 23), which I note in more detail in the next chapter. In other words, given the Song of Song's postexilic date, its male protagonist perhaps serves to prefigure the king that would rule postexilic "Israel," in other words, the divine king enthroned in Jerusalem. Thus on one level the book may celebrate the political-religious centrality of Jerusalem, with the deity as king and the city as spouse. This foundational theme was the well-spring of later rabbinic and Christian allegorical readings of the book.[237] This female personification of the city of Jerusalem is well attested in vari-ous biblical passages, as we see in the final chapter.

6 The Royal City and Its Gods

I now examine notions of city as spaces for gods beyond the geographical identifications that I examined in Chapter 5. At the end of that chapter, it was suggested that the portrait of the female protagonist in the Song of Songs draws on the idea of the city personified as a woman. As examples, I noted Jerusalem personified in this manner elsewhere in the Hebrew Bible.[1] This idea has roots in traditional notions about ancient cities.

1. Terms for the City

Scholars such as C. H. J. De Geus caution against identifying the biblical Hebrew word *'ir* as "city."[2] De Geus notes that the word applies to various sorts of settlements, as indicated by its double usage in 2 Kgs 17:9: "at all their towns, from watchtower to fortified city."[3] He surmises that no place in ancient Israel perhaps apart from Samaria could be considered a city in the modern sense.[4] The apparent exception of Samaria shows just how different this so-called city is from a city in modern terms. According to a study of Iron II Samaria by Ron E. Tappy, it was about 4.8 acres (1.96 hectares) in size, and it would have been home to about five hundred people.[5] In modern terms it was hardly a city. The kingdom of Ugarit covered about 770 square miles (2,000 square kilometers),[6] and the city-state's population has been estimated as between thirty-one thousand and thirty-three thousand people, with approximately six thousand to eight thousand people in the town of Ugarit itself.[7] Samaria and Ugarit may be regarded as small cities, but whatever word in English is used, it is important to bear in mind the scale of these places.

The ancient words for "city" bear a number of cultural associations. According to J. David Schloen, the main terms in the ancient Semitic languages (BH *'ir*, Ugaritic *qrt*, and Akkadian *ālum*) denote permanent settlements of various sizes, whether walled or unwalled (Deut 3:5; Esth 9:19).[8] Daniel E. Fleming similarly observes: "Every social category embodied by an English word carries with it the wrong identity or an inaccurate range of identities. Our 'city' and 'town' are essentially large settlements, defined especially by their concentrated populations.... A 'town' thus spans everything from a rural crossroads settlement to the center of a major city, so I have preferred 'town' as a translation for Akkadian *ālum*, which has a similar range."[9] Fleming also notes, "Both cities and towns are concentrated settlements, defined at least in part by population."[10] He elaborates:

> Although every *ālum* had a physical aspect, and one could definitely speak of the city, town, or village in concrete terms, the only physical feature that was essential to its definition was the clustering of permanent buildings that served some group of people. An *ālum* did not have to have fortifications or any particular size, and it is not even clear that an *ālum* had to include "houses," buildings whose primary use was for residence. The *ālum* was therefore the physical expression of a political reality, the clustering of some group of people for the shared use of the *ālum* structures, whether for homes, mutual defense, celebration, or economic exchange.[11]

Finally, Fleming observes that the parallelism of "city" and "house" in biblical and Mesopotamian literature suggests that "house" or temple points to the city as the home of the temple and that the temple lies at the heart of the city.[12]

The etymologies of some of these words provide further information. John Huehnergard notes the two singular forms in Ugaritic *qrt*[13] (cf. Hebrew *qāret*) and *qryt* (cf. Hebrew *qiryat*).[14] The latter derives from **qry*, "to meet," perhaps suggesting a place of meeting. In other words, it may connote a population center, relative to the surrounding towns or area.[15] The former's base seems to compare with the Moabite word *qr*, "city" (*KAI* 181:11),[16] possibly to be connected with Hebrew *qîr* and Phoenician *qr*, "wall" (*KAI* 7:1). In this case, this form of the word would have developed metonymically from the term denoting its outer perimeter. In short, the outer part signifies the inner whole.

While the ancients do not have a particular word for city, they made distinctions by means of four modifiers. A number of cities or towns are called "great" (*gĕdôlâ).[17] Nineveh is called "the great city" in Jonah 1:2; 3:2; and 4:11; and famously it is characterized in Jonah 3:3 as 'îr-gĕdôlâ lē'lōhîm, literally, "a large city to God" (NJPS, "an enormously large city"). Ugaritic likewise uses rbt for large towns or cities (KTU 1.14 III 5, 30, IV 47, V 41 [reconstructed], VI 11; 1.15 IV 8, 19, V 25).[18] This usage apparently informs "Hamath the great" (Amos 6:2) and "Sidon the great" (Josh 11:8), as well as the name of the Ammonite capital, Rabbah (2 Sam 12:26–27; cf. 2 Sam 11:1; Amos 1:14, etc.; 2 Sam 12:29). The town Rabutu seems to lie between Gezer and Jerusalem (EA 289:13, 290:11, and the geographical lists of Thutmose III and Shishak).[19] Akkadian also attests to a cognate, rebītum, "metropolis."[20] Finally, the difficult verse Isa 6:12 uses rabbâ, perhaps as a reference to Jerusalem (cf. Lam 1:1).[21]

Third, the Phoenician word 'm, "mother," is used for the city of Tyre; it is called "mother of the Sidonians."[22] Biblical Hebrew likewise uses the word "mother" for the town of Abel in 2 Sam 20:18.[23] This usage is implicit in the description of Jerusalem in Ps 48:11, with "the daughters of Judah" following the mention of Zion noted in the preceding chapter. Fourth and finally, the term mamlākâ, "kingdom," is applied to cities. While this modifier does not mark size as such, the scale is suggested contextually by the comparison of Gibeon in Josh 10:2, where it is said to be "a great city like one of the royal cities."

These four modifiers suggest that capital cities or large towns were recognized as standing in a hierarchy of settlement compared with other towns in a polity. What we might call cities (or large towns) were permanent settlements distinguished by a modifier. In addition, the sense of a city is expressed by its architecture distinguishing what is *outside* from what is *inside*, namely the walls. The city walls offer protection (Deut 28:52; Josh 2:15; 6:5, 20)[24] and a warning to outsiders by what may be hung on them (1 Sam 31:10, 12; Ezek 27:11; 1 Macc 4:57).[25] Basic to the identity of a town is what is *inside*, in particular the palace or "house" of the deity within the city (see Ps 48).[26]

2. The Political City: Divine and Human Agency

Beyond its physical size and reality, the city holds a range of symbolic associations. It is attributed a number of images and symbols that place the divine in relation to space.[27] Any number of deities may be city deities.[28] Yahweh is Jerusalem's city god (see Isa 45:13; 60:14; Pss 46:4–5; 48:1, 9; 87:1–3;

101:8; Dan 9:16–19).[29] Political agency is also attributed collectively to "the gods of Ugarit." These gods also offer blessing (*KTU* 2.16.4–5).[30] This divine collective is paralleled at Emar in a title for a diviner, called "Diviner of the Gods of the Town."[31] According to Sophie Démare-Lafont, this particular diviner was at the center of scribal training and not attached to a particular deity.[32] She also views this figure as responsible for overseeing the rituals of the town, as labeled in the heading of Emar 446: "[tablet of the rit]uals of the town."[33] The Akkadian deity listing in RS 92.2004.27, paralleled in the Ugaritic list in *KTU* 1.148.40, would have presupposed some sort of similar ritual or set of rituals on behalf of Ugarit sponsored by the gods of the town. Furthermore, they may be little different from "the gods of Ugarit," the appellation found in the letter (*KTU* 2.16.4–5) noted above. In the ritual realm at Ugarit, such religious or ritual activity would have been subsumed under or assimilated to royal authority and cult. In *KTU* 1.148.40, the "gods of the city" (reconstructed from RS 92.2004.27) receive an offering collectively along with the other deities under the heading of "the gods of Sapan."[34]

The political importance of the city deity is related to its important human agents. The city is particularly central to the identity of members of the royal family, especially the king: "king of Jerusalem" (Josh 10:1–5, 23; 12:10), "king in Jerusalem" (Eccl 1:1), and "king over Jerusalem" (Eccl 1:12) (compare "king of Ugarit" particularly in letters).[35] The usage is expressive of royal authority and authorization. A comparable term for the queen does not occur in the biblical corpus, but the "queen of Ugarit" appears in Ugaritic letters.[36] The city is also involved in the inventory list of Queen Ahatmilku's trousseau: "one city of gold."[37] This item of jewelry is a royal crown found in ancient iconography on the heads of goddesses.[38] In this instance, the queen wears a crown associated with the city or at least its image.

The political agency of the city appears in broader terms in what may be called the socio-political collective.[39] Elders of a city constitute a common marker of such a collectivity associated often with the city gates (Deut 21:3–4, 6; 22:15–18; Josh 20:4; Judg 8:16; 1 Sam 16:4; Ruth 4:2; Job 29:7; Prov 31:23; Ezra 10:14).[40] In Judg 9:2, 46–47, 51, this collective is presented in terms of "lords" (*bĕʿālîm*).[41] The term appears also for a number of other towns (Josh 24:11; Judg 20:5; 1 Sam 23:11; 2 Sam 21:12).[42] This collective is represented as "the 'fathers' of Ugarit" in one of the Akkadian texts from this city.[43] In some cases, the political context is interesting. One king, probably of Tyre,[44] writes to the prefect of Ugarit to contest customs duties placed on its merchants.[45] In making his claim, the Tyrian king asks the prefect to make inquiry of "the fathers of Ugarit" to see what they think. It is thought that the fathers represent elders.[46] This would not be unusual in a legal matter,[47] but the expression "fathers of Ugarit" is not the regular term used for such elders,[48] and the phrase might denote ancestors, as it apparently does elsewhere.[49] In either case, it is notable that the foreign ruler does not ask the prefect of Ugarit to consult the king of Ugarit, but another body from whom he perhaps hopes to receive a more favorable hearing.

The city itself is sometimes personified as a socio-political collective (e.g., "the spoil of the city," in Josh 8:27; 2 Sam 12:30). It is the place of assembly (Isa 33:20). The Ugaritic word *qrt* similarly represents a city collective in a letter: "my mother will/ought to speak before the city [*qrt*] [its assembly]."[50] Documents from Tall Munbaqa (Ekalte) represent the city speaking as well.[51] The political composition of such a gathering or the precise legal representation is unclear, but the passage apparently involves a public acknowledgment pronounced before a political body represented as the city. Such a legal figuration of the town is not without parallel. One of the legal texts from Emar awards an allocation by "the king and the town of Emar."[52] Political authority is evidently broader than the royal family or royal officials of Ugarit. As suggested in the following section, the city embodies the political authority of its divine and human agents.

3. Rituals of the Political City

Like temples, cities were stages for the performance of divine power and presence. In a sense, cities were temples writ large. At the core of this conceptualization of the city was a corresponding notion about the temple's central importance: the fate of the one was not uncommonly the fate of the other, in historical reality, cultural perception, and literary representation.[53] The temple's zone of holiness could expand to the city (2 Kgs 16:18; Jer 31:38–40). The gate of the temple precinct was a liminal space and site of ritual acknowledgment between the temple and the city (Pss 15; 24; 118:19–20; cf. Ezek 8:3, 5). The city itself served as a site for moral performance—or a lack thereof (Ps 55:9–11).

Two royal rituals belonged to the temple-palace complex. Royal coronations took place in the temple (2 Kgs 11:11–12, 15–16; see also Ps 110:1),[54] but sites outside of the temple were also recalled as sites of coronation (the Gihon spring, in 1 Kgs 1:38, 45; cf. the stone of Zoheleth in 1 Kgs 1:9). The coronation was a ritual function ("before Yahweh," 1 Sam 11:15) as well as a public function involving public offerings (1 Sam 11:15; 16:5, 13) and celebration (1 Kgs 1:9, 41, 45). A coronation would be an occasion for acknowledging the god's choice of both the king and his city, as suggested by two oracles quoted in Psalm 2.[55] One celebrates the god's "king on Zion, my holy hill" (v. 6); the other shows the deity referring to the king as becoming the god's son on the day of coronation: "today I have begotten you" (v. 7). Elsewhere royal altars were on the temple's roof by the upper chamber of Ahaz (2 Kgs 23:12), presumably serving royal ritual purposes.[56]

The death of the king was likewise an occasion of city ritual, entailing great mourning (1 Sam 31:13; 2 Sam 1:11–12) and royal burial. In Jerusalem, the city of David had a traditional royal burial site (initially in 1 Kgs 2:10 and 11:43, and later in 2 Kgs 15:38; 16:20; 20:11). Later, the garden of the king's palace became the home of royal burials (2 Kgs 21:18, 26; Ezek 43:7–9; cf. 2 Kgs 23:30).[57] Royal burial itself was likely a locus of ritual activity, as suggested by an Ugaritic funerary ritual in which the recently deceased king is mourned.[58] This ritual (*KTU* 1.161) ends with a wish for the well-being of the new king and his spouse (lines 31–34):

> Peace to Ammur[api],
> and peace to his house;
> Peace to [Tha]riyelli,
> peace to her house;
> Peace to U[ga]rit,
> peace to her gates.

The wish for blessing extends from the king and his household as well as the queen and her household to the city as a whole and its gates. This ritual involves no prayer to a deity who answers it with blessing. Instead, the ritual creates a "channel" or connection between the dead ancestors in the underworld and the living king[59] in the royal palace on the earthly level.[60] With this "channel" open, the ritual links the king above with the royal ancestors below. With the king and his ancestors as their focus, the ritual actions move from the center of the palace and out to the city and its gates.

There are other settings for the city as a zone of ritual activity. A good deal of this religious activity is no less political in nature. According to 2 Sam 1:20a, lament and celebration of victory take place in city public space:

> Make no proclamation[61] in Gath,[62]
> No announcement in Ashkelon's streets.[63]

This verse represents "oral proclamation" in a central, communal space.[64] As imagined in this verse, the news of victory would be proclaimed in a specific "outside" space (ḥûṣôt).[65] The association of this term with "broad places, squares" (rĕḥōbôt) in later texts (e.g., Prov 1:20; 7:12; 22:13, Jer 5:1; 9:20),[66] likewise suggests public space for ḥûṣôt (often translated as "streets").[67] Proverbs 1:20 mentions these two terms, along with the wall and the gate, specifically as communal spaces where female Wisdom personified speaks out.[68]

As represented in 2 Sam 1:20a, the communal spaces of the town outside of the temple serve for the announcement of news and the communal celebration of it. The opposite of this type of public celebration is public lamentation, and this, too, may transpire in this public setting (Amos 5:16; Isa 15:3; 24:11).[69] Thus this shared space of the town, used for public passage and commerce, functions as the location for the public performance of celebration and lamentation, activities that affirm and shape shared identity over and against enemies. In turn, such locations served as one of the places of communal reception of such news and the site of the initial social interpretation of the news. Such expressions not only reflect the setting; the communal space served as the spatial vessel for communicating such events and shaped the form of verbal communications. What is expressed in such a public context, whether it entails victory or defeat, is a matter of life and death for the people gathered there, and often it is the deity whose help would be celebrated in victory and whose absence would be lamented in defeat.

The celebration of the new king could entail a procession through the city (1 Kgs 1:38–40). The praxis of ritual procession may also inform the instructions in Ps 48:12–14: "Walk about Zion, go all around it, count its towers, consider well its ramparts, go through its citadels, that you may tell the next generation that this is God, our God forever and ever. He will be our guide forever." The tower, ramparts, and citadels all witness to the city's divine support. The ritual worldview here moves outward from temple precincts or public plazas to the outer boundaries of the city. Accordingly, the city gate and walls are foci of ritual activity.[70] According to 2 Kgs 23:8, high places were maintained at the left-hand side of the city gate.[71] Such high places would be sites for ritual activity. At the site of Bethsaida, a stele depicting a standing bull with a weapon in its belt[72] was found on a platform located at the northern tower of the outer city gate, which the excavators regard as a high place.[73] Along with this stele were two undecorated steles on either side of the outer gate. Thus the gate was literally marked as a zone of passage between outside and inside. The city gate is similarly to be marked by the commandments (Deut 6:4–9).[74]

One ritual function of the city gate was for prayer and offerings for military success, whether for a campaign or for the city's defense. The kings of Judah and Israel listen to prophetic oracles about undertaking a military campaign while sitting on their thrones at the threshing floor at the entrance of the gate of Samaria (1 Kgs 22:10). It is on the tower of the city wall that Kirta makes offerings in preparation for a battle campaign.[75] An instruction for prayer found at Ugarit is for the expulsion of the enemy from the city gate.[76] It is thus unsurprising to see God metaphorically figured as a tower (Prov 18:10) or to see Wisdom calling at the city gates (Prov 8:3) and from the heights of the city (Prov 9:3, 14; cf. Isa 14:31).

4. The City as the God's Home and Female Counterpart

Jerusalem as the mountain of theophany was the subject of Jörg Jeremias's important monograph *Theophanie*,[77] followed by Frank Moore Cross in his classic *Canaanite Myth and Hebrew Epic*.[78] The basic template of the divine warrior manifest on Jerusalem as his holy mountain is represented by many biblical texts.[79] Studies usually focus on examples from Psalms or Isaiah. Here I note some cases from the minor prophets. Zephaniah 3:11–15 and 16–20 announce divine support and human celebration. The passage refers to Jerusalem as the "holy mountain" (3:11), with the image of the divine warrior explicit in v. 17. The city here is called "daughter Zion" and "daughter Jerusalem" (v. 14), a motif that does not appear in the Ugaritic version of the template and represents one of its prominent biblical expansions. I return to this point below.

Zechariah 9:14–16 announces the manifestation of the divine warrior in the context of Zion's salvation. According to v. 14b, "he will advance in storms of Teman," an apparent echo of the deity's southern abode.[80] The context of Zech 9:9 and 9:13 also makes it evident that Jerusalem-Zion is the recipient of this good news. Zechariah 14 likewise attests to a series of the motifs from the template: the conflict centered on Jerusalem, with the manifestation of Yahweh and his retinue of "holy ones" (vv. 1–5). This passage also contains the motif of the splitting of the mountains as the result of the theophany at Jerusalem.[81] In Zech 12:3–4 and 14:2, this template includes the motif of the foreign enemies opposing the divine warrior at the divine mountain (*Volkerkampf*), a motif known from the Baal Cycle (*KTU* 1.3 II, 1.4 VII 35–36) and other passages in the Hebrew Bible (e.g., Joel 4:9–14).[82]

Another representative of this city template comes from the ending of Joel, in 4:16–21. Yahweh will roar from Zion (v. 16), an image that also marks Amos 1:2 and 9:1. The idiom "to give the voice" is precisely Baal's expression delivered in opening the window in his palace (*KTU* 1.4 VII 29, known also in Ps 18:13//2 Sam 22:14; Ps 46:6; Jer 25:30; cf. EA 147:13–15).[83] This takes place on the god's holy mountain (Joel 4:17), issuing in agricultural fertility (v. 18) and the destruction of the enemies (v. 19 and evidently v. 21). The city is promised long life (v. 20). The section closes with the statement that undergirds all the other statements, namely that Yahweh dwells in Zion (v. 21c). In addition, the darkening of the sun and moon in v. 15 has been associated with the sirocco, which is followed by the agricultural fertility of v. 18. Aloysius Fitzgerald accordingly proposed that the summer dry season echoed in the imagery of v. 15 is thus followed by the early fall fruit harvest.[84] I return to the question of this imagery below.

The themes shared by Baal Sapan and Yahweh in association with Jerusalem lead to a further comparison. As noted in Chapter 5, the Ugaritic texts attribute a complex of themes to Mount Sapan and not to the city of Ugarit; at the same time, it has been argued that in the Ugaritic texts, Baal Sapan represents a complex of religious ideas important to the temple of Baal in the city of Ugarit. Baal Sapan looms over and informs the figure of Baal of Ugarit and contributes to the power of the cult of his temple in Ugarit. By comparison, Jerusalem embodies both identities, as royal capital and temple and as the holy mountain of the god. Where Sapan offers a mirror image for Ugarit, these twin realities form a single set of images for Jerusalem's identity.

This difference may hold some implications for understanding the female personification of Jerusalem in the Hebrew Bible. It has also been common to seek a background for this representation in the Ugaritic texts. It is clear that the Ugaritic texts do not offer a straightforward personification along the lines of personified Jerusalem. According to Fitzgerald, the personification of the city specifically as a goddess can be gleaned from the imagery of the city on royal crowns worn by queens or goddesses as well as the epithets shared by West Semitic cities and goddesses.[85] This proposal has met with a variety of responses, including strong criticism.[86] In her judicious assessment, Christl Maier opines that this idea may be seen in the titles *rbt* and *b'lt* used for Byblos.[87] One of the problems in Fitzgerald's proposal, besides the lack of data, is the different terms or figures being compared. With the personification of the city, it is not always clear whether its imagery stems from goddesses or from queens. The evidence noted by

Shalom Paul (followed by Maier) for the image of the city on the queen's crown suggests a homology not between the city and goddess, but between the city and queen, an imaging that may run in both directions (e.g., city as queen and queen as city).[88] As noted above, the "daughters of Judah" following "Mount Zion" in 48:11 suggests an image for Jerusalem as mother and not necessarily as queen or goddess; this usage also informs the description of Abel as "mother" in 2 Sam 20:18 and perhaps 2 Sam 8:1. Other contexts for Zion, such as the opening of Lamentations 1, would suggest a queen. Thus there is no particularly clear or strong evidence for the goddess as the specific model for the biblical imagery. Instead, the imagery seems pliable, operating in different possible models and in multiple directions of influence.

The distribution of the evidence in Ugaritic and biblical sources is notable. The Ugaritic texts are focused on the mountain and not on the city. By implication, it may be unsurprising that the evidence for female personification is lacking in the Ugaritic texts. The closest we come in Ugaritic to the sort of personification of the city as "sitting" (*yšb) in lament in Lam 1:1 is the same root used in a Ugaritic letter (*KTU* 2.72.20–22) to refer to the condition of a city: "if now the city 'sits' [*yṯbt*] not in distress" (i.e., if the city is not in distress).[89] By contrast, with the city and the mountain both informing the identity of Jerusalem, traditional city imagery comes to the fore in the biblical material. Moreover, as Christl Maier shows, the biblical material expands on this theme in different ways, for example in the metaphor of Jerusalem as a mother (Ps 87:4–6; Isa 49:14–26; 60:4 and 9; 66:7–11) or the broader image of "young woman Israel" (Amos 5:2) for the "House of Israel" (Amos 5:1). These cases extend the imagery of the city personified.

As several of these passages suggest, the city of God embodied ritually by its inhabitants became God's city as embodied female. The deity ritually celebrated in anthropomorphic form helped to inspire the anthropomorphism of the city. The traditional ritual spaces of cities informed anthropomorphic perceptions of deities, and in turn, anthropomorphic deities associated with cities helped to generate the anthropomorphism of city space. The city personified as a woman remained a powerful, enduring image. In Gal 4:26, Jerusalem is the heavenly city that is "our mother" (see also Rev 21:2). The city of God would continue long after Jerusalem's destruction by the Romans. For Christians, it would be enshrined by St. Augustine's classic work *City of God.*

Epilogue
Ancient Theorizing About
Anthropomorphism and Space

I now take a retrospective look at this book's chapters in an effort to tease out the theorizing embedded in ancient sources. Rather than suggesting a full-scale theory, the following remarks offer some basic observations concerning ancient theorizing about anthropomorphism and spaces.

In Chapter 1, we saw how three types of location correlate with three types of human form for deities. The first two bodies of God mark the most focused spatial points of contact with humanity played out in homes and temples, while the third divine body evokes a more diffuse sense of the divine over the universe. These three bodily forms with their types of locations suggest a fundamental correlation between deities and places. In the biblical world, deities have little existence apart from space and place. The human places of deities mark deities as human, and in turn their human locations are marked as divine. As a matter of theorizing, I indicate in this chapter that correlation is a key component of ancient thinking about spaces and places in relation to human forms of divinity.

The correlation between spaces and deities as seen in Chapter 1 extends to temples when they are attributed features of the divine, as seen in Chapter 2. The qualities of deities were given expression by the very places represented as sites of their ritual. In other words, not only are space and divinity correlated, but space serves as an analogy to divinity. To some extent, this analogy is modeled on human characteristics, yet such analogizing also shows a capacity to express how deities are not the same as humans; rather, deities are represented as inherently more than humans. Temples serve also as spatial markers for mediating the sense of deities as both like and unlike humans. Thus along with a correlation between divine bodies and spaces, mediation is key to the ancient sense of place.

As we saw in Chapter 3, divine anthropomorphism and theriomorphism are often represented as operative ritually at temples, serving as bifocal lenses for viewing gods. Various combinations of anthropomorphic and theriomorphic imagery are represented in both literary and iconographic sources. Physiomorphic imagery provides yet a third way of viewing deities. Taken together, these forms suggest not simply a kaleidoscopic understanding of deities, but also a sense of their irreducibility to the human. The combination of forms represents a maximal *via positiva* that implies how different deities were understood relative to humans. (This approach would contrast with occasional biblical statements that deities are not human or later theological descriptions that deploy a minimal *via negativa* to speak about God.) Deities were intensely anthropomorphic and nonanthropomorphic at the same time. This duality of like and unlike perhaps fundamentally underlies what may be more familiar dualities of divine presence and absence and of divine immanence and transcendence. The multiplicity of divine forms gave expression to the fundamental sense that deities can be "both" human and nonhuman in human locations. Thus, with respect to deities and their spaces, correlation and mediation entail a degree of paradox.

This representation of the divine is at once religious and political. It does not operate apart from human politics. Rather, it is richly invested in a wide array of political activities and social energies. It is not simply expressive of human politics; it serves as one of its most politically charged realizations. In Chapter 4, I examined the calves at Bethel, a royal sanctuary that served to assert the political status of Israel, the northern kingdom, in opposition to the southern kingdom of Judah. In using the language of freedom from Egypt, the northern kingdom claimed a freedom for itself over and against the southern kingdom. The representation of freedom from the royal, political order of Egypt served to convey the northern kingdom's separation from the political order of Judah. This representation inspired a counterreaction that regarded the calf cult as idolatrous. Stated differently, the theory of idolatry as it developed in the Bible was shaped by the space and place of Dan and Bethel. In this case, idolatry did not entail worshipping other gods; rather, it involved the use of the wrong symbols for the right god. The power invested in royal shrines by these symbols of the divine was thus turned on its head: the symbols of these places eventually became the biblical icon for idolatry, so much so that many modern readers mistakenly assume that the calves of Dan and Bethel in 1 Kgs 12:28, refracted through the "Golden Calf" story in Exodus 32, were originally symbols not of Yahweh, but of the god Baal. Correlation and mediation of the divine, with their potential for paradox, are fully embedded in social and political relations.

Just as stories and poems associate deities with temples and shrines, the names of deities are associated with cities. In Chapter 5, we saw how deities are recalled in association with specific cities. The grammatical forms associating deities with these places suggest a number of spatial concepts. Such places are the homes or residences of deities or sites of their enthronement where they exercise lordship. Different sites with their manifestations of the same deity may compete with one another or exercise influence over one another. Divine competition could entail two gods in a single place, or two places of a single god. Thus the same god at different cult sites hardly signals political or ritual uniformity. A deity's site as marked by his or her name may also lie outside of his or her traditional sphere, thus serving as international expressions of the deity considerably earlier than biblical expressions of monotheism. In these various ways, the social and political orders name deities in spatial terms.

The character of the deity is performed not only in a temple, as I noted in Chapter 2, but also in a city, as we observed in Chapter 6. The city, like the temple, is a stage of performance for divine-human communication. The city, we might say, performs what and who the deity is to and for humans. While the deity is made present ritually at the city temple, the deity's association with the city in a sense makes the city into a temple. Analogy between these types of spaces functioned to extend the sense of divinity, as the temple served as a model for the god's city. The city rituals that I noted in Chapter 6 also show invocation of the divine between the city temple and the city walls; deities encompass both. Together, temples and cities serve as performance spaces for deities' presence and power. Both were homes for deities, and just as domestic space provided the model for the earthly temple, the earthly temple provided the model for the heavenly Jerusalem (Gal 4:26; Heb 12:22; Rev 21:2; cf. Phil 3:20; Heb 11:10–16).

A thread running through these chapters is the implicit, yet fundamental, perception that human spaces make divinity possible for human communities. Whether divine-human relations were cast in terms of model or analogy, it is evident that without human spaces and places, there is no mediation; without such space, there is neither divine contact with humans nor human knowledge of divinity. This implicit theory presupposes that divinity can be grasped in association with the human or in nature, not apart from the human or the natural; nor can it be reduced to either. Using a place for divinity could arise from either a human impulse or a perceived divine initiative, or both. In the case of Bethel, the same place is marked as a sacred space both under human initiative (Gen 28:16–19) and by divine command (Gen 35:1, 7). Place and space belong to a human desire to honor the deity sometimes without divine prompting, an impulse considered constitutive of humanity in Gen 4:26: "At that time people began to invoke the name of Yahweh." Robert S. Kawashima observes, "The very fact that Yahweh has always been known by name (4,1.26) all but turns Yahwism into a type of 'natural religion'—analogous to 'natural law'—premised, in turn, on the universal receptivity within all humans towards this universal God."[1]

This is a critical and fundamental matter of ancient theory. As Kawashima notes, this verse points to a theory of "natural religion," while divinely commanded religion elsewhere in the Bible reflects a theory of "revealed religion." Thus the Bible itself offers (at least) two theories of religion, and both are related to the spaces where the deity resides or visits. On one hand, people may give place to divinity in their lives without divine imperative.[2] On the other hand, deities are understood as seeking their place in the world among humans by commanding them to construct spaces or mark particular places. This tension between natural and revealed religion continues to shape modern perceptions of deities and their spaces; if God is revealed at all, it is debated whether this takes places in religious settings or through nature, and whether it is caused by revelation or by natural means (e.g., natural law in some religious traditions). These questions remain central to the task of religious understanding. The contemporary sense of divine anthropomorphism and the spaces linked to it are an integral dimension of the issue. In the end, the ancient sources provide the oldest theory in this debate, namely that making places and visiting spaces are acts of humanity and divinity directed with vital intention to—and for—one another, despite their significant similarities and mysterious differences.

Notes

Introduction

1. Cf. Martin Luther's denunciation of "chapels in forests and the churches in field," in his 1520 treatise "To the Christian Nobility of the German Nation Concerning the Reform of the Christian Estate," in *A Reformation Reader: Primary Texts with Introductions*, ed. Denis R. Janz (Minneapolis: Fortress, 1999), 97, para. 20.

2. Ömür Harmanşah, *Cities and the Shaping of Memory in the Ancient Near East* (Cambridge: Cambridge University Press, 2013), 190.

3. *DCH* V:461; see also Carey A. Moore, *Esther: A New Translation with Introduction and Commentary*, AYB 7B (New York: Doubleday, 1971), 50; and J. Gamberoni, "*māqôm*," *TDOT* VIII:544.

4. A. E. Cowley, *Aramaic Papyri of the Fifth Century B.C.* (Oxford: Clarendon, 1923), 147, #44:3.

5. Compare the address spoken to the altar in m. Sukkah 4:5, discussed by Jeffrey H. Tigay, "A Second Temple Parallel to the Blessings from Kuntillet 'Ajrud," *IEJ* 40 (1990): 218.

6. For the epithet in rabbinic literature, see A. Marmorstein, *The Old Rabbinic Doctrine of God: II. The Names and Attributes of God* (New York: KTAV, 1968 [originally published in 1927]), 92–93; E. E. Urbach, *The Sages: Their Concepts and Beliefs*, 2 vols. (Jerusalem: Magnes, 1975), 1.66–77. See more recently Noam J. Zohar, "'Maqom'—the Indwelling God and Rabbinic Reshaping of Sacrificial Ritual," in *Essays in the Social Scientific Study of Judaism and Jewish Society*, ed. Simcha Fishbane et al., 2 vols. (Hoboken, N.J.: KTAV, 1992), 2.13–19.

7. For Akkadian, see *CAD* A/2:458–59. For Ugaritic, see *KTU* 1.17 I 28, 46, II 2, 17, in *COS* 1.344–45 and n. 344 n. 8; cf. *DULAT* 125. For Phoenician and Aramaic, see *DNWSI* 129.

8. For references, see Peter Brown, *The Cult of the Saints: Its Rise and Function in Latin Christianity* (Chicago: University of Chicago Press, 1981), 11, 86, and 135–36 n. 42.

9. Braudel, "History and the Social Sciences: *The Longue Durée*," in his volume *On History*, trans. Sarah Matthews (Chicago: University of Chicago Press, 1980), 51.

10. For a partial exception, see *Sacred Time, Sacred Place: Archaeology and the Religion of Israel*, ed. Barry Gittlen (Winona Lake, Ind.: Eisenbrauns, 2002). Contrast Richard Jenkyns, *God, Space, and City in the Roman Imagination* (Oxford: Oxford University Press, 2013). Note also *Redefining the Sacred: Religious Architecture and Text in the Near East and Egypt, 1000 BC–AD 300*, ed. Elizabeth Frood and Rubina Raja (Turnhout: Brepols, 2014).

11. For recent defenses of this view, see Mark S. Smith, "Biblical Narrative between Ugaritic and Akkadian Literature: Part I: Ugarit and the Hebrew Bible: Consideration of Recent Comparative Research," *RB* 114 (2007): 5–29; Edward L. Greenstein, "Texts from Ugarit Solve Biblical Puzzles," *Biblical Archaeology Review* 36/6 (2010): 48–53; and Dennis Pardee, *The Ugaritic Texts and the Origins of West Semitic Literary Composition*, Schweich Lectures of the British Academy 2007 (Oxford: Oxford University Press, 2012), 79–80.

12. For example, the tradition of Yahweh coming from Edom/Seir/Paran, as found in older texts such as Judg 5:4–5 and Ps 68:7–8 and refracted in later passages, such as Deut 33:2–5 and Hab 3:3; see Mark S. Smith, "Remembering God: Collective Memory in Israelite Religion," *CBQ* 64 (2002): 631–51. For some key differences with respect to genre, see Mark S. Smith, "Biblical Narrative between Ugaritic and Akkadian Literature: Part II," *RB* 114 (2007): 189–207.

13. This information is summarized by Christl M. Maier, *Daughter Zion, Mother Zion: Gender, Space, and the Sacred in Ancient Israel* (Minneapolis: Fortress, 2008), 10–14.

14. Lefebvre, *The Production of Space*, trans. Donald Nicholson-Smith (Malden, Mass.: Blackwell, 1991). See also the essays in *Space, Difference, Everyday Life: Reading Henri Lefebvre*, ed. Henri Lefebvre and Kanisha Goonewardena (New York: Routledge, 2008).

15. Soja, *Thirdspace: Journeys to Los Angeles and Other Real-and-Imagined Places* (Malden, Mass.: Blackwell, 1996). For a précis, see Jon Berquist, "Spaces of Jerusalem," in *Constructions of Space II: The Biblical City and Other Imagined Spaces*, ed. Jon L. Berquist and Claudia V. Camp, LHB/OTS 490 (New York: T & T Clark, 2008), 40–52. See further *Constructions of Space I: Theory, Geography, and Narrative*, ed. Jon L. Berquist and Claudia Camp, LHB/OTS 481 (London: T & T Clark, 2007); and *Constructions of Space V: Place, Space and Identity in the Ancient Mediterranean World*, ed. Gert T. Prinsloo and Christl M. Maier, LHB/OTS 576 (London: Bloomsbury, 2013). Note also the field of "geography of religion"; see Justin K. H. Tse, "Grounded Theologies: 'Religion' and the 'Secular' in Human Geography," *Progress in Human Geography* 2013: 1–20.

16. Maier, *Daughter Zion, Mother Zion*, 10–14. For an important, early interpreter of this theory for biblical studies, see James W. Flanagan, "Ancient Perceptions of Space/Perceptions of Ancient Space," in *The Social World of the Hebrew Bible: Twenty-Five Years of the Social Sciences in the Academy*, ed. Ronald A. Simkins and Stephen L. Cook, Semeia 87 (Atlanta: SBL, 1999), 15–43. Note

also the essays recognizing Flanagan's work in *Imagining Biblical Worlds: Studies in Spatial, Social, and Historical Constructs in Honor of James W. Flanagan*, ed. James W. Flanagan, David M. Gunn, and Paula M. McNutt (London: Sheffield Academic, 2002).

17. For a recent "Firstspace" study of divine architectural spaces, see William E. Mierse, *Temples and Sanctuaries from the Early Iron Age Levant: Recovery after Collapse*, History, Archaeology, and Culture of the Levant (Winona Lake, Ind.: Eisenbrauns, 2012). For an application of this theoretical approach to the cultic complex at Tel Dan, see Andrew R. Davis, *Tel Dan in Its Northern Cultic Context*, SBL Archaeology and Biblical Studies 20 (Atlanta: SBL, 2013).

18. This study does not engage "Thirdspace" as a "space of radical openness, the space of social struggle," discussed by Claudia Camp, "Introduction," in *Constructions of Space II*, 4. Jeroboam's calves studied in Chapter 4 might be viewed as an example of "liberationist iconography" vis-à-vis the Jerusalem monarchy.

19. Cf. Jeremiah W. Cataldo, *Breaking Monotheism: Yehud and the Material Formation of Monotheistic Identity*, LHB/OTS 565 (New York: Bloomsbury, 2012), 154.

20. For temples in the Levant, see Magnus Ottoson, *Temples and Cult Places in Palestine*, Acta Universitatis Upsaliensis, Uppsala Studies in Ancient Mediterranean and Near Eastern Civilizations 12 (Uppsala: Academia Upsaliensis, 1980); Wolfgang Zwickel, *Der Tempelkult in Kanaan und Israel: Ein Betrag zur Kultgeschichte Palästinas von der Mittelbronzezeit bis zum Untergang Judas*, FAT 10 (Tübingen: Mohr Siebeck, 1994); Bertram Herr, *"Deinem Haus gebührt Heiligkeit, Jhwh, alle Tage": Typen und Funktionen von Sakralbauten im vorexilischen Israel*, Bonner biblische Beiträge 124 (Berlin: Philo, 2000); Michael B. Hundley, *Gods in Dwellings: Temples and Divine Presence in the Ancient Near East*, WAWSup 3 (Atlanta: SBL, 2013).

21. For recent study of anthropomorphism in the biblical world, see Esther J. Hamori, *"When Gods Were Men": The Embodied God in Biblical and Near Eastern Literature*, BZAW 384 (Berlin: de Gruyter, 2008); Anne K. Knafl, *Forming God: Divine Anthropomorphism in the Pentateuch*, Siphrut 12 (Winona Lake, Ind.: Eisenbrauns, 2014); Benjamin D. Sommer, *The Bodies of God in Ancient Israel and Its World* (Cambridge: Cambridge University Press, 2009); Andreas Wagner, *Gottes Körper: Zur alttestamentlichen Vorstellung des Menschengestaltigkeit Gottes* (Gütersloh: Gütersloher, 2010); Andreas Wagner, ed., *Göttliche Körper— Göttliche Gefühle: Was leisten anthropomorphe und anthropapathische Götterkonzepte im Alten Orient und im Alten Testament?* OBO 270 (Fribourg: Academic Press; Göttingen: Vandenhoeck & Ruprecht, 2014). For approaches invested with postbiblical theological concerns, see Brian Howell, *In the Eyes of God: A Contextual Approach to Biblical Anthropomorphic Metaphors* (Eugene, Ore.: Wipf and Stock, 2013); and Mark Sheridan, O.S.B., *Language for God in Patristic Tradition: Wrestling with Biblical Anthropomorphism* (Downer's Grove, Ill.: IVP Academic, 2015).

22. This point has been emphasized by Hamori, *"When Gods Were Men,"* 54; and Wagner, *Gottes Körper,* 156. See also Knafl, *Forming God,* 254.

23. Greene, *Natural Knowledge in Preclassical Antiquity* (Baltimore: Johns Hopkins University Press, 1992), xii.

24. *CMHE* 91–194; and Patrick D. Miller, *The Divine Warrior in Early Israel* (Cambridge, Mass.: Harvard University Press, 1973; repr., Atlanta: SBL, 2006). For further discussion and secondary literature, see Mark S. Smith, *The Early History of God: Yahweh and the Other Deities of Ancient Israel,* 2nd ed. Biblical Resource Series (Grand Rapids, Mich.: Eerdmans; Dearborn, Mich.: Dove, 2002), 43–47, 65–101.

25. These passages and several others are studied in Aloysius Fitzgerald, F.S.C., *The Lord of the East Wind,* CBQMS 34 (Washington, D.C.: Catholic Biblical Association of America, 2002). See also *UBC* 1.98–99, 352–53.

26. For divine imagery of patriarchy, see Erhard Gerstenberger, *Yahweh the Patriarch: Ancient Images of God and Feminist Theology,* trans. F. J. Gaiser (Minneapolis: Fortress, 1996). For the broader West Semitic context of the patriarchal household, see J. David Schloen, *The House of the Father as Fact and Symbol: Patrimonialism in Ugarit and the Ancient Near East,* Studies in the Archaeology and History of the Levant 2 (Winona Lake, Ind.: Eisenbrauns, 2001). For the impact of the patriarchal household on the imagery of the divine family, see Mark S. Smith, *The Origins of Biblical Monotheism: Israel's Polytheistic Background and the Ugaritic Texts* (Oxford: Oxford University Press, 2001), 54–66, 163–65.

27. For maternal images of God, see Mayer I. Gruber, *The Motherhood of God and Other Studies,* South Florida Studies in the History of Judaism 57 (Atlanta: Scholars, 1992); Sarah Dille, *Mixing Metaphors: God as Mother and Father in Deutero-Isaiah* (London: T & T Clark, 2004); Hanne Løland, *Silent or Salient Gender: The Interpretation of Gendered God-Language in the Hebrew Bible Exemplified in Isaiah 42, 46, and 49,* FAT 2/32 (Tübingen: Mohr Siebeck, 2008); L. Juliana M. Claasens, *Mourner, Mother, Midwife: Reimagining God's Delivering Presence in the Old Testament* (Louisville, Ky.: Westminster John Knox, 2012). Note also the older classic by Phyllis Trible, *God and the Rhetoric of Sexuality,* Overtures to Biblical Theology (Philadelphia: Fortress, 1978).

28. Karel van der Toorn, *Family Religion in Babylonia, Syria and Israel: Continuity and Change in the Forms of Religious Life,* Studies in the History and Culture of the Ancient Near East VII (Leiden: Brill, 1996).

29. The standard synthesis on this topic is Dennis J. McCarthy, *Treaty and Covenant: A Study in Form in the Ancient Oriental Documents and in the Old Testament,* new ed. AnBib 21A (Rome: Biblical Institute, 1978), followed up by his student, Paul Kalluveettil, *Declaration and Covenant: A Comprehensive Review of Covenant Formulae from the Old Testament and the Ancient Near East,* AnBib 88 (Rome: Pontifical Biblical Institute, 1982). See also Frank M. Cross, *From*

Epic to Canon: History and Literature in Ancient Israel (Baltimore: Johns Hopkins University Press, 1998), 3–21; Gary N. Knoppers, "Ancient Near Eastern Royal Grants and the Davidic Covenant," *JAOS* 116 (1996): 670–97; Robert A. Oden, "The Place of Covenant in the Religion of Ancient Israel," in *Ancient Israelite Religion: Essays in Honor of Frank Moore Cross*, ed. P. D. Miller, Jr., P. D. Hanson, and S. D. McBride (Philadelphia: Fortress, 1987), 427–47; Theodore J. Lewis, "The Identity and Function of El/Baal Berith," *JBL* 115 (1996): 401–23, and "Covenant and Blood Rituals: Understanding Exodus 24:3–8 in Its Ancient Near Eastern Context," in *Confronting the Past: Archaeological and Historical Essays on Ancient Israel in Honor of William G. Dever*, ed. S. Gitin, J. E. Wright, and J. P. Dessel (Winona Lake, Ind.: Eisenbrauns, 2006), 341–50; Saul M. Olyan, "Honor, Shame, and Covenant Relations in Ancient Israel," *JBL* 115 (1996): 201–18; and S. David Sperling, *The Original Torah: The Political Intent of the Bible Writers* (New York: New York University Press, 1998), 61–74. The older classic study of "love" as covenant/treaty term is William L. Moran, "The Ancient Near Eastern Background of the Love of God in Deuteronomy," *CBQ* 25 (1963): 77–87. See also Susan Ackerman, "The Personal Is Political: Covenantal and Affectionate Love (*'ĀHĒB, 'AHĂBĂ*) in the Hebrew Bible," *VT* 52 (2002): 437–58; and Jacqueline E. Lapsley, "Feeling Our Way: Love for God in Deuteronomy," *CBQ* 65 (2003): 350–69.

30. For a synchronic approach to royal imagery for God, see Marc Zvi Brettler, *God Is King: Understanding an Israelite Metaphor*, JSOTSup 76 (Sheffield: Sheffield Academic, 1989). For a diachronic approach, see Shawn W. Flynn, *YHWH Is King: The Development of Divine Kingship in Ancient Israel*, VTSup 159 (Leiden: Brill, 2013).

31. For the biblical passages, see *CMHE* 37 n. 147, and 186–88. For a recent survey, see Ellen White, *Yahweh's Council: Its Structure and Membership*, FAT 2/65 (Tübingen: Mohr Siebeck, 2014). The divine council setting in prophetic visions occurs not only in several biblical passages, but also in the Deir 'Alla inscription and in a Mari letter (*Archives royales de Mari* 26 196). For this Mari letter and the Deir 'Alla inscription, see Martti Nissinen, with contributions by C. L. Seow and Robert K. Ritner, *Prophets and Prophecy in the Ancient Near East*, ed. Peter Machinist, WAW 12 (Atlanta: SBL, 2003), 26–27 and 207–12; and Mark S. Smith, *God in Translation: Deities in Cross-Cultural Discourse in the Biblical World*, FAT I/57 (Tübingen: Mohr Siebeck, 2008; repr., Grand Rapids, Mich.: Eerdmans, 2010), 137–39.

32. For the royal audience as the paradigm for temple ritual, see Jeffrey H. Tigay, "On Some Aspects of Prayer in the Bible," *AJSR* 1 (1976): 363–79; Friedhelm Hartenstein, *Das Angesicht JHWHs: Studien zu seinem höfischen und kultischen Bedeutungshintergrund in den Psalmen und in Exodus 32–34*, FAT 55 (Tübingen: Mohr Siebeck, 2009); and Simeon B. Chavel, "The Face of God and the Etiquette of Eye-Contact: Visitation, Pilgrimage and Prophetic Vision in

Ancient Israelite and Early Jewish Imagination," *JSQ* 19 (2012): 1–55. For an iconographic approach to this theme, see Christoph Uehlinger, "Audienz in der Götterwelt: Anthropomorphismus und Soziomorphismus in der Ikonographie eines altsyrischer Zylindersiegels," *UF* 24 (1992): 339–59. For some sacrificial terms as deriving from the royal or political sphere, see Baruch A. Levine, *In the Presence of the Lord: A Study of Cult and Some Cultic Terms in Ancient Israel* (Leiden: Brill, 1974), 16, 17, and 29.

33. For the following, see Smith, *Early History of God,* 205–6.

34. See Chapter 1.

35. See Kirsten Nielsen, *Yahweh as Prosecutor and Judge* (Sheffield: Sheffield Academic, 1978); Karin Finsterbuch, *JHWH als Lehrer der Menschen: Ein Beitrag zur Gottesvorstellung der Hebräischen Bibel,* Biblisch-Theologische Studien 90 (Neukirchen-Vluyn: Neukirchener, 2007).

36. For a survey, see Hamori, *"When Gods Were Men,"* 35–64.

37. Stewart E. Guthrie redefines religion as "systematic anthropomorphism." See Guthrie, *Faces in the Clouds: A New Theory of Religion* (Oxford: Oxford University Press, 1993).

38. The discussion is vast. See Hamori, *"When Gods Were Men,"* 40–44; and Warren Zev Harvey, "Maimonides and Aquinas on Interpreting the Bible," *Proceedings of the American Academy of Jewish Research* 55 (1988): 59–77.

39. Hamori, *"When Gods Were Men,"* 53.

40. Hamori, *"When Gods Were Men,"* 55, 56.

41. Hamori, *"When Gods Were Men,"* 64.

42. See also Elliot R. Wolfson, "'Imago Templi' and the Meeting of the Two Seas: Liturgical Time-Space and the Feminine Imaginary in Zoharic Kabbalah," *RES: Anthropology and Aesthetics* 51 (2007): 121–35.

43. Metaphor has become a major topic in biblical studies. See the surveys of Andrea L. Weiss, *Figurative Language in Biblical Prose Narrative: Metaphor in the Book of Samuel,* VTSup 107 (Leiden: Brill, 2006), 20–34; Job Y. Jindo, *Biblical Metaphor Reconsidered: A Cognitive Approach to Poetic Prophecy in Jeremiah 1–24,* HSM 64 (Winona Lake, Ind.: Eisenbrauns, 2010), 8–23. Note also William P. Brown, *Seeing the Psalms: A Theology of Metaphor* (Louisville, Ky.: Westminster John Knox, 2002), 3–14; Edward L. Greenstein, "Some Metaphors in the Poetry of Job," in *Built by Wisdom, Established by Understanding: Essays on Biblical and Near Eastern Literature in Honor of Adele Berlin,* ed. Maxine L. Grossman (Bethesda, Md.: University Press of America, 2013), 179–95; and Bernd Janowski, *Arguing with God: A Theological Anthropology of the Psalms,* trans. Armin Siedlecki (Louisville, Ky.: Westminster John Knox, 2013), 22–35. Some linguistic work has pushed back against the distinction made between the literal (or mundane) and the metaphorical; see Ellen van Wolde, *Reframing Biblical Studies: When Language and Text Meet Culture, Cognition, and Context* (Winona Lake, Ind.: Eisenbrauns, 2009), 32.

44. See George Lakoff and Mark Johnson, *Metaphors We Live By* (Chicago: University of Chicago Press, 1980). For biblical work that draws on Lakoff and Johnson, see Alec Basson, *Divine Metaphors in Selected Hebrew Psalms of Lamentation*, FAT 2/15 (Tübingen: Mohr Siebeck, 2006); and Ellen van Wolde, "Sentiments as Culturally Constructed Emotions: Anger and Love in the Hebrew Bible," *Biblical Interpretation* 16 (2008): 1–24. For a critique of the theory of metaphor of Lakoff and Johnson as overly broad, see Weiss, *Figurative Language in Biblical Prose Narrative*, 16–17 n. 72.

45. Perkins, *Archimedes' Bathtub: The Art and Logic of Breakthrough Thinking* (New York: Norton, 2000). In the interests of full disclosure, I mention that in 1979 I helped with the research for this book.

46. Perkins, *Archimedes' Bathtub*, 187.

47. Perkins, *Archimedes' Bathtub*, 255.

48. Piaget, *The Child's Conception of the World* (New York: Harcourt Brace, 1929).

49. Jay S. Blanchard, "Anthropomorphism in Beginning Readers," *Reading Teacher* 35/5 (1982): 586–91, here 587.

50. Barrett and Richert, "Anthropomorphism or Preparedness? Exploring Children's God Concepts," *Review of Religious Research* 44/3 (2003): 300–312.

51. Boyer, "What Makes Anthropomorphism Natural: Intuitive Ontology and Cultural Representations," *Journal of the Royal Anthropological Institute* 2/1 (1996): 83–97.

52. Boyer, "What Makes Anthropomorphism Natural," 88.

53. Boyer, "What Makes Anthropomorphism Natural," 93.

54. For the body in recent biblical scholarship, see *Menschenbilder und Körperkonzepte im Alten Israel, in Ägypten und im Alten Testament*, ed. Angelika Berlejung, Jan Dietrich, and Joachim Friedrich Quack, ORA 9 (Tübingen: Mohr Siebeck, 2012); and *Hebrew Bible and Ancient Israel* 4/2 (2013) devoted to "Body and Religion." For the divine body in particular, see also the works cited in Chapter 1.

55. For the body in English metaphor, see George Lakoff and Mark Johnson, *Metaphors We Live By* (Chicago: University of Chicago Press, 1980), and *More Than Cool Reason: A Field Guide to Poetic Metaphor* (Chicago: University of Chicago Press, 1989). See further the reflections of Christl M. Maier, "Body Space as Public Space," in *Constructions of Space II*, 119–38, esp. 121–25.

56. For these meanings, see these words in *BDB* and *DCH*.

57. For a cognitive approach exploring links between biblical language and culture, see van Wolde, *Reframing Biblical Studies*.

Chapter 1. The Three Bodies of God in the Hebrew Bible

1. Esther Hamori, *"When Gods Were Men": The Embodied God in Biblical and Near Eastern Literature*, BZAW 384 (Berlin: de Gruyter, 2008); Benjamin D. Sommer, *The Bodies of God in Ancient Israel and Its World* (Cambridge: Cambridge

University Press, 2009); Andreas Wagner, *Gottes Körper: Zur alttestamentlichen Vorstellung des Menschengestaltigkeit Gottes* (Gütersloh: Gütersloher, 2010); and Anne K. Knafl, *Forming God: Divine Anthropomorphism in the Pentateuch,* Siphrut 12 (Winona Lake, Ind.: Eisenbrauns, 2014). See also *Göttliche Körper— Göttliche Gefühle: was leisten anthropomorphe und anthropapathische Götterkonzepte im Alten Orient und Alten Testament?,* ed. Andreas Wagner, OBO 270 (Fribourg: Universitätsverlag; Göttingen: Vandenhoeck & Ruprecht, 2014). For a comparative study, note *Menschenbilder und Körperkonzepte im Alten Israel, in Ägypten und im Alten Orient,* ed. Angelika Berlejung, Jan Dietrich, and Joachim F. Quack, ORA 9 (Tübingen: Mohr Siebeck, 2012). See also the following: Esther J. Hamori, "Divine Embodiment in the Hebrew Bible and Some Implications for Jewish and Christian Incarnational Theologies," in *Bodies, Embodiment, and Theology of the Hebrew Bible,* ed. S. Tamar Kamionkowski and Wonil Kim, LHB/OTS 465 (New York: T & T Clark, 2010), 161–83; Friedhelm Hartenstein, "Wolkendunkel und Himmelfeste: Zur Genese und Kosmologie des himmlischen Heiligtums JHWHs," in *Das biblische Weltbild und seine altorientalischen Kontexte,* ed. Ego Beate and Bernd Janowski, with Annette Krüger FAT 1/32 (Tübingen: Mohr Siebeck, 2001), 125–79; Ronald S. Hendel, "Aniconism and Anthropomorphism in Ancient Israel," in *The Image and the Book: Iconic Cults, Aniconism, and the Rise of Book Religion in Israel and the Ancient Near East,* ed. Karel van der Toorn, Biblical Exegesis and Religion 21 (Leuven: Peeters, 1997), 205–28; Marjo C. A. Korpel, *A Rift in the Clouds: Ugaritic and Hebrew Descriptions of the Divine* (Münster: Ugarit-Verlag, 1990); Stephen D. Moore, "Gigantic God: Yahweh's Body," *JSOT* 70 (1996): 87–115; Mark S. Smith, "Divine Form and Size in Ugaritic and Israelite Religion," *ZAW* 100 (1988): 424–27, and "Like Deities, Like Temples (Like People)," in *Temple and Worship in Biblical Israel,* ed. John Day, LHB/OTS 422 (London: T & T Clark, 2005), 3–27 (see also Chapter 2 below); Elliot Wolfson, *Through a Speculum That Shines: Vision and Imagination in Medieval Jewish Mysticism* (Princeton, N.J.: Princeton University Press, 1994), 16–28; and Ziony Zevit, "Taking the Measure of the Ten Cubit Gap, Isaiah's Vision, and Iron Age Bones," in *Marbeh Ḥokmah: Studies in the Bible and the Ancient Near East in Loving Memory of Victor Avigdor Hurowitz,* ed. Shamir Yonah, Ed Greenstein, Mayer Gruber, Peter Machinist, and Shalom Paul (Winona Lake, Ind.: Eisenbrauns, 2015), 633–55. (I thank Professor Zevit for bringing his essay to my attention.) Important older studies include Jonas C. Greenfield, "Ba'al's Throne and Isa. 6:1," in *Mélanges bibliques et orientaux en l'honneur de M. Mathias Delcor,* ed. André Caquot, Simon Légasse, and Michel Tardieu, AOAT 215 (Kevelaer: Butzon und Bercker; Neukirchen-Vluyn: Neukirchener, 1985), 193–98; and James Barr, "Theophany and Anthropomorphism in the Old Testament," in *Congress Volume—Oxford 1959,* VTSup 7 (Leiden: Brill, 1960), 31–38. Note also the issues raised by Howard Eilberg-Schwartz, "Does God Have a Body? The Problem of

Metaphor and Literal Language in Biblical Interpretation," in *Bodies, Embodiment, and Theology of the Hebrew Bible*, ed. S. Tamar Kamionkowski and Wonil Kim, LHB/OTS 465 (New York: T & T Clark, 2010), 201–37.

2. Hendel ("Aniconism and Anthropomorphism in Ancient Israel," 207, 223) includes several references under the rubric of "transcendent anthropomorphism." This felicitous phrase applies well to the third type of divine body.

3. Hamori (*"When the Gods Were Men"*) addresses passages about God's body where God is referenced as a "man." Assuming four traditional sources (plus H) rather unproblematically, Knafl focuses on references in the Pentateuch (see *Forming God*, 22–33). Knafl's discussion also decouples the divine body and divine space as different "types" of anthropomorphism.

4. See notes 1 and 2 above for references.

5. See Smith, "Divine Form and Size."

6. For scholarship on this point, see Sommer, *Bodies of God*, 2 and 175 n. 3.

7. For examples from Jewish mystical tradition, see Martin Samuel Cohen, *The Shi'ur Qomah: Texts and Recensions*, Texte und Studien zum Antiken Judentum 9 (Tübingen: Mohr Siebeck, 1985). Such texts use biblical passages depicting the third, cosmic body of God; for example, not only the famously cited Ezekiel 1 (e.g., Cohen, *Shi'ur Qomah*, 39, 41, 100–102, 103, 104) and Daniel 7 (e.g., Cohen, *Shi'ur Qomah*, 42, 77, 107), but also notably Isa 40:12 (e.g., Cohen, *Shi'ur Qomah*, 28, 37, 51, 52, 71, 72, 95, 217), as well as Isa 66:1 (e.g., Cohen, *Shi'ur Qomah*, 59, 87); for discussion of these biblical passages, see Section 4 below.

8. Following Hendel (see note 2), Wesley Williams ("A Body Unlike Bodies: Transcendent Anthropomorphism in Ancient Semitic Tradition and Early Islam," *JAOS* 129 [2009]: 28–44) argues that early Islam also attests to "transcendent anthropomorphism."

9. Recent work on scribalism in ancient Israel suggests that the scribal setting represented an important, further setting for many literary works in addition to their traditional social *Sitz im Leben*. Among the many works on scribalism in ancient Israel, see David M. Carr, *Writing on the Tablet of the Heart: Origins of Scripture and Literature* (Oxford: Oxford University Press, 2005); Karel van der Toorn, *Scribal Culture and the Making of the Hebrew Bible* (Cambridge, Mass.: Harvard University Press, 2007); and Seth Sanders, *Textual Production and Religious Experience: The Transformation of Scribal Cultures in Judah and Babylon*, in press.

10. Sommer, *Bodies of God*, 80. See also the discussion on p. 60.

11. *The Compact Edition of the Oxford English Dictionary: Complete Text Reproduced Micrographically. Volume I. A–O* (Glasgow: Oxford University Press, 1971), 963.

12. *The American Heritage Dictionary of the English Language*, ed. William Morris (New York: American Heritage Publishing/Houghton Mifflin, 1969), 147.

13. The distinction between Pentateuchal priestly passages and Ezekiel 1 on this score is seen correctly by Wolfson, *Speculum*, 22. *Kābôd* may be a quality of

the presence of the divine body (as in Exod 33:18–23, discussed below), but no priestly passage in the Pentateuch indicates that *kābôd* is the divine body, as Sommer argues, *Bodies of God,* 60. Pentateuchal priestly passages do not mention a divine body or body parts in their presentation of *kābôd.* As C. A. Strine has made the point, "Ezekiel and P possess a family resemblance, but they are not identical twins." See Strine, "Ezekiel's Image Problem: The Mesopotamian Cult Statue Induction Ritual and the *Imago Dei* Anthropology in the Book of Ezekiel," *JBL* 133 (2014): 272.

14. The secondary literature is enormous. For two important studies, see Terje Stordalen, *Echoes of Eden: Genesis 2–3 and Symbolism of the Eden Garden in Biblical Hebrew Literature,* CEBT 25 (Kampen: Kok Pharos, 2000); and Tryggve N. D. Mettinger, *The Eden Narrative: A Literary and Religio-historical Study of Genesis 2–3* (Winona Lake, Ind.: Eisenbrauns, 2007).

15. For 2 Kgs 4:34–35 on this point, see Mark S. Smith, "Recent Study of Israelite Religion in Light of the Ugaritic Texts," in *Ugarit at Seventy-Five,* ed. K. Lawson Younger, Jr. (Winona Lake, Ind.: Eisenbrauns, 2007), 1–25, here 12–13. Note also Gregorio del Olmo Lete, *Incantations and Anti-Witchcraft Texts from Ugarit,* Studies in Ancient Near Eastern Records 4 (Boston: de Gruyter, 2014), 181–82.

16. See Lawrence E. Stager, "Jerusalem as Eden," *Biblical Archaeology Review* 26/3 (2000): 41–43.

17. The greater size of kings relative to other humans is a classic motif found in many well-known pieces of iconography. For Egyptian examples, see *ANEP* #296–297 for the Narmer palette; *ANEP* #312 for Tutmoses III smiting captives in battle; note also *ANEP* #338 for Ramses II on a cylinder seal from Bethshan. For Mesopotamian examples, see *ANEP* #303 for the royal standard of Ur, and *ANEP* #309 for Naram-Sin in battle.

18. For this usage, see further Lena-Sofia Tiemeyer, "YHWH, the Divine Beings, and Zechariah 1–6," in *Monotheism in Late Prophetic and Early Apocalyptic Literature,* ed. Nathan MacDonald and Ken Brown, Studies of the Sofja Kovalevskaja Research Group on Early Jewish Monotheism III, FAT 2/72 (Tübingen: Mohr Siebeck, 2014), 77–78.

19. Cf. a human analogy in 1 Kgs 14:6 involving the hearing of "the sound of her feet."

20. For this passage, see Hamori, *"When Gods Were Men,"* 65–96; Ronald Hendel, Chana Kronfeld, and Ilana Pardes, "Gender and Sexuality," in *Reading Genesis: Ten Methods,* ed. Ronald Hendel (Cambridge: Cambridge University Press, 2010), 77–90; and Ellen J. van Wolde, "Outcry, Knowledge, and Judgment in Genesis 18–19," in *Universalism and Particularism at Sodom and Gomorrah: Essays in Memory of Ron Pirson,* ed. Diana Lipton (Atlanta: SBL, 2012), 71–100.

21. The core of the hospitality theme with "the three men" might have evoked for an early Israelite audience the type-scene of human hospitality to deities, as seen

not only in the Aqhat story (*KTU* 1. 17 V, in *UNP* 58–59) as commonly noted (see the discussion below), but also in the Kirta story (*KTU* 1.15 II–III, in *UNP* 24–27); cf. Thomas Römer, "Quand les dieux rendent visite aux hommes (Gn 18–19). Abraham, Lot et la mythologie grecque et proche-orientale," in *Dans le laboratoire de l'historien des religions. Mélanges offerts à Philippe Borgeaud*, ed. F. Prescendi and Y. Volokhine, Religions en perspectives 24 (Geneva: Labor et Fides, 2011), 615–26. If so, the narrative framing in Gen 18:1 may be designed to clarify that this is an appearance of Yahweh, and the parallel narrative framing in Gen 19:1 similarly serves to identify the other two figures as angels. In this view, the narrator provides clarification about what sort of beings all three are, as the audience might have known a *topos* of the hospitality to deities that appeared "less monotheistic" (I owe this point to Raik Heckl).

22. Hamori, *"When Gods Were Men,"* 1–2, 101, and 109.

23. Josh 5:13–15 and Judges 13 are two other examples involving angels that are called "man" (see also Ezek 40:3, 4, 5; 43:6; 47:3; Zech 1:10, 2:5). See Hendel, "Aniconism and Anthropomorphism in Ancient Israel," 220–21; and Hamori, *"When Gods Were Men,"* 111–14. Hamori would differentiate these angel passages from the "*'îš* [man]-theophanies" for God in Genesis 18 and 32 for their "anthropomorphic realism." However, the angels in Genesis 18–19 are no less realistic than Yahweh (note their speech in Gen 19 and Yahweh's in Gen 18, as well as their eating with Yahweh in Gen 18). The fact of being called "man" (*'îš*) or "men" (*'ănāšîm*) would thus not seem to be so distinctive. To be sure, the use of these terms contributes to the human portrait of both Yahweh and the angels (here I agree with Hamori), but this usage is not specific to God, applying also to angels. See Chapter 3, Section 5. For further criticisms, see Knafl, *Forming God*, 109–13.

24. Cf. the effect of wine on gods and on people in Judg 9:13.

25. So Michael Carasik, "The Limits of Omniscience," *JBL* 119 (2000): 221–32.

26. Mordechai Cogan and Hayim Tadmor, *II Kings: A New Translation with Introduction and Commentary*, AYB 11 (Garden City, N.Y.: Doubleday, 1988), 74; Hayim ben Yosef Tawil, *An Akkadian Lexical Companion for Biblical Hebrew: Etymological-Semantic and Idiomatic Equivalents with Supplement on Biblical Hebrew* (Jersey City, N.J.: KTAV, 2009), 264. This surmise concerning the date of the story, if correct, would represent a further problem for Hamori's claims about it as "early and authentically Israelite." See Hamori, *"When Gods Were Men,"* 96.

27. See Roland de Vaux and Benjamin Mazar, cited by Peter Machinist, "Biblical Traditions: The Philistines and Israelite History," in *The Sea Peoples and Their World: A Reassessment*, ed. Eliezer D. Oren, University Museum Monograph 108, University Museum Symposium Series 11 (Philadelphia: University Museum, University of Pennsylvania, 2000), 53–83, here 58 and 71 n. 29. I am grateful to Peter Machinist for bringing this point and reference to my attention.

28. For the "convergence" of divine roles attributed to El-Yahweh in early Israelite religion, see Mark S. Smith, *The Early History of God: Yahweh and the Other Deities in Ancient Israel,* 2nd ed., Biblical Resource Series (Grand Rapids, Mich.: Eerdmans; Dearborn, Mich.: Dove, 2002), xxii, xxxvii, 7–9, 11, 54–59, 184, and 195–202.

29. For literary-critical questions, see Matthias Köckert, "War Jacobs Gegner in Gene 32,23–33 ein Dämon?," in *Die Dämonen—Demons: Die Dämonologie der israelitisch-jüdischen und frühchristlichen Literatur im Kontext ihrer Umwelt,* ed. Armin Lange, Hermann Lichtenberger, and K. F. Diethard Römheld (Tübingen: Mohr Siebeck, 2003), 160–83; and Jeremy M. Hutton, "Jacob's 'Two Camps' and Transjordanian Geography: Wrestling with Order in Genesis 32," *ZAW* 122 (2010): 20–32. For this passage, see also Ronald S. Hendel, *The Epic of the Patriarch: The Jacob Cycle and the Narrative Traditions of Canaan and Israel,* HSM 42 (Atlanta: Scholars, 1987), 101–9; and Hamori, *"When Gods Were Men,"* 96–101.

30. For this verbal root in a request for release in other conflict narratives, see Gen 30:25 and 1 Sam 19:17.

31. Note the LXX: "for you have prevailed with a god, and with humans you are powerful" (NETS). Hendel (*Epic of the Patriarch,* 103) suggests that the LXX here may have been the original text.

32. In theory, this word in both vv. 28 and 30 could be translated as "God," "gods," "divinities," or "divine beings," and indeed, a plural translation of the word in v. 28 might go well with the plural "men," which would fit the figure's renaming of Jacob in v. 29, "for you have striven with gods and men." Cf. Judg 9:9 and 13. The combination is attested elsewhere: Akkadian "god and man" in Shurpu V–VI 182, etc. (*CAD* A/2:49b; see also (*CAD* A/2:59)); Hittite "humans and gods" in the "Disappearance of Telepinu" (A i 16–20), in Harry A. Hoffner, Jr., *Hittite Myths,* ed. G. A. Beckman, 2nd ed., WAW 2 (Atlanta: Scholars, 1998), 15; Ugaritic "gods and men" (*KTU* 1.4 VII 51 in *UNP* 137; see *UBC* 2.692); Zinjirli Aramaic "before gods and before men" (*KAI* 215:23); and Greek "gods and men" (Odyssey XX:112; see also Odyssey XVI:265, XVIII:135).

33. For the literary relation between the two passages, see Steven L. McKenzie, "The Jacob Tradition in Hosea 12:4–5," *VT* 36 (1986): 311–22; Hamori, *"When Gods Were Men,"* 99–101; Erhard Blum, "Hosea 12 und die Pentateuchüberlieferungen," in *Die Erzväter in der biblischen Tradition: Festschrift für Matthias Köckert,* ed. Anselm C. Hagedorn and Henrik Pfeiffer, BZAW 400 (Berlin: de Gruyter, 2009), 291–321, esp. 312–18.

34. The preposition is a problem; it would seem smoother to have either *'im,* "with" (as in Gen 32:29) or *'ēt,* "with" (as in Hos 12:5). Several commentators read the MT preposition *'el* as the noun *'ēl,* "god/God," and delete or bracket *mal'āk* as a gloss. See *BHS;* Hans Walter Wolff, *Hosea: A Commentary on the Book of the Prophet Hosea,* ed. Paul D. Hanson, trans. Gary Stansell, Hermeneia (Phila-

delphia: Fortress, 1974), 206 and 212–13; Francis I. Andersen and David Noel Freedman, *Hosea: A New Translation with Introduction and Commentary*, AYB 24 (Garden City, N.Y.: Doubleday, 1980), 609; Ehud Ben Zvi, *Hosea*, Forms of Old Testament Literature XXIA/1 (Grand Rapids, Mich./Cambridge: Eerdmans, 2005), 249–50; and R. Scott Chalmers, *The Struggle of Yahweh and El for Hosea's Israel*, Hebrew Bible Monographs 11 (Sheffield: Sheffield Phoenix, 2008), 101, 106–10, 113. The resulting rereading would also make "God"/"El" the subject rather than the object, which would resolve a number of problems. However, there is little versional evidence for this emendation, and it arguably detracts from the parallelism of the two lines. Still the verb-preposition combination in the MT is not a simple matter (Chalmers, *Struggle of Yahweh and El*, 108). However, some preposition appears indicated by Chalmers's citation of the parallel idiom *wayyāśar . . . 'al* in Judg 9:22. Thus it would be simpler to see the MT preposition *'el* in Hos 12:5 as a variant of or mistake for the preposition *'al* or *'ēt*.

35. For the problem of the MT pointing of the verb as **śrr*, "to be a prince," rather than **śrh*, "strive, contend," as in Gen 32:29, see Wolff, *Hosea*, 212; *DCH* VIII:190 and 199; and Hamori, *"When Gods Were Men,"* 99–100.

36. That the word "angel" is the parallel B-term to "divine being" as the A-term is also suggested by the **qatal/**wayyaqtul* parallelism of the same verbal root in these two lines, a poetic phenomenon insightfully discussed a half-century ago by Moshe Held, "The YQTL-QTL (QTL-YQTL) Sequence of Identical Verbs in Biblical Hebrew and in Ugaritic," in *Studies and Essays in Honor of A. A. Neumann*, ed. M. Ben-Horin, B. D. Weinryb, and S. Zeitlin (Leiden: Brill, for the Dropsie College, Philadelphia, 1962), 281–90.

37. For the possibilities, see Hendel, *Epic of the Patriarch*, 104–6; Hamori, *"When Gods Were Men,"* 13–23. See also Mark S. Smith, "Remembering God: Collective Memory in Israelite Religion," *CBQ* 64 (2002): 641–44.

38. Common among older exegetes is the view (see Hutton, "Jacob's 'Two Camps,'" 31) that "an earlier story" was "incorporated" into these verses. Cf. Köckert, "War Jacobs Gegner in Gene 32,23–33 ein Dämon?," 160–83; and John Barton, "Jacob at the Jabbok," in *Die Erzväter in der biblischen Tradition: Festschrift für Matthias Köckert*, ed. Anselm C. Hagedorn and Henrik Pfeiffer, BZAW 400 (Berlin: de Gruyter, 2009), 187–95.

39. So the theory associated with Hermann Gunkel, *Genesis*, trans. Mark E. Biddle (Macon, Ga.: Mercer University Press, 1997), 352–53, discussed by Hendel, *Epic of the Patriarch*, 104–5; and Hamori, *"When Gods Were Men,"* 13–18.

40. For example, see Tob 3:8. For the issues with this view for Genesis 32, see Köckert, "War Jacobs Gegner in Gene 32, 23–33 ein Dämon?," 160–83. For Mesopotamian night demons, see Frans A. M. Wiggerman, "Lamaštu, Daughter of Anu. A Profile," in M. Stol, *Birth in Babylonia and the Bible: Its Mediterranean Setting*, Cuneiform Monographs 14 (Groningen: Styx, 2000), 217–52, here 246–47, and

"Some Demons of Time and Their Functions in Mesopotamian Iconography," in *Die Welt der Götterbilder,* ed. Brigitte Groneberg and Hermann Spieckermann, BZAW 376 (Berlin: de Gruyter, 2007), 102–16, here 107–8.

41. See Hermann Wohlstein, "Zu einigen altisraelitischen Volksvorstellungen von Toten-und Ahnengeistern in biblischer Überlieferung," *Zeitschrift für Religions- und Geistesgeschichte* 19 (1967): 353, cited by Hamori, *"When Gods Were Men,"* 19. A displeased deceased family member might seem a lesser possibility, more at home in Mesopotamian literature than in the Levant. See Jean Bottéro, "Les morts et l'au-delà dans rituels en accadien contre l'action des 'revenants,'" *Zeitschrift für Assyriologie* 73 (1983): 153–203.

42. A Hittite parallel involving a deity that supports the royal protagonist has been proposed by Matitiahu Tsevat, "Two Old Testament Stories and Their Hittite Analogues," *JAOS* 103 (1983 = *Studies in Literature from the Ancient Near East, by Members of the American Oriental Society, Dedicated to Samuel Noah Kramer*): 321–22.

43. J. Glenn Taylor reads "the man" as "a pre-dawn phase of the sun," with the sun "presumed to be the face of God." See Taylor, *Yahweh and the Sun: Biblical and Archaeological Evidence for Sun Worship in Ancient Israel* JSOTSup 111 (Sheffield Academic, 1993), 241.

44. See Hendel, *Epic of the Patriarch,* 105–8.

45. Cf. the Ugaritic story of Kirta (*KTU* 1.14 I–III, in *UNP* 12–18), where the king falls asleep at night, and his personal god, El, appears to him in a dream.

46. The classic study of the divine mountain is Richard J. Clifford, *The Cosmic Mountain in Canaan and the Old Testament* HSM 4 (Cambridge, Mass.: Harvard University Press, 1972). See also L. M. Morales, *The Tabernacle Pre-figured: Cosmic Mountain Ideology in Genesis and Exodus,* Biblical Tools and Studies 15 (Leuven: Peeters, 2012).

47. For literary issues, see Ernest W. Nicholson, "The Antiquity of the Tradition in Exodus 24:9–11," *VT* 26 (1976): 148–60; Ronald S. Hendel, "Sacrifice as a Cultural System: The Ritual Symbolism of Exodus 24:3–8," *ZAW* 101 (1989): 366–90; Jean-Louis Ska, "Le repas de Ex 24,11," *Bib* 74 (1993): 305–27; Hartenstein, "Wolkendunkel und Himmelfeste," 136–37; and William H. C. Propp, *Exodus 19–40: A New Translation with Introduction and Commentary,* AYB 2A (New York: Doubleday, 2006), 147–48. The composition of Exod 24:1–11 is complex. Verses 1–2 appear to have been written as the preface to both vv. 3–8 and 9–11, as v. 1 shares information with v. 9, while v. 2 serves to set up the scene for vv. 3–8. Moreover, vv. 1–2 are to be seen as somewhat separate from vv. 9–11, given the use of different divine names and titles in these two subunits. It is also to be noted that the beginning of v. 1 omits a named subject for the verb (note also *wĕʾel...*, suggesting continuity with the preceding unit). On the whole, vv. 9–11, whether or not they are to be linked to vv. 1–2, seem to represent a fragment of an older visionary account, recontextualized within Exod 24:1–11, perhaps to

help introduce what follows. With the tabernacle narrative in Exodus 25–40 in mind, Thomas B. Dozeman (*Exodus*, Eerdmans Critical Commentary [Grand Rapids, Mich.: Eerdmans, 2009], 567) notes that vv. 9–11 "begin the process of addressing the need for a sanctuary by introducing the image of the heavenly temple as the model for an earthly sanctuary to contain the holiness of God."

48. Otto, *The Idea of the Holy: An Inquiry into the Non-rational Factor in the Idea of the Divine and Its Relation to the Rational,* trans. John W. Harvey (London: Oxford University Press, 1928); Jacobsen, *The Treasures of Darkness: A History of Mesopotamian Religion* (New Haven, Conn.: Yale University Press, 1976), 1. See also Hendel, "Aniconism and Anthropomorphism in Ancient Israel," 220–21.

49. So Dozeman, *Exodus,* 567.

50. See the discussion below for comparative evidence.

51. Childs, *The Book of Exodus: A Critical, Theological Commentary,* OTL (Philadelphia: Westminster, 1974), 506.

52. Hartenstein, "Wolkendunkel und Himmelfeste," 140.

53. See Philip J. King and Lawrence E. Stager, *Life in Biblical Israel* (Louisville, Ky.: Westminster John Knox, 2001), 335–36; John M. Monson, "The 'Ain Dara Temple and the Jerusalem Temple," in *Text, Artifact, and Image: Revealing Ancient Israelite Religion,* ed. Gary M. Beckman and Theodore J. Lewis, Brown Judaic Studies 346 (Providence, R.I.: Brown Judaic Studies, 2006), 273–99, esp. 281.

54. Cf. the temple setting for the divine feet in Pss 99:5; 132:7; Isa 60:13; Lam 2:1; and Ezek 43:7.

55. For parallels, see Gen 31:54 and 1 Kgs 18:42–43, discussed by Kathryn L. Roberts, "God, Prophet, and King: Eating and Drinking on the Mountain in First Kings 18:41," *CBQ* 62/4 (2000): 632–44.

56. Sommer (*Bodies of God,* 41, 78, 232, and 254) assumes that "avatars" of God's body are located in more than one place at the same time. For discussion, see Chapter 5.

57. In this passage, it is not clear whether the superhuman divine body is composed of fire or light or some other phenomenon (cf. Ps 104:1: "wrapped in light as with a garment"). See Mark S. Smith, "Divine Form and Size in Ugaritic and Israelite Religion," *ZAW* 100 (1988): 424–27. Sommer (*Bodies of God,* 2) speaks of this body as being "made of energy rather than matter" (see also Sommer, *Bodies of God,* 71). See the emphasis on fire for the divine appearance in Theodore J. Lewis, "Divine Fire in Deuteronomy 33:2," *JBL* 132 (2013): 791–803; and Deena Grant, "Fire and Body of Yhwh," *JSOT* 40/2 (2015): 139–61.

58. For the literary-critical issues, see Friedhelm Hartenstein, *Die Unzugänglichkeit Gottes im Heiligtum: Jesaja 6 und der Wohnort JHWHs in der Jerusalemer Kulttradition,* WMANT 75 (Neukirchen-Vluyn: Neukirchener, 1997); and Torsten Uhlig, *The Theme of Hardening in the Book of Isaiah: An Analysis of Communicative Action,* FAT 2/39 (Tübingen: Mohr Siebeck, 2009), 73–143. For the iconographic repertoire represented by this passage, see Othmar Keel, *Jahwe-Visionen und*

Siegelkunst: Eine neue Deutung der Majestätschilderungen in Jes 6, Ez 1 und 10 und Sach 4, Stuttgarter Bibel—Studien 84/85 (Stuttgart: Katholisches Bibelwerk, 1977), 46–124. Note also Othmar Keel and Christoph Uehlinger, *Gods, Goddesses, and Images of God in Ancient Israel,* trans. Thomas H. Trapp (Minneapolis: Fortress, 1998), 273–74 and 401; and Friedhelm Hartenstein, "Cherubim and Seraphim in the Bible and in the Light of Ancient Near Eastern Sources," in *Angels: The Concept of Celestial Beings,* ed. Friedrich V. Reiterer, Tobias Nicklas, and Karin Schöpflin (Berlin: de Gruyter, 2007), 155–88.

59. For this usage, see also v. 8; note "Yahweh of hosts" in vv. 3 and 5.

60. For *šûlāyw* in v. 1b instead as the god's extremities, see G. R. Driver, "Isaiah 6:1 'his train filled the temple,'" in *Near Eastern Studies in Honor of William Foxwell Albright,* ed. Hans Goedicke (Baltimore: Johns Hopkins University Press, 1971), 87–96. See also Lyle Eslinger, "The Infinite in a Finite Organical Perception (Isaiah VI 1–5)," *VT* 45 (1995): 145–73, followed by N. Wyatt, *Myths of Power: A Study of Royal Myth and Ideology in Ugaritic and Biblical Tradition* (Münster: Ugarit-Verlag, 1996), 5, 342. Eslinger and Wyatt understand the term to refer to God's genitals. Cf. Smith, *Origins of Biblical Monotheism,* 246 n. 36.

61. For a detailed discussion of the divine body in Isaiah 6 by reference to the temple description in 1 Kings 6, see Zevit, "Taking the Measure."

62. For the cherubs, see Hartenstein, "Cherubim and Seraphim in the Bible," 156–63 and 169–72.

63. For this phrase as applied to this representation, see Hartenstein, "Cherubim and Seraphim in the Bible," 163. A cherub elsewhere is what the storm-god rides on (2 Sam 22:11//Ps 18:10).

64. Cf. Zevit ("Taking the Measure," 650): "Accordingly, from the floor of the *debir* to the top of the seated figure's head, the height was 3 (height of legs) + 1.5 (height of ark) + 3.7 (stature of the seated figure) = 8.2 cubits."

65. Later Jewish mystical texts describe God in terms of the third, cosmic body. They also assimilate elements of biblical texts describing the second body into their descriptions of the third. For example, the description of the heavenly throne in Merkavah Rabbah (lines 21–22) draws on the earthly temple scene in Isaiah 6 (Cohen, *Shi'ur Qomah,* 56). Within its account of the cosmic divine body, Siddur Rabbah (lines 36–44) renders the heavenly court with elements drawn from Isaiah 6 as well as Ezekiel 1 and Daniel 7 (Cohen, *Shi'ur Qomah,* 41–42).

66. Cf. Ps 139:7–12; Jer 23:23–24; and Amos 9:2.

67. For the iconographic repertoire represented by this passage, see Keel, *Jahwe-Visionen und Siegelkunst,* 125–273; Christoph Uehlinger and Suzanne Müller Trufaut, "Ezekiel 1, Babylonian Cosmological Scholarship and Iconography: Attempts at Further Refinement," *TZ* 57 (2001): 140–71; and Hartenstein, "Wolkendunkel und Himmelfeste," 141–44. Note also Jill Middlemas, "Exclusively YHWH: Aniconism and Anthropomorphism in Ezekiel," in *Prophecy*

and the Prophets in Ancient Israel: Proceedings of the Oxford Old Testament Seminar, ed. John Day, LHB/OTS 531 (New York: T & T Clark, 2010), 309–24.

68. For seraphim, see Hartenstein, "Cherubim and Seraphim in the Bible," 163–72.

69. For this type of storm (here called *rûaḥ sĕ'ārâ*), elsewhere a dry, desiccating storm from the east, see Aloysius Fitzgerald, F.S.C., *The Lord of the East Wind,* CBQMS 34 (Washington, D.C.: Catholic Biblical Association of America, 2002), 136–39.

70. For cherubim here, see Hartenstein, "Cherubim and Seraphim in the Bible," 155–88. Hartenstein rightly stresses their role as guardians.

71. For this word *rāqîa',* see the discussion below.

72. Comparing the same usage in Judg 13:6, Moshe Greenberg contends that *mar'eh* in Ezekiel 1 "does not signify a reservation with respect to looks but with respect to substance." Greenberg, *Ezekiel 1–20: A New Translation with Introduction and Commentary,* AYB 22 (Garden City, N.Y.: Doubleday, 1983), 53. The basis for Greenberg's distinction is not quite clear, as the semantics of *mar'eh* may include the appearance or looks of a figure, whether divine or human (cf. 1 Sam 16:7; Isa 52:14).

73. For Greenberg (*Ezekiel 1–20,* 53), the comparative particle "signifies unwillingness to commit oneself to the substantial identity of the seen with the compared."

74. "Loins" here refers to the midsection of the body, comparable to "waist."

75. This cosmic body is comparable to Marduk's in Enuma Elish, tablet 1, lines 93–100 ("impossible to understand"), as noted by Hendel ("Aniconism," 207). For the passage, see W. G. Lambert, *Babylonian Creation Myths,* MC 16 (Winona Lake, Ind.: Eisenbrauns, 2013), 55–57; and Thomas R. Kämmerer and Kai A. Metzler, eds., *Das babylonische Weltschöpfungsepos Enūma eliš,* AOAT 375 (Münster: Ugarit-Verlag, 2012), 133–34.

76. Note Ben Sira (Ecclesiasticus) 49:8 (NRSV), where the prophet's vision is characterized for the first time in terms of a "chariot." Ezekiel 1 was the subject of reuse, for example in "Pseudo-Ezekiel," in the Dead Sea Scrolls (4Q385, fragment 6), in Devorah Dimant, "Pseudo-Ezekiel," in *Outside the Bible: Ancient Jewish Writings Related to Scripture,* ed. Louis H. Feldman, James L. Kugel, and Lawrence H. Schiffman, 3 vols. (Philadelphia: Jewish Publication Society/ University of Nebraska Press, 2013), 2.1526–27.

77. John J. Collins, *Daniel: A Commentary on the Book of Daniel,* ed. Frank Moore Cross, Hermeneia (Minneapolis: Fortress, 1993), 299–303.

78. For these passages, see Collins, *Daniel,* 300; and Wolfson, *Speculum,* 28–33. Note also the chariot-throne in Songs of the Sabbath Sacrifice 12.3–4, in Carol A. Newsom and James H. Charlesworth, with Brent A. Strawn and Henry W. L. Rietz, "Angelic Liturgy: Songs of the Sabbath (4Q400–4Q107, 11Q17, Masīk)," in *Hebrew, Aramaic, and Greek Texts with English Translations: Volume 4B. Angelic Liturgy: Songs of the Sabbath Sacrifice,* ed. James H. Charlesworth and

Carol A. Newsom, Princeton Theological Seminary Dead Sea Scrolls Project 4B (Tübingen: Mohr Siebeck; Louisville, Ky.: Westminster John Knox, 1999), 182–83. See also Ascension of Isaiah, chapter 9, esp. 27–32 (*OTP* 2.171).

79. For example, Isa 40:12 is echoed in 4Q511 (4QShirb), fr. 30 lines 4–5 (*DSSR* 2.896–97) and The Greek Apocalypse of Ezra 7:5 (*OTP* 1.578), and Isa 66:1 in 1 Enoch 84:2 (*OTP* 1.62), Sibylline Oracles 1:139 (*OTP* 1.338), and Aristobulus, fr. 4:5 (*OTP* 2.840). First Kings 8:27 is paralleled in Chronicles in 2 Chr 6:18 and is used in 2 Chr 2:5.

80. For these views, see Michael Shenkar, "The Coin of the 'God on the Winged Wheel,'" *BOREAS—Münstersche Beiträge zur Archäologie* 30/31 (2007/2008): 13–25, with a photographic image of the coin (Talfel 7.1); and Izaak J. de Hulster, *Iconographic Exegesis and Third Isaiah*, FAT 2/36 (Tübingen: Mohr Siebeck, 2009), 194–205. Shenkar ("Coin," 22) suggests that the coin might not be Yehudean but Samarian: "the god of Samaria, 'Samarian Yahweh,' worshipped on Mount Gerizim, probably is the deity depicted on the BM drachm" (the high admixture of copper in the coin contributes to this view). However, as noted by Zachary Margulies (personal communication), there are Samaritan coins from this period that explicitly name their deity Zeus (obverse) and that use a distinctive Samaritan Hebrew alphabet (reverse).

81. Wolfson, *Speculum*, 28.

82. For this point, see Barr, "Theophany and Anthropomorphism," 38.

83. See Paolo Xella, "L'épisode de Dnil et Kothar (*KTU* 1.17 [= *CTA* 17] v 1–31 et Gen. xviii 1–16," *VT* 28 (1978): 483–88; Simon B. Parker, *The Pre-Biblical Narrative Tradition: Essays on the Ugaritic Poems Keret and Aqhat*, SBLRBS 24 (Atlanta: Scholars, 1989), 109–11; and Hamori, *"When Gods Were Men,"* 78–96. For the passage, see *UNP* 58–59.

84. In his journeying to Danil in *KTU* 1.17 V (in *UNP* 58), Kothar might seem superhuman in scale as he is seen by Danil across "a thousand fields, ten thousand acres" (line 10), but with Kothar's eating and drinking at Danil's tent, this superhuman size is less evident.

85. For the former, see *KTU* 1.15 II–III, in *UNP* 24–27; for the latter, see *KTU* 1.17 II 26–40, in *UNP* 57.

86. Genesis 2 and 32 depart somewhat from this pattern, perhaps deliberately: in Genesis 2, the deity is the host to the humans (as in the temple model of the second body), while in Genesis 32 the hostility of the passage perhaps suggests Jacob as an anti-host, reflecting his worry over meeting his brother, Esau.

87. See Karel van der Toorn, *Family Religion in Babylonia, Syria and Israel: Continuity and Change in the Forms of Religious Life*, Studies in the History and Culture of the Ancient Near East 7 (Leiden: Brill, 1996), 220–22; and Theodore J. Lewis, "Teraphim," *DDD* 844–50. Lewis surveys scholarly proposals, including van der Toorn's view of them as ancestral figurines or statues as well as other scholars who understand them as household gods. William Foxwell Albright

believed that the two words, *tĕrāpîm* and *rĕpā'îm*, were possibly related etymologically; see Albright, *Yahweh and the Gods of Canaan: A Historical Analysis of Two Contrasting Faiths* (Winona Lake, Ind.: Eisenbrauns, n.d.), 168 n. 43. This does not appear to be the case. Despite their different etymological origins (see *DDD* 844–45), the two similar sounding words, *tĕrāpîm* and *rĕpā'îm*, may have been associated as a popular or folk etymology; in this case, *tĕrāpîm* might be figurines of the *rĕpā'îm*, the deceased, "divine" ancestors. However, household gods would better fit the context of Genesis 31; perhaps a conflation of both household deities and ancestors underlies biblical *tĕrāpîm*. Note the cautionary remarks of P. R. S. Moorey, *Idols of the People: Miniature Images of Clay in the Ancient Near East*, Schweich Lectures of the British Academy 2001 (Oxford: Oxford University Press, 2003), 49. The contexts for the *tĕrāpîm* in Genesis 31 and 1 Samuel 19 imply images of very different sizes, the former small enough to sit on and the latter nearly life-size. In view of the difficulty of identifying household male figurines (see the following note), Robert D. Miller II identifies *tĕrāpîm* as masks ("Shamanism in Early Israel," *WZKM* 101 [2011]: 326–27). Van der Toorn observes that masks were not part of domestic cult.

88. The literature is vast. See Othmar Keel and Christoph Uehlinger, *Gods, Goddesses, and Images of God in Ancient Israel*, trans. Thomas Trapp (Minneapolis: Fortress, 1998); and Christoph Uehlinger, "Anthropomorphic Cult Statuary in Iron Age Palestine and the Search for Yahweh's Cult Images," in *The Image and the Book: Iconic Cults, Aniconism, and the Rise of Book Religion in Israel and the Ancient Near East*, ed. Karel van der Toorn, Biblical Exegesis and Theology 21 (Leuven: Peeters, 1997), 97–156.

89. Male figurines for Iron Age Israel, apart from the horse and rider type, are virtually unknown (Liz Bloch-Smith and Beth Alpert-Nakhai, personal communications). The relative lack of male figurines in the archaeological record is noted also by Karel van der Toorn, who identifies *tĕrāpîm* as male and female figurines; see van der Toorn, "Israelite Figurines: A View from the Texts," in *Sacred Time, Sacred Place: Archaeology and the Religion of Israel*, ed. Barry Gittlen (Winona Lake, Ind.: Eisenbrauns, 2002), 45–62. There is evidence for male and female figurines from Tell Jawa, summarized by Rainer Albertz, "Family Religion in Ancient Israel," in *Household and Family Religion in Antiquity*, ed. John Bodel and Saul M. Olyan (Malden, Mass.: Blackwell, 2008), 89–112, here 96. A sanctuary room at Khirbat 'Ataruz also yielded a fragmentary Iron II cult stand (or shrine model) depicting two males. See Chang-Ho Ji, "Khirbat 'Ataruz: An Interim Overview of the 10 Years of Archaeological Architectural Findings," *ADAJ* 55 (2011): 561–79, here 566–67 (my thanks to Elizabeth Bloch-Smith for this reference). For a broad consideration of anthropomorphic and zoomorphic figurines in domestic installations, see Beth Alpert-Nakhai, "Varieties of Religious Expression in the Domestic Setting," in *Household Archaeology in Ancient Israel and Beyond*, ed. A. Yasur-Landau,

J. R. Ebeling, and L. B. Mazow, CHANE 50 (Leiden: Brill, 2011), 347–60, here 350 and 354 (reference courtesy of Alpert-Nakhai).

90. Hamori, *"When Gods Were Men,"* 111–14. As noted above, Hamori believes this feature to pertain to God in these passages and not angels elsewhere, but this overlooks the fact that angels no less than God appear in Genesis 18.

91. See Barr, "Theophany and Anthropomorphism in the Old Testament," 38. For further discussion, see Chapter 2 below.

92. For Baal's abode, see Clifford, *Cosmic Mountain,* 57–73.

93. The pertinent section of the Baal Cycle concerning Baal's palace is *KTU* 1.4 V–VII, in *UNP* 129–36. For the elements of the heavenly palace in the Bible and the Dead Sea Scrolls, see Mark S. Smith, "Biblical and Canaanite Notes to the Songs of the Sabbath Sacrifice from Qumran," *RdQ* 12 (1987): 585–88. For a comparison with Mesopotamian sources, see Hartenstein, "Wolkendunkel und Himmelfeste," 138–40. On the basis of these parallels, as well as Ezek 1:26, Hartenstein believes that the lapis lazuli in Exod 24:10 is the material for a pedestal for the feet of God, as noted above. It is also possibly the flooring (also discussed above), in view of the Ugaritic evidence.

94. For the royal audience as the temple-paradigm, see Jeffrey H. Tigay, "On Some Aspects of Prayer in the Bible," *AJSR* 1 (1976): 363–79; and Mark S. Smith, *The Pilgrimage Pattern in Exodus,* with contributions by Elizabeth M. Bloch-Smith, JSOTSup 239 (Sheffield: Sheffield Academic, 1997), 100–109. For more recent studies, see Friedhelm Hartenstein, *Das Angesicht JHWHs: Studien zu seinem höfischen und kultischen Bedeutungshintergrund in den Psalmen und in Exodus 32–34,* FAT 1/55 (Tübingen: Mohr Siebeck, 2009); and Simeon B. Chavel, "The Face of God and the Etiquette of Eye-Contact: Visitation, Pilgrimage and Prophetic Vision in Ancient Israelite and Early Jewish Imagination," *JSQ* 19 (2012): 1–55. For an iconographic treatment, see Christoph Uehlinger, "Audienz in der Götterwelt: Anthropomorphismus und Soziomorphismus in der Ikonographie eines altsyrischer Zylindersiegels," *UF* 24 (1992): 339–59.

95. Hartenstein, *Das Angesicht JHWHs,* 55–56. For depictions and discussion of Mesopotamian sources, see Christopher G. Frechette, *Mesopotamian Ritual-prayers of "Hand-lifting" (Akkadian Šuillas): An Investigation of Function in Light of the Idiomatic Meaning of the Rubric,* AOAT 379 (Münster: Ugarit-Verlag, 2012), 30–31, 71–77.

96. Greenfield, "Ba'al's Throne and Isa. 6:1," 193–98. For the text, see *UNP* 154.

97. Louvre AO 15.775 = RS 4.427, in *ANEP* 168, #490; *UBC* 1.107.

98. For this evidence, see the references in note 53 above.

99. Monson, "New 'Ain Dara Temple," 28.

100. For the perception of the deity in these psalms, see Mark S. Smith, "'Seeing God' in the Psalms: The Background to the Beatific Vision in the Hebrew Scriptures," *CBQ* 50 (1988): 171–83; Hendel, "Aniconism and Anthropomorphism in Ancient Israel," 222; and Hartenstein, *Das Angesicht JHWHs.* For divine embodiment within the thematic complex of seeing God, see S. Tamar

Kamionkowski, "The Erotics of Pilgrimage: A Fresh Look at Psalms 84 and 63," in *Gazing on the Deep: Ancient Near Eastern and Other Studies in Honor of Tzvi Abusch*, ed. Jeffrey Stackert, Barbara Nevling Porter, and David P. Wright (Bethesda, Md.: CDL, 2010), 467–78. See also Job 42:5.

101. For a case with the first body, see Gen 32:31. In this text, no danger is suggested in seeing the mysterious figure, unlike many cases for seeing the second divine body. For a case for the third body, see Ezekiel 1 (esp. vv. 26–28). The appearance of the motif there may be playing off its evident reuse of Isa 6:1, but seeing the deity is a matter raised with other passages involving the third body, as noted below.

102. Meyer, "Placing and Tracing Absence: A Material Culture of the Immaterial," *Journal of Material Culture* 17/1 (2012): 103–10, here 103.

103. Ingold, "Culture on the Ground: The World Perceived Through the Feet," *Journal of Material Culture* 9/3 (2004): 315–40, here 328. Note also his comment (p. 333): "pedestrian movements thread a tangled network of personalized trails through the landscape itself. Through walking, in short, landscapes are woven into life, and lives are woven into the landscape, in a process that is continuous and never-ending ... pedestrian activities can mark the landscape. When the same paths are repeatedly trodden ... the consequences may be quite dramatic. . . . Surfaces are indeed transformed. But these are surfaces *in* the world, not the surface *of* the world. Indeed strictly speaking, the world has no surface. Human beings live in the world, not on it, and as beings in the world the historical transformations they effect are part and parcel of the world's transformation of itself." The point applies analogously to deities in the world.

104. *OTP* 1.21 and 136, respectively. Perhaps reflecting this problem of seeing the third body, the Songs of the Sabbath Sacrifice praise "the form of God" (Song 7:39) and refer to the divine throne in heaven (e.g., Song 11:23; 12:3–4), but they do not describe the deity as such, as noted by Newsom in Newsom and Charlesworth, "Angelic Liturgy," 6.

105. Halpern, *From Gods to God: The Dynamics of Iron Age Cosmologies*, ed. Matthew J. Adams, FAT 1/63 (Tübingen: Mohr Siebeck, 2009), 429–42.

106. Christoph Uehlinger and Suzanne Müller Trufaut, "Ezekiel 1, Babylonian Cosmological Scholarship and Iconography: Attempts at Further Refinement," *TZ* 57 (2001): 140–71.

107. Uehlinger and Müller Trufaut, "Ezekiel 1," 153, also citing Keel, *Jahwe-Visionen und Siegelkunst*, 210–12, figures 159–162; see also Hartenstein, "Wolkendunkel und Himmelfeste," 139 and 170 Tafel 2/1. Uehlinger and Müller Trufaut ("Ezekiel 1," 158–59) also note that divine garments of Babylonian deities represented on monuments include major celestial bodies and spheres. See further Irit Ziffer, "Iconography," in Raz Kletter, Irit Ziffer, and Wolfgang Zwickel, *Yavneh I: The Excavation of the 'Temple Hill' Repository Pit and the Cult Stands*,

OBO, Series Archaeologica 30 (Fribourg: Academic Press; Göttingen: Vandenhoeck & Ruprecht, 2010), 64–65.

108. CT 13 34 41:2, cited in *CAD* B:244. For further references, see *CAD* B:244–45; and Alasdair Livingstone, *Court Poetry and Literary Miscellanea*, SAA III (Helsinki: Helsinki University Press, 1989), 4–5 (*ABRT* 1 32, lines 21, 24) and 7 (*ABRT* 1 29f. also cited in the *CAD* entry); Erica Reiner, *Astral Magic in Babylonia* (Philadelphia: American Philosophical Society, 1995), 9; and Wayne B. Horowitz, *Mesopotamian Cosmic Geography*, Mesopotamian Civilizations 8 (Winona Lake, Ind.: Eisenbrauns, 1998), 214, 226–27, and 260. Horowitz (*Mesopotamian Cosmic Geography*, 226) derives the word from *barāmu* B, "to be speckled" (referring to stars "as specks on a dark background"). Cf. Akkadian *qiddu*, possibly "celestial firmament," attested in a lexical series (*CAD* Q:251).

109. VAT 9656, lines 7–8 and 10, cited in L. Kataja and R. Whiting, *Grants, Decrees and Gifts of the Neo-Assyrian Period*, States Archives of Assyria XII (Helsinki: Helsinki University Press, 1995), 104.

110. *ABRT* 1 29:8, cited in *CAD* B:244–45.

111. AWOL—The Ancient World Online, http://ancientworldonline.blogspot.com/2014/02/online-etymological-dictionary-of.html, letter B.

112. Horowitz, *Mesopotamian Cosmic Geography*, 226. For this term, see also Horowitz, "Stars, Cows, Semicircles and Domes," in *A Woman of Valor: Jerusalem Ancient Near Eastern Studies in Honor of Joan Goodnick Westenholz*, ed. Wayne Horowitz, U. Gabbay, and F. Vukosavović, Biblioteca del Próximo Oriente Antiguo 8 (Madrid: Consejo Superior de Investigaciones Científicas, 2010), 75.

113. See Horowitz, *Mesopotamian Cosmic Geography*, 243–52, and "Stars, Cows, Semicircles and Domes," 73–86. Cf. *ANEP* #529 and Hartenstein, "Wolkendunkel und Himmelfeste," 139 and 170, Tafel 2/2, for the enthronement of Shamash in his shrine on the heavenly ocean.

114. Uehlinger and Müller Trufaut, "Ezekiel 1," 144 and 164–65. See also Keel, *Jahwe-Visionen und Siegelkunst*, 252.

115. For discussion, see Mark S. Smith, *The Priestly Vision of Genesis 1* (Minneapolis: Fortress, 2010), 213–15 nn. 2–5.

116. For the priestly scribal background of Genesis, see Smith, *Priestly Vision of Genesis 1*, 117–37; for a discussion of "priestly mystical thinking," see Smith, *Priestly Vision of Genesis 1*, 84–87.

117. See Mark S. Smith, *The Origins of Biblical Monotheism: Israel's Polytheistic Background and the Ugaritic Texts* (Oxford: Oxford University Press, 2003). For a complementary approach also concerned with anthropomorphism and space, see Martin Leuenberger, "Jhwh, 'der Gott Jerusalems' (BLay 1,2): Konturen der Jerusalemer Tempeltheologie aus religions- und theologiegeschichtlicher Perspektive," *EvT* 74 (2014): 245–60.

118. Hendel, Review of Benjamin Sommer, *The Bodies of God*, *AJSR* 34 (2010): 407–10, here 409. I thank Ron Hendel for discussion of these points and for his suggestions, which I have included here.

119. For this point, see Hendel, *The Book of Genesis: A Biography,* Lives of Great Religious Books (Princeton, N.J.: Princeton University Press, 2013), 151–52. On this point Hendel cites Francesca Rochberg, "'The Stars Their Likenesses': Perspectives on the Relation Between Celestial Bodies and Gods in Mesopotamia," in *What Is a God? Anthropomorphic and Non-Anthropomorphic Aspects of Deity in Ancient Mesopotamia,* ed. Barbara Porter (Winona Lake, Ind.: Eisenbrauns, 2009), 89. See also Rochberg, *The Heavenly Writing: Divination, Horoscopy, and Astronomy in Mesopotamian Culture* (Cambridge: Cambridge University Press, 2004), 168–69, which supplies details for the case of Sin.

120. Reiner, *Astral Magic in Babylonia,* Transactions of the American Philosophical Society 85/4 (Philadelphia: American Philosophical Society, 1995), 1–2.

121. Rochberg, *Heavenly Writing,* 169.

122. Rochberg, *Heavenly Writing,* 171; see also p. 175. The general point applies also to West Semitic deities: the Ugaritic word for Shapshu is the sun-goddess and also the sun; and the Ugaritic word for Yarikh is the moon-god and also the moon. Cf. Steve A. Wiggins, "What's in a Name? Yariḫ at Ugarit," *UF* 30 (1998): 761–79.

123. See the preceding note, and Smith, *Origins of Biblical Monotheism,* 61–66.

124. See Keel and Uehlinger, *Gods, Goddesses, and Images of God,* 288, 290–91, 294–95, 316–17, 320–23, 357–58, 374–77; Keel, *Goddesses and Trees, New Moon and Yahweh: Ancient Near Eastern Art and the Hebrew Bible,* JSOTSup 261 (Sheffield: Sheffield Academic, 1998), 59–109.

125. See T. N. D. Mettinger, *The Dethronement of Sabaoth: Studies in the Shem and Kabod Theologies,* trans. F. H. Cryer, ConBOT 18 (Lund: Gleerup, 1982), 80–124; and John Kutsko, *Between Heaven and Earth: Divine Presence and Absence in the Book of Ezekiel,* Biblical and Judaic Studies 7 (Winona Lake, Ind.: Eisenbrauns, 2000), 77–100.

126. Sommer (*Bodies of God,* 80–81) views Pentateuchal priestly *kābôd* as a body. Cf. Steven Weitzman, "New Light on God's Opacity," in *Shai le-Sara Japhet: Studies in the Bible, Its Exegesis and Its Language,* ed. M. Bar Asher, E. Tov, D. Rom-Shiloni, and N. Wazana (Jerusalem: Mosad Bialik, 2007), 379*. According to Sommer (*Bodies of God,* 69–70), the proof that priestly *kābôd* in the Pentateuch involves a body is Gen 1:26–28. However, the image and likeness of God hardly need to entail a physical body. The immediate context suggests that humanity is like God with respect to creation and dominion. For this point, see W. Randall Garr, *In His Own Image and Likeness: Humanity, Divinity, and Monotheism,* CHANE 15 (Leiden: Brill, 2003), 174–76; and Smith, *Priestly Vision of Genesis 1,* 134–35. Knafl (*Forming God,* 127) rightly notes that Pentateuchal priestly material uses verbs that imply a body yet elsewhere labels this material as "the least anthropomorphic" of Pentateuchal sources (*Forming God,* 168). In any case, I regard verbal usages as different from the representation of a divine body, a point that to my mind is not sufficiently addressed in Knafl's discussion.

127. See Shawn Zelig Aster, *The Unbeatable Light: Melammu and Its Biblical Parallels*, AOAT 384 (Münster: Ugarit-Verlag, 2013), 315.

128. See Moshe Weinfeld, *Deuteronomy and the Deuteronomic School* (Oxford: Clarendon, 1972), 198; Mettinger, *Dethronement of Sabaoth*, 47. Note also the survey of views in Sandra L. Richter, *The Deuteronomistic History and the Name Theology: ľšakkēn šᵉmô šām in the Bible and the Ancient Near East*, BZAW 318 (Berlin: de Gruyter, 2002), 7–40. Despite her critique against a name "hypostasis" in many Deuteronomic and Deuteronomistic texts, "name theology" of various sorts seems attested in biblical and extra-biblical texts (note Sommers, *Bodies of God*, 190 n. 101; cf. Knafl, *Forming God*, 207). The divine name is personified as a divine warrior in Isa 30:27, and the divine name in Ps 29:1 has "glory" (*kābôd*); these lie beyond the purview of Richter's study. For the West Semitic background of the name as a divine warrior, see Smith, *Origins of Biblical Monotheism*, 74–76.

129. See Stephen Cook, "God's Real Absence and Real Presence in Deuteronomy and Deuteronomists," in *Divine Presence and Absence in Exilic and Post-Exilic Judaism*, ed. Nathan MacDonald and Izaak J. de Hulster, Studies of the Sofja Kovalevskaja Research Group on Early Jewish Monotheism II, FAT 2/61 (Tübingen: Mohr Siebeck, 2013), 121–50. See also Knafl, *Forming God*, 100–109 and 184–87.

130. See J. Edward Wright, *The Early History of Heaven* (New York: Oxford University Press, 2000), 98–184. See also Alexander Kulik, "Apocalypse of Abraham," in *Outside the Bible*, 2.1480 n. 46.

131. Hamori ("Divine Embodiment," 161–83) cautions against characterizing the first body as "incarnation." Sommer (*Bodies of God*, 136) likewise would avoid "incarnation," preferring "embodiment" for Jewish notions of the divine body. Elliot Wolfson (*Giving Beyond the Gift: Apophasis and Overcoming Theomania* [New York: Fordham University Press, 2013], 262 n. 9) responds: "the semantic distinction between embodiment and incarnation as presented by Sommer is a distinction without a difference." It is unclear why Sommer's distinction applies to the ancient evidence for the first divine body, especially in Genesis 18–19, compared with New Testament representations of incarnation. This issue remains a problem for both scholarly and religious consideration.

Chapter 2. Like Deities, Like Temples (Like People)

1. For a recent survey of temple structures and the ways deities are present in them, see Michael B. Hundley, *Gods in Dwellings: Temples and Divine Presence in the Ancient Near East*, WAWSup 3 (Atlanta: SBL, 2013).

2. For the royal audience as the temple-paradigm, see the literature cited in Chapter 1 n. 94.

3. *KTU* 1.4 VII 17–19, 25–28, in *UNP* 136.

4. Moshe Weinfeld, "Gen. 7:11, 8:1–2 Against the Background of Ancient Near Eastern Tradition," *WO* 9 (1977): 242–48. The rains are also experienced in the context of the temple, as dramatized in Psalm 29 as Yahweh's easterly procession. In v. 9 of this psalm, the storm issues in the community's recognition of the theophany indicated by *kābôd* ("glory" or "effulgence"). The final clause of the verse is usually translated, "and in his temple all say glory" or the like, but it may be understood, "and in his temple, all of it, effulgence is visible." For this translation, see Mark S. Smith, *Untold Stories: The Bible and Ugaritic Studies in the Twentieth Century* (Peabody, Mass.: Hendrickson, 2001), 160–61.

5. *KTU* 1.4 V 6–9, in *UNP* 129. For discussion, see *UBC* 2.535, 537, 542, and 556–63.

6. Charles Virolleaud, "Un nouveau chant du poème d'Alein-Baal," *Syria* 13 (1932): 133–41, here 133 and 141; and Theodore H. Gaster, "The Ritual Pattern of a Ras-Shamra Epic," *Archiv Orientální* 5 (1933): 118–23.

7. See *BDB* 727; Jonas C. Greenfield, *'Al Kanfei Yonah: Collected Studies of Jonas C. Greenfield on Semitic Philology,* ed. Shalom M. Paul, Michael E. Stone, and Avital Pinnick, 2 vols. (Leiden: Brill; Jerusalem: Hebrew University Magnes Press, 2001), 750–55; and Alan R. Millard, "The Etymology of Eden," *VT* 34 (1984): 103–10.

8. For this point, see Greenfield, *'Al Kanfei Yonah,* 750–55; and Jonas C. Greenfield and Aaron Shaffer, "Notes on the Akkadian-Aramaic Bilingual Statue from Tell Fekherye," in *'Al Kanfei Yonah,* 217–24. For the text, see Ali Abou-Assaf, Pierre Bordreuil, and Alan R. Millard, *La statue de Tell Fekherye et son inscription bilingue assyro-araméenne,* Études Assyriologiques 10 (Paris: Éditions Recherche sur les Civilisations, 1982).

9. *KTU* 1.6 III 12–13, in *UNP* 158.

10. McCarter, "The Garden of Eden" (unpublished essay, used with permission, for which I thank Professor McCarter). Cf. Edward Lipiński, "El's Abode. Mythological Traditions Related to Mt. Hermon and the Mountains of Armenia," *OLP* 2 (1971): 13–69.

11. See also Nahum Waldman, "The Wealth of the Mountain and Sea: The Background of a Biblical Image," *JQR* 71 (1981): 176–80; and Avigdor (Victor) Hurowitz, *I Have Built You an Exalted House: Temple Building in the Bible in Light of Mesopotamian and Northwest Semitic Writings,* JSOTSup 115, JSOT/ASOR Monographs 5 (Sheffield: Sheffield Academic, 1992), 171–223.

12. Gilgamesh SB tablet V, line 6, in *ANET* 82, in A. R. George, *The Babylonian Gilgamesh Tablet: Introduction, Critical Edition and Cuneiform Texts,* 2 vols. (Oxford: Oxford University Press 2003), 1.602–3 (see also 466 and 822 n. 6).

13. The so-called OB Bauer fragment, tablet V, C, reverse, line 20 in *ANET* 504, and as line 38' in George, *Babylonian Gilgamesh Tablet,* 1.264–65. For an iconographic representation of the cedars in Gilgamesh, see Wilfred G. Lambert, "Gilgamesh in Literature and Art: The Second and First Millennia," in *Gilgamesh: A Reader,* ed. J. Maier (Wauconda, Ill.: Bolchazy-Carducci, 1994), 55 figure 9.

14. For these themes in both the Jerusalem temple and the temple narrative of the Baal Cycle, see Elizabeth Bloch-Smith, "'Who Is the King of Glory?' Solomon's Temple as Symbol," in *Scripture and Other Artifacts: Essays on the Bible and Archaeology in Honor of Philip J. King,* ed. Michael D. Coogan, Cheryl Exum, and Lawrence E. Stager (Louisville, Ky.: Westminster/John Knox, 1994), 19–23.

15. *KTU* 1.4 VI 16–21, in *UNP* 133. See also *KTU* 1.4 V 12–18, in *UNP* 130.

16. Mark S. Smith, "Biblical and Canaanite Notes to the Songs of the Sabbath Sacrifice from Qumran," *RdQ* 12 (1987): 585–88.

17. Josephus, *Ant.* 8.145, citing Menander; cf. Apion 1.118. See H. St. J. Thackeray and R. Marcus, *Josephus V. Jewish Antiquities, Books V–VIII,* Loeb Classical Library (London: Heinemann; Cambridge, Mass.: Harvard University Press, 1934), 648–49. For Apion, see Thackeray, *The Life/Against Apion,* Loeb Classical Library (London: Heinemann; Cambridge, Mass.: Harvard University Press, 1926), 210–11.

18. PE 1.1.9. For the text and translation of these lines, see Harold A. Attridge and Robert A. Oden, *Philo of Byblos. The Phoenician History: Introduction, Critical Text, Translation, Notes,* CBQMS 9 (Washington, D.C.: Catholic Biblical Association of America, 1981), 42–43.

19. *KAI* 15; see Otto Eissfeldt, "Schamemrumim," 123–26, cited in Attridge and Oden, *Philo of Byblos,* 82 n. 56.

20. Weinfeld, "Semiramis: Her Name and Her Origin," in *Ah, Assyria . . . : Studies in Assyrian History and Ancient Near Eastern Historiography Presented to Hayim Tadmor,* ed. M. Cogan and I. Eph'al, Scripta hierosolymitana 33 (Jerusalem: Magnes, 1991), 99–103, esp. 100 n. 12. Weinfeld also notes the name of the queen Semiramis, identified with Sammuramat, the queen mother of Adad-nirari III, attested for example in Lucian of Samosata's *De Dea Syria* 14 and 39; for text and translation, see Harold A. Attridge and Robert A. Oden, *The Syrian Goddess (De Dea Syria) Attributed to Lucian,* Texts and Translations 9, Greco-Roman Religion 1 (Missoula, Mont.: Scholars for the SBL, 1979), 20–21 and 48–49, respectively. According to the first passage, Semiramis's mother is known as Derketo. Both names are reminiscent of Anat's titles in *KTU* 1.108.6–7, *b'lt drkt b'lt šmm rmm* (cf. reading *rḫpt [bšm]m rm<m>,* so *KTU* 1.108.9–10), in *RCU* 194; and Gregorio del Olmo Lete, *Canaanite Religion According to the Liturgical Texts of Ugarit,* trans. Wilfred G. E. Watson, 2nd ed., AOAT 408 (Münster: Ugarit-Verlag, 2014), 151.

21. *KTU* 1.3 III 20–31, in *UNP* 110. For discussion, see *UBC* 2.223–37.

22. See Bloch-Smith, "'Who Is the King of Glory?,'" 18–31. See also her remarks in Mark S. Smith, *The Pilgrimage Pattern in Exodus,* with contributions by Elizabeth M. Bloch-Smith, JSOTSup 239 (Sheffield: Sheffield Academic, 1997), 84–86.

23. Bloch-Smith, "'Who Is the King of Glory?,'" 27.

24. Bloch-Smith, "'Who Is the King of Glory?,'" 27.

25. Stordalen, *Echoes of Eden: Genesis 2–3 and Symbolism of the Eden Garden in Biblical Hebrew Literature*, CEBT 25 (Leuven: Peeters, 2000); and Lawrence E. Stager, "Jerusalem and the Garden of Eden," *EI* 26 (1999 = Frank Moore Cross Volume): 183–94, and "Jerusalem as Eden," *Biblical Archaeology Review* 26/3 (2000): 41–43. See also Howard N. Wallace, *The Eden Narrative*, HSM 32 (Atlanta: Scholars, 1985), 28–29.

26. Stordalen, *Echoes of Eden*, 410–17; Stager, "Jerusalem as Eden," 41–43.

27. Olyan, *Asherah and the Cult of Yahweh in Israel*, SBLDS 34 (Atlanta: Scholars, 1988), 71 n. 4. See also Marjo C. A. Korpel and Johannes C. de Moor, *Adam, Eve, and the Devil: A New Beginning*, Hebrew Bible Monographs 65 (Sheffield: Sheffield Phoenix, 2014), 53. The opening of the inscription has been recently interpreted differently, e.g., Philip C. Schmitz, *The Phoenician Diaspora: Epigraphic and Historical Studies* (Winona Lake, Ind.: Eisenbrauns, 2012), 69–84.

28. See also Nicholas Wyatt, "The Hollow Crown: Ambivalent Elements in West Semitic Royal Ideology," *UF* 18 (1986): 421–36, with some rather speculative elements.

29. See David Bokovoy, "Did Eve Acquire, Create, or Procreate with Yahweh? A Grammatical and Contextual Reassessment of Genesis 4:1," *VT* 63 (2013): 19–35; "Yahweh as a Sexual Deity in J's Prehistory," Ph.D. diss., Brandeis University, 2012. For **qny*, see also Patrick D. Miller, "Creator of Earth," *BASOR* 239 (1980): 43–46. These authors also note the title of her consort El, **qny 'rṣ*, which is not only in Late Bronze Age material, but also known in biblical tradition, attached to the founding myth of Jerusalem in Genesis 14.

30. For a more expansive reconstruction, see Korpel and de Moor, *Adam, Eve, and the Devil*.

31. See Mark S. Smith, *The Origins of Biblical Monotheism* (Oxford: Oxford University Press, 2001), 41–66.

32. *KTU* 1.3 III 31, in *UNP* 110; and *KTU* 1.10 III 31, in *UNP* 185.

33. Holtz, "God as Refuge and Temple Refuge in the Psalms," in *The Temple of Jerusalem: From Moses to the Messiah. In Honor of Louis H. Feldman*, ed. Steven Fine, Brill Reference Library of Judaism 29 (Leiden: Brill, 2011), 17–26.

34. For more detail, see Mark S. Smith, "God and Zion: Form and Meaning in Psalm 48," *SEL* 6 (1989): 67–77.

35. See Smith, *Origins of Biblical Monotheism*, 144, and the secondary literature cited there. In the second translation *qdš* might be regarded as the title of a specific deity, but this view is debated. For discussion, see *UBC* 1.294–95; Paolo Merlo, "Note critiche su alcune presunte iconografie della dea Ašera," *SEL* 14 (1997): 43–64, esp. 50. See *KTU* 1.2 I 20–21, 38; 1.17 I 3, 8, 10–11, 13, 22; cf. 1.2 III 19–20. See, respectively, *UNP* 99, 101, 51, 52, and 97.

36. *KAI* 4.4–5.

37. For the divine retinue, see Mark S. Smith, *The Early History of God: Yahweh and the Other Deities of Ancient Israel*, 2nd ed., Biblical Resource Series (Grand Rapids, Mich.: Eerdmans; Dearborn, Mich.: Dove, 2002), 122–23 n. 64.

38. For the former, see *KTU* 1.3 III 30; 1.16 I 7, in *UNP* 110 and 31, respectively; for the latter, see *KTU* 1.3 III 29, in *UNP* 110.

39. As noted by Wright, "Holiness, Sex, and Death," 305–29.

40. These points are made in van der Toorn, *Sin and Sanction in Israel and Mesopotamia: A Comparative Study*, Studia semitica neerlandica 22 (Assen: Van Gorcum, 1985), 28–29, and "La pureté rituelle au proche-orient ancien," *Revue de l'histoire des religions* 206 (1989): 339–56. For clarifications of the Mesopotamian evidence, see Mark J. Geller, "Taboo in Mesopotamia: A Review Article," *JCS* 42 (1990): 105–17.

41. *KTU* 1.4 V 19, in *UNP* 130.

42. For discussion of this Ugaritic passage and Exod 24:10, see Chapter 1.

43. *UBC* 1.xxvii, 355–56, and Smith, "Biblical and Canaanite Notes," 585–88.

44. Van der Toorn, *Sin and Sanction*, 23, 29.

45. Jacobsen, *Treasures of Darkness* (New Haven, Conn.: Yale University Press, 1976), 3. To be sure, Otto's *mysterium tremendum et fascinosum* has been influential in the analysis of other religions. For only one example, see R. C. Zaehner, *Hinduism*, 2nd ed. (Oxford: Oxford University Press, 1966), 86.

46. *KTU* 1.4 VII, in *UNP* 136–37.

47. *UNP* 136–37.

48. Jacobsen, *Treasures of Darkness*, 16.

49. For a similar view of the divinity as numinous, see Robert A. de Vito, *Studies in Third Millennium Sumerian and Akkadian Personal Names: The Designation and Conception of the Personal God*, Studia Pohl: Series Maior 16 (Rome: Pontificio Istituto Biblico, 1993), 256–57.

50. Franz A. M. Wiggerman, *Mesopotamian Protective Deities: The Ritual Texts*, Cuneiform Monographs 1 (Groningen: Styx and PP, 1992), 151–54; Smith, *Origins of Biblical Monotheism*, 27–40.

51. Daniel Merkur, "The Numinous as a Category of Values," in *The Sacred and the Scholars: Comparative Methodologies for the Study of Primary Religious Data*, ed. T. A. Idinipulos and E. A. Yonan, Numen 73 (Leiden: Brill, 1996), 104–23.

52. For the ideological use of holiness of temples and other sacred spaces, see Guthrie, "The Sacred: A Skeptical View," in *The Sacred and the Scholars*, 124–38.

53. Guthrie, "The Sacred," 135.

54. Paden, "Sacrality as Integrity: 'Sacred Order' as a Model for Describing Religious Worlds," in *The Sacred and the Scholars*, 15.

55. Paden, "Sacrality as Integrity," 13.

56. *BDB* 871–74.

57. The priestly conceptualization of holiness is a broad topic. See the summary of Michael B. Hundley, "Sacred Spaces, Objects, Offerings, and People in the Priestly Texts: A Reappraisal," *JBL* 132 (2013): 749–67.

58. Smith, *Early History of God*, 205–6. See also Tikva Frymer-Kensky, *In the Wake of the Goddesses: Women, Culture, and the Biblical Transformation of Pagan Myth* (New York: Basic Books, 1992), 189–90; Erhard S. Gerstenberger, *Yahweh the*

Patriarch: Ancient Images of God and Feminist Theology, trans. F. J. Gaiser (Minneapolis: Fortress, 1996), vi, 90; and Wright, "Holiness, Sex, and Death," 314.

59. Sexual impurity includes menstruation (Lev 15:19–30; 18:19), pregnancy (Lev 12), and emission of semen (Lev 15:1–18). The connection between these sorts of impurity and the holiness of Yahweh is made explicitly in Lev 15:31. See Eve Levavi Feinstein, *Sexual Pollution in the Hebrew Bible* (Oxford: Oxford University Press, 2014).

60. For restrictions on priestly contact with the dead, see Lev 21:1–3, 11; 22:4b; Num 6:6–7. The statement in Lev 21:3 stands in tension with 22:4b. See Elizabeth Bloch-Smith ("The Cult of the Dead in Judah: Interpreting the Material Remains," *JBL* 111 [1992]: 213–24, here 222–23), who emphasizes the financial benefit gained through these prohibitions.

61. For the degrees of holiness between the people, the priesthood, and the chief priest, see Jacob Milgrom, *Studies in Cultic Theology and Terminology* (Leiden: Brill, 1983), 75–84; and Hundley, "Sacred Spaces," 759–64.

62. Hundley, "Sacred Spaces," 767 and 762, respectively.

63. The reading, "we will die," in the MT is one of the eighteen "corrections of the scribes."

64. For text and translation, see Attridge and Oden, *Syrian Goddess*, 56–57.

65. Smith, *Early History of God*, 206.

66. *KTU* 1.4 IV 38–39, in *UNP* 128.

67. For discussion of this text, see Mark S. Smith, *The Sacrificial Rituals and Myths of the Goodly Gods, KTU/CAT 1.23: Royal Constructions of Opposition, Intersection, Integration and Domination*, SBLRBS 51 (Atlanta: SBL; Leiden: Brill, 2006).

68. For the inscriptions, see Zeev Meshel, *Kuntillet ʿAjrud (Horvat Teman): An Iron Age II Religious Site on the Judah-Sinai Border* (Jerusalem: Israel Exploration Society, 2012). Note also the syntheses in Othmar Keel and Christoph Uehlinger, *Gods, Goddesses, and Images of God in Ancient Israel*, trans. Thomas Trapp (Minneapolis: Fortress, 1998), 226–28; and F. W. Dobbs-Allsopp, J. J. M. Roberts, C. L. Seow, and R. E. Whitaker, *Hebrew Inscriptions: Texts from the Biblical Period of the Monarchy with Concordance* (New Haven, Conn.: Yale University Press, 2005), 293–96.

69. For example, see Susan Ackerman, *Under Every Green Tree: Popular Religion in Sixth-Century Judah*, HSM 46 (Atlanta: Scholars, 1992), 37–66. Note also Meindert Dijkstra, "El, the God of Israel—Israel, the People of YHWH: On the Origins of Ancient Israelite Yahwism," in *Only One God? Monotheism in Ancient Israel and the Veneration of the Goddess Asherah*, ed. Bob Becking et al., Biblical Seminar 77 (Sheffield: Sheffield Academic, 2001), 118; and Judith M. Hadley, *The Cult of Asherah in Ancient Israel and Judah: Evidence for a Hebrew Goddess*, University of Cambridge Oriental Publications 57 (Cambridge: Cambridge University Press, 2001), 201–2. Cf. Nadav Naʾaman, "The Inscriptions of Kuntillet ʿAjrud Through the Lens of Historical Research," *UF* 43 (2011): 299–324, here 304–6.

70. For example, Frank M. Cross, "The Phoenician Ostracon from Acco, the Ekron Inscriptions and אשרתה," *EI* 29 (2009 = Ephraim Stern Festschrift): 20*–22*; Patrick D. Miller, "The Absence of the Goddess in Israelite Religion," *HAR* 10 (1986): 239–48; Maryo C. A. Korpel, "Asherah Outside of Israel," in *Only One God?*, 145–50; Shmuel Aḥituv, *Echoes from the Past: Hebrew and Cognate Inscriptions from the Biblical Period* (Jerusalem: Carta, 2008), 315–19; Smith, *Early History of God*, 108–37; and Bernard Lang, *The Hebrew God: Portrait of an Ancient Deity* (New Haven, Conn.: Yale University Press, 2002), vii.

71. Zevit, *The Religions of Ancient Israel: A Synthesis of Parallactic Approaches* (New York: Continuum, 2000), 403 n. 10 (Zevit's italics).

72. Regarding 2 Kgs 23:4, Day (*Yahweh and the Gods and Goddesses of Canaan*, JSOTSup 265 [Sheffield: Sheffield Academic, 2000], 42–43) considers "Contra Mark S. Smith," that "it would be extremely forced not to understand Asherah here as the name of the deity likewise." Although I continue to harbor doubts for reasons that go unanswered by Day, I grant that it could be the name of the goddess. Unfortunately, Day does not consider the larger cultural issue of whether polemic is involved in these passages and if so, whether scholars should presume that the cult of the goddess Asherah was a historical reality in the seventh century.

73. Frymer-Kensky, *In the Wake of the Goddesses*, 168–78.

74. See Chapter 1, Section 3.

75. Bloch-Smith, "'Who Is the King of Glory?,'" 18–31.

76. A further development of the homology of god and house involves the representation of the temple as cosmos, especially in priestly works of the Bible (Gen 1 and Exod 39–40). See Moshe Weinfeld, "Sabbath, Temple and the Enthronement of the Lord—The Problem of the *Sitz im Leben* of Genesis 1:1–2:3," in *Mélanges bibliques et orientaux en l'honneur de M. Henri Cazelles*, ed. A. Caquot and M. Delcor, AOAT 212 (Kevelaer: Butzon und Bercker; Neukirchen-Vluyn: Neukirchener, 1981), 501–12; Jon D. Levenson, *Creation and the Persistence of Evil: The Jewish Drama of Divine Omnipotence* (San Francisco: Harper and Row, 1988), 78–87; and Bernd Janowski, "Tempel und Schöpfung. Schöpfungstheologische Aspekte der priesterschriftlichen Heiligtumskonzeption," *Jahrbuch für Biblisch Theologie* 5 (1990): 37–69. This particular topic lies beyond the scope of the discussion.

77. *KTU* 1.14 III 41–42, in *UNP* 17; paralleled in *KTU* 1.14 VI 26–28, in *UNP* 23.

78. *KTU* 1.23.1 (largely reconstructed), 23, 58 (partially reconstructed), 60, 67, in *UNP* 208–14. For the semantics, see Smith, *Sacrificial Rituals*, 33–34. For the contexts, see Smith, *Sacrificial Rituals*, 31, 65, 105, 109, 116.

79. *KTU* 1.23.2, in *UNP* 208; Smith, *Sacrificial Rituals*, 33–34. See also *KTU* 1.5 III 15, in *UNP* 145.

80. *KTU* 1.108.27, in *RCU* 195.

81. *KTU* 1.19 I 42–46, in *UNP* 69. See also *KTU* 1.16 III 4–11, in *UNP* 35–36.

82. *KTU* 1.3 III 30–31, in *UNP* 110; see also 1.10 III 31, in *UNP* 185.

83. *KTU* 1.4 V 19, in *UNP* 130.
84. Cf. Jon D. Levenson, "A Technical Meaning for *N'M* in the Hebrew Bible," *VT* 35 (1985): 61–67. Levenson does not mention that *n'm* is one of the terms used for the inheritance of the god in *KTU* 1.3 III 28–31. This usage also suits the sanctuary context of Ps 27:13, as noted by Greenfield, *'Al Kanfei Yonah*, 794.
85. Karel van der Toorn, *Family Religion in Babylonia, Syria and Israel: Continuity and Change in the Forms of Religious Life*, Studies in the History and Culture of the Ancient Near East 7 (Leiden: Brill, 1996), 210–11; Raymond J. Tournay, "À propos du Psaume 16, 1–4," *RB* 108 (2001): 21–25; and A. Aparicio Rodríguez, *Tú Eres Mi Bien: Análisis exegético y teológico del Salmo 16. Aplicación a la vida religiosa* (Madrid: Clarentianas, 1993); and Klaas Spronk, *Beatific Afterlife in Ancient Israel and in the Ancient Near East*, AOAT 219 (Kevelaer: Butzon und Bercker; Neukirchen-Vluyn: Neukirchener, 1986), 334–38.
86. For another Ugaritic example, see Chapter 4, Section 2. The text in question, *KTU* 1.101, encapsulates the major themes associated with the god as known from the Baal Cycle, yet it may further preserve explicitly what many temple texts perhaps only imply or presuppose, namely that the god's erotic magnetism is conveyed through the literary presentation of the human experience of his temple-mountain.
87. See Smith, *Origins of Biblical Monotheism*, 83–103.
88. Smith, *Origins of Biblical Monotheism*, 103.

Chapter 3. The Construction of Anthropomorphism and Theriomorphism

1. *KTU* 1.114 (*UNP* 193–96; *RCU* 167–70; Gregorio del Olmo Lete, *Canaanite Religion According to the Liturgical Texts of Ugarit*, trans. Wilfred G. E. Watson, 2nd ed., AOAT 408 [Münster: Ugarit-Verlag, 2014], 335–37) illustrates a further way a text constructs anthropomorphism, namely by correlating its medical concerns with traditional anthropomorphic notions. The words separated at the end of this text by a scribal line (lines 29–31) relate the ingredients to be used for handling the deleterious effects of drinking. The topic of the cure, namely heavy drinking, is given expression in El's severe inebriation. More specifically, "the hair of the dog," probably a plant name of the sort found in Mesopotamian medicinal texts, correlates with the discussion of the dog in the narrative. The other ingredients are the material for which Anat and Astarte are said to go hunting in lines 26–27, as these seem to refer to healing (**rp'*) and reviving (**hr* in the *N*-stem). In sum, the narrative portion of the text works out its specific medicinal concern against the canvas of traditional anthropomorphism.
2. Marjo Christina Annette Korpel, *A Rift in the Clouds: Ugaritic and Hebrew Descriptions of the Divine*, UBL 8 (Münster: Ugarit-Verlag, 1990). For criticism, see Ziony Zevit, *The Religions of Ancient Israel: A Synthesis of Parallactic Approaches*

(London: Continuum, 2001), 608–9 n. 96. See also Evelyne Martin, "Therio-morphismus im Alten Testament und im Alten Orient: Eine Einführung," in *Tiergestaltigkeit der Göttinen und Götter zwischen Metapher und Symbol,* ed. Evelyne Martin, Biblischer-theologische Studien 129 (Neukirchener-Vluyn: Neukirchener, 2012), 1–36. Note also the suggestion of Robert D. Miller II that theriomorphic imagery for deities should be situated in the shamanistic practice of using animal cult masks; see Miller, "Shamanism in Early Israel," *WZKM* 101 (2011): 309–42, here 331–32. While West Semitic texts are unfortunately lacking in terms for shamans or evidence of tying masks to theriomorphic representation of deities, such a (distant?) background is hardly impossible.

3. Pughat in *KTU* 1.19 II 27 (*UNP* 70), Athirat in 1.4 II 12 (*UNP* 122), Baal in 1.10 II 14 (*UNP* 183), and Anat in 1.10 II 26–27 (*UNP* 184).

4. Kothar seen by Danil in *KTU* 1.17 V 9–11 (*UNP* 58), and Baal and Anat seen by Athirat in 1.4 II 12–16 (*UNP* 122).

5. Human messengers in *KTU* 1.19 II 40 (*UNP* 71), divine messengers in 1.5 II 16–17 (*UNP* 144), El in 1.5 VI 22 (*UNP* 150), and Anat in 1.6 I 39 (*UNP* 153).

6. Danil in *KTU* 1.19 IV 8–9 (*UNP* 75), Horon in 1.100.67–68 (*RCU* 178), and El in 1.114.17–18 (*UNP* 195).

7. Pughat in *KTU* 1.19 IV 41–43 (*UNP* 77) and Anat in 1.3 III 1–2 (*UNP* 109).

8. Baal in *KTU* 1.5 II 6–7 (*UNP* 143), and Mot in 1.6 VI 30–31 (*UNP* 163).

9. Danil receives bad news of Aqhat's death in *KTU* 1.19 II 44–47 (*UNP* 71); Anat fears that Baal has been defeated in 1.3 III 32–35 (*UNP* 111); and Athirat fears that her children have been murdered by Baal in 1.4 II 16–20 (*UNP* 122); cf. the expression of Pughat's slaying of her enemies in 1.19 IV 34–35 (*UNP* 77).

10. Danil in *KTU* 1.19 III 20–21, 40–41 (*UNP* 73 and 74, respectively) and Anat in 1.6 I 15–18 (*UNP* 152).

11. Aqhat in *KTU* 1.17 II 10–12 (*UNP* 55); El in 1.6 III 16 (*UNP* 158); cf. El in 1.12 I 12–13 (*UNP* 188).

12. Kirta's children in *KTU* 1.16 I 15 (*UNP* 31), Danil in 1.17 II 8–9 (his face lights up, *UNP* 55), Anat in 1.3 II 26 (*UNP* 108), El in 1.6 III 14 (*UNP* 158), Baal in 1.10 III 37 (*UNP* 186).

13. Kirta in *KTU* 1.14 I 37–III 51 (*UNP* 13–18), and El in 1.6 III 1–13 (*UNP* 157–58). Cf. Aqhat in 1.17 I 15–II 8 (*UNP* 52–55).

14. *KTU* 1.10 I 3 (*UNP* 182); cf. 1.114.7 (*UNP* 194).

15. *KTU* 1.3 III 27–28 (*UNP* 110) and IV 15–16 (*UNP* 113).

16. *KTU* 1.169.6 (*RCU* 160; cf. del Olmo Lete, *Canaanite Religion,* 332 n. 192).

17. *KTU* 1.2 IV 18, 26 (*UNP* 104).

18. For *'adn,* "father," in *Ugaritica V,* see John Huehnergard, *Ugaritic Vocabulary in Syllabic Transcription,* rev. ed., HSS 32 (Winona Lake, Ind.: Eisenbrauns, 2008), 104. Note also the parallelism of Ugaritic *'adn* with *'um,* "mother," in *KTU* 1.24.33–34, in *UNP* 217; and *'adn* in RS 96.2039.13 (see Pierre Bordreuil and Dennis Pardee, *Une bibliothèque au sud de la ville: Textes 1994–2002 en cunéiforme*

alphabétique de la maison d'Ourtenou, RSO XVIII [Lyon: Maison de l'Orient et de la Méditeranée—Jean Pouilloux, 2012], 174–75).

19. *KTU* 4.360.1–3, in Kevin McGeough, *Ugaritic Economic Tablets: Text, Translation and Notes,* ed. Mark S. Smith, Ancient Near Eastern Studies Supplement 32 (Leuven: Peeters, 2010), 246. For discussion, see Mark S. Smith, *The Origins of Biblical Monotheism: Israel's Polytheistic Background and the Ugaritic Texts* (Oxford: Oxford University Press, 2001), 59. Cf. Ps 92:10.

20. NRSV and NJPS take *lô* in functional terms, "for them," rather than the possessive "to him" (i.e. "he has . . ."). NABRE reads Israel rather than God as the referent.

21. *KTU* 1.17 I 1–15, in *UNP* 51–52.

22. *KTU* 1.17 II 29–38, in *UNP* 57.

23. *KTU* 1.17 I 16–34, in *UNP* 52–53.

24. *KTU* 1.17 I 31–32, II 4–5, in *UNP* 53, 55.

25. *KTU* 1.17 II 26 and 39–40, in *UNP* 56 and 57.

26. *KTU* 1.17 V 10–13, in *UNP* 58.

27. Cf. William Foxwell Albright, *From the Stone Age to Christianity: Monotheism and the Historical Process,* 2nd ed. (Baltimore: John Hopkins University Press, 1957), 272.

28. *KTU* 1.6 I 39–41, in *UNP* 153.

29. *KTU* 1.4 III 17–18, in *UNP* 124.

30. *KTU* 1.17 I 16, in *UNP* 52.

31. *KTU* 1.3 III 5–6, in *UNP* 109.

32. *KTU* 1.6 II 13–14, in *UNP* 155.

33. *KTU* 1.6 II 28–30, in *UNP* 156.

34. See *KTU* 1.3 II 25–27, as well as 1.4 V 25, 1.17 VI 41–42, and 1.18 I 22, in *UNP* 108, 130, 62, 64, respectively. For discussion, see *UBC* 2.164–74.

35. *KTU* 1.18 I 22, in *UNP* 64.

36. *KTU* 1.4 V 25, in *UNP* 130.

37. *KTU* 1.4 IV 27–28, in *UNP* 127.

38. *KTU* 1.12 I 12, in *UNP* 188.

39. *KTU* 1.4 VII 21–22, in *UNP* 136.

40. See J. J. M. Roberts, *The Bible and the Ancient Near East: Collected Essays* (Winona Lake, Ind.: Eisenbrauns, 1992), 132–42; and David Bosworth, "The Tears of God in the Book of Jeremiah," *Bib* 94 (2013): 24–46.

41. "The elohim are understood to be existent as gods," according to Peter Machinist, "How Gods Die, Biblically and Otherwise: A Problem of Cosmic Restructuring," in *Reconsidering the Concept of Revolutionary Monotheism,* ed. Beate Pongratz-Leisten (Winona Lake, Ind.: Eisenbrauns, 2011), 230. I would emphasize also that it is specifically God who is expressing this understanding of the gods. The background of Psalm 82 thematically fits with Isa 41:23, as noted by Machinist, "How Gods Die," 228–30.

42. *KTU* 1.23.51–52 and 57–58, in *UNP* 213.

43. For *bn 'il(m)*, see *KTU* 1.4 III 14, in *UNP* 124; 1.10 I 3, in *UNP* 182; 1.17 VI 29, in *UNP* 61; 1.40.8, 25, 34, 41, 42, in *RCU* 79–80 (with slightly different line numbering); 1.65.1, 2, 3, in *RCU* 22; and perhaps 1.123.15, cf. *RCU* 151. The god Mot many times is called *bn 'ilm*: *KTU* 1.4 VII 45, in *UNP* 137; 1.4 VIII 16, 30, in *UNP* 139; 1.5 I 7, 12, in *UNP* 141; 1.5 II 8, 11, 14, 19, 20, in *UNP* 143, 144; 1.6 II 13, 25, 31, in *UNP* 155, 156; 1.6 V 9, in *UNP* 160; 1.6 VI 7, 9, 24, 30, in *UNP* 162–63; see *UBC* 1.287 n. 116. For Kirta as *bn 'il*, see *KTU* 1.16 I 20, in *UNP* 31. Cf. *bn 'ily* in a scribal list of PNs in *KTU* 5.18.3–4. See also Pss 29:1 and 89:6–7.

44. *KTU* 1.23.30–61 generally (specifically line 30 reconstructed), in *UNP* 210–13; and *KTU* 1.24, in *UNP* 216–17.

45. Baal in *KTU* 1.5 VI–1.6 II, in *UNP* 148–56. Baruch A. Levine and Jean-Michel de Tarragon have argued that the mourning for Baal, the search for this god in the underworld, the descent of the sun into the underworld, and the funerary offerings in the Baal Cycle have been modeled on ideas about deceased kings as found in royal funerary ritual as in *KTU* 1.161. See Levine and de Tarragon, "Dead Kings and Rephaim: The Patrons of the Ugaritic Dynasty," *JAOS* 104 (1984): 649–59, followed by Mark S. Smith, "The Death of 'Dying and Rising Gods' in the Biblical World: An Update, with Special Reference to Baal in the Baal Cycle," *Scandinavian Journal of the Old Testament* 12/2 (1998): 257–313, and *Origins of Biblical Monotheism*, 104–31.

46. See Smith, *Origins of Biblical Monotheism*, 97–102. The situation in Mesopotamian texts differs on this score. For a recent summary, see Machinist, "How Gods Die," 189–240.

47. Cf. Albright, *From the Stone Age to Christianity*, 261.

48. For this point, see Introduction, Section 3, and Chapter 2, Section 3.

49. *KTU* 1.4 II 3–9, in *UNP* 122. See Mark S. Smith, in "Discussions," in *Symbiosis, Symbolism, and the Power of the Past: Canaan, Ancient Israel, and Their Neighbors—From the Late Bronze Age Through Roman Palaestina*, ed. W. G. Dever and S. Gitin, W.F. Albright Institute of Archaeological Research Anniversary Volume (Winona Lake, Ind.: Eisenbrauns, 2003), 558. See further Kevin M. McGeough, *Exchange Relationships at Ugarit*, Ancient Near Eastern Studies Supplement 26 (Leuven: Peeters, 2007), 168–69.

50. See Mark S. Smith, *Poetic Heroes: The Literary Commemoration of Warriors and Warrior Culture in the Early Biblical World* (Grand Rapids, Mich.: Eerdmans, 2014), 73–74, 116, 118, 132–35, 174, 175, 187–95, 199, 201, and 325–26.

51. *KTU* 1.17 VI 40, in *UNP* 62. See Smith, *Poetic Heroes*, 131–33.

52. For an effort to address the latter development, see Smith, *Poetic Heroes*, 308–32.

53. Cf. Albright's claim that Yahweh has no mythology (*From the Stone Age to Christianity*, 272). To my mind, this difference is overstated by Ellen F. Davis, "'And Pharaoh Will Change His Mind . . .' (Ezekiel 32:31): Dismantling Mythical Discourse," in *Theological Exegesis: Essays in Conversation with Brevard S.*

Childs, ed. Christopher Seitz and Kathryn Greene-McCreight (Grand Rapids, Mich.: Eerdmans, 1999), 224–39. Davis's canonical approach seems to mute the diachronic depth of biblical anthropomorphism. On the other hand, Davis's canonical perception that the Bible revises such mythic language is on target; see further below.

54. See Mark S. Smith, "Myth and Myth-making in Ugaritic and Israelite Literatures," in *Ugarit and the Bible,* Proceedings of the International Symposium on Ugarit and the Bible, Manchester, September 1992, ed. G. J. Brooke, A. H. W. Curtis, and J. F. Healey, UBL 11 (Münster: Ugarit-Verlag, 1994), 293–341, and "Mythmaking and Mythology in Canaan and Israel," in *Civilizations of the Ancient Near East,* ed. J. Sasson, 4 vols. (New York: Scribner, 1995), 3.2031–41.

55. See Peter Machinist, "Order and Disorder: Some Mesopotamian Reflections," in *Genesis and Regeneration,* ed. Shaul Shaked (Jerusalem: Israel Academy of Sciences and Humanities, 2005), 31–61. See also Mark S. Smith, "Ancient Near Eastern 'Myths' and the Hebrew Bible: Interim Reflections," in *Was ist der Mensch, dass du seiner gedenkst? (Psalm 8,5): Aspekte einer theologischen Anthropologie. Festschrift für Bernd Janowski zum 65. Geburstag,* ed. Michaela Bauks, Kathrin Liess, and Peter Riede (Neukirchen-Vluyn: Neukirchener, 2008), 487–501.

56. Note also the consideration of the deity in terms of space and place for the activity of prayer in J. Gerald Janzen, *When Prayer Takes Place: Forays into a Biblical World,* ed. Brent A. Strawn and Patrick D. Miller (Eugene, Ore.: Cascade, 2012).

57. For a detailed discussion of this range, see Andreas Wagner, *Gottes Körper: Zur alttestamentlichen Vorstellung des Menschengestaltigkeit Gottes* (Gütersloh: Gütersloher, 2010), 110–34 and 135–58, which includes his theory of "Synthetisches Bedeutungsspektrum." As Wagner notes, his approach has its intellectual antecedent in Hans Wolter Wolff's notion that "stereometric-synthetic thinking sees a part of the body together with its particular activities and capacities"; see Wolff, *Anthropology of the Old Testament,* trans. Margaret Kohl (Philadelphia: Fortress, 1974), 11.

58. For comparative *k-,* see *DULAT* 415–16, and for *km,* see *DULAT* 438–40. Cf. Akkadian similes with *kīma,* discussed by Giorgio Buccellati, "Towards a Formal Typology of Akkadian Similes," in *Kramer Anniversary Volume: Cuneiform Studies in Honor of Samuel Noah Kramer,* ed. Barry L. Eichler, with the assistance of Jane W. Heimerdinger and Ake W. Sjöberg, AOAT 25 (Kevelaer: Butzon und Bercker; Neukirchen-Vluyn: Neukirchener, 1976), 59–70.

59. *KTU* 1.15 I 5–7, in *UNP* 24.

60. *KTU* 1.6 II 6–7, in *UNP* 155.

61. *KTU* 1.114.21–22, in *RCU* 168–70; and del Olmo Lete, *Canaanite Religion,* 337. For a recent study, see Smith, *Poetic Heroes,* 190–93. Cf. JoAnn Scurlock, "'Whirling (*ṣâdu*) in the Month of Marzaḥani at Emar' or 'Why Did El Get, So To

Speak, Drunk as a Lord in *KTU* 1.114,'" *UF* 44 (2013 = In memoriam Pierre Bordreuil): 285–308.

62. *KTU* 1.6 II 22, in *UNP* 156.
63. *KTU* 1.5 II 5, in *UNP* 143.
64. *KTU* 1.14 I 41–43, in *UNP* 13.
65. *KTU* 1.14 III 41–42 = 1.14 VI 26–28, in *UNP* 17, 23.
66. *KTU* 1.16 VI 1–2, in *UNP* 36.
67. *KTU* 1.101.1–9. See Dennis Pardee, *Les textes paramythologiques de la 24e campagne (1961)*, RSO IV, Mémoire no. 77 (Paris: Éditions Recherche sur la Civilisations, 1988), 119–52, esp. 120–21, 125; *UBC* 1.3–4; David M. Clements, "*KTU* 1.45 and 1.6 I 8–18, 1.161, 1.101," *UF* 33 (2001): 65–116, esp. 105–13; and Katie M. Heffelfinger, "Like the Sitting of a Mountain: The Significance of Metaphor in *KTU* 1.101's (recto) Description of Ba'l," *UF* 39 (2007 = In Memoriam Kurt Bergerhof): 381–97; Robert Hawley, "On the Alphabetic Scribal Curriculum at Ugarit," in *Proceedings of the 51st Rencontre Assyriologique Internationale Held at the Oriental Institute of the University of Chicago July 18–22, 2005*, ed. R. D. Biggs, J. Myers, and M. T. Roth, Studies in Ancient Oriental Civilization 62 (Chicago: Oriental Institute of the University of Chicago, 2008), 66. Note also the older studies of M. H. Pope and J. H. Tigay, "A Description of Baal," *UF* 3 (1971): 117–30; and W. H. Irwin, "The Extended Simile in RS 24.245 obv.," *UF* 15 (1983): 54–57; and *RTU*, 388–90. See also Chapter 2, Section 4.
68. Pardee, *Les textes paramythologiques*, 127 n. 12 and 128 n. 16.
69. See *KTU* 1.3 I 24–25, in *UNP* 106; *KTU* 1.3 III 7, in *UNP* 109; *KTU* 1.3 IV 51, in *UNP* 115; 1.3 V 42, in *UNP* 118; 1.4 I 17, in *UNP* 120; and 1.4 IV 56, in *UNP* 128.
70. See Chapter 1, Section 4, for discussion of this passage.
71. Barr, "Theophany and Anthropomorphism in the Old Testament," in *Congress Volume: Oxford 1959*, VTSup VII (Leiden: Brill, 1960), 36–37 (Barr's italics).
72. Hendel, "Aniconism and Anthropomorphism in Ancient Israel," in *The Image and the Book: Iconic Cults, Aniconism, and the Rise of Book Religion in Israel and the Ancient Near East*, ed. Karel van der Toorn, CBET 21 (Leuven: Peeters, 1997), 205–28. Hendel's expression occurs on p. 207, where he also mentions Ezekiel 1. See also "transcendent Baal" used in *RTU*, 388–90, cited by Theodore J. Lewis, "Syro-Palestinian Iconography and Divine Images," in *Cult Image and Divine Representation in the Ancient Near East*, ed. Neal H. Walls, ASOR 10 (Boston: ASOR, 2005), 76. According to Hamori, in Hendel's discussion such representations are less anthropomorphic; she would prefer to label such cases "transcending anthropomorphism" (Esther J. Hamori, *"When Gods Were Men": The Embodied God in Biblical and Near Eastern Literature*, BZAW 384 [Berlin: de Gruyter, 2008], 32 n. 11). In those cases where Mesopotamian deities are represented as various parts of Marduk or Ninurta, the texts are not less anthropomorphic; they are very anthropomorphic. Thus in these instances, Hendel's label is accurate. Ezekiel 1 seems to reflect an effort to qualify not simply

anthropomorphic representation, but also the sense of immanent divinity. See Chapter 1 above.

73. For some of the theoretical issues bearing on theriomorphism discussed here, see Martin, "Theriomorphismus im Alten Testament und im Alten Orient," 11–16. For an extensive listing of theriomorphic descriptions of deities, see Korpel, *Rift in the Clouds*, 523–59.

74. *KTU* 1.18 IV 29–33, in *UNP* 66.

75. *KTU* 1.10 II 10–12, in *UNP* 183. For a recent survey of the iconographic evidence, see Akio Tsukimoto, "'In the Shadow of Thy Wings': A Review of the Winged Goddess in Ancient Near Eastern Iconography," in *Transformations of a Goddess: Ishtar—Astarte—Aphrodite*, ed. David T. Sugimoto, OBO 263 (Fribourg: Academic Press; Göttingen: Vandenhoeck & Ruprecht, 2014), 15–31. The winged goddess is a well-known motif in glyptic. For Ugarit, see Claude F. A. Schaeffer, *Corpus des cylindres-sceaux de Ras Shamra-Ugarit et d'Enkomi-Alasia: Tome I* (Paris: Éditions Recherche sur les Civilisations, 1983), 16–21, and RS 5.089 (according to Schaeffer, this seal relates to *KTU* 1.10: the winged goddess is Anat and the bull is Baal). For the motif in glyptic from Enkomi, see Schaeffer, *Corpus des cylindres-sceaux*, 62. For the motif at Emar, see Dominique Beyer, *Emar IV: Les sceaux*, OBO 20 (Fribourg: Editions Universitaires; Göttingen: Vandenhoeck & Ruprecht, 2001), 318. For further examples, see Beatrice Teissier, *Ancient Near Eastern Cylinder Seals from the Marcopoli Collection* (Berkeley: University of California Press; Beverly Hills, Calif.: Summa, 1984), 80–81, and #476, #483, #489, #490. Teissier notes the view of Edith Porada that in the Syrian glyptic the goddess depicted was Anat; Teissier (*Ancient Near Eastern Cylinder Seals*, 372 n. 109) cites Porada, "Cylinder Seal with Camel," *Journal of the Walters Art Gallery* 36:2–3.

76. *KTU* 1.10 II 21–24, in *UNP* 183. Note also her epithet "Milk Cow," in Egyptian texts; see James E. Hoch, *Semitic Words in Egyptian Texts of the New Kingdom and Third Intermediate Period* (Princeton, N.J.: Princeton University Press, 1994), 67–68, #73. This representation may correspond to Baal as a young bull.

77. *KTU* 1.5 V 18–22, in *UNP* 148; cf. *KTU* 1.86.3–4, in *COS* 1.293–94.

78. *KTU* 1.101.6–7, discussed below and also in Chapter 5.

79. For this characterization, see Othmar Keel and Christoph Uehlinger, *Gods, Goddesses, and Images of God in Ancient Israel*, trans. Thomas Trapp (Minneapolis: Fortress, 1998), 146.

80. Aicha Rahmouni, *Divine Epithets in the Ugaritic Alphabetic Texts*, trans. James N. Ford (Leiden: Brill, 2008), 318–30.

81. The contexts are unclear. The god may be so referenced with a simile in *KTU* 1.2 III 20 (in *UNP* 97) and perhaps with a title in *KTU* 1.24.30 (in *UNP* 217).

82. See Dennis Pardee, "Preliminary Presentation of a New Ugaritic Song to 'Attartu (RIH 98/02)," in *Ugarit at Seventy-Five*, ed. K. Lawson Younger, Jr. (Winona Lake, Ind.: Eisenbrauns, 2007), 27–39; and Smith, *Poetic Heroes*, 204–7. For this passage, see further the discussion below. Note also PNs *'bdlb't* in

Ugaritic and on an Iron I arrowhead, discussed by Richard S. Hess, "Arrow-heads from Iron Age I," in *Ugarit at Seventy-Five*, 119–20. For the problems of assigning feline iconography to a specific goddess, see Steve A. Wiggins, "The Myth of Asherah: Lion Lady and Serpent Goddess," *UF* 23 (1991): 386–89.

83. RIH 98/02 = *KTU* 1.180, lines 1–5, in Smith, *Poetic Heroes*, 204, with prior bib-liography and discussion.

84. See the discussion in Smith, *Poetic Heroes*, 204–8.

85. To judge from the comparable phrasing in Deut 33:17, the image denotes power in warfare in Num 23:22 and 24:8, more specifically El's victory over the Egyp-tians in warfare. Victory over enemies also seems to be the force of Anat's anointed horns (*KTU* 1.10 II 21–24, in *UNP* 183) noted above (for oil in con-nection with horns, see Ps 92:10). Note also that Baal and Mot "gore each other like wild oxen" (*KTU* 1.6 VI 17–18, in *UNP* 162). For horns for victory, see also 1 Kgs 22:11//2 Chr 18:10; Mic 4:13; Ps 89:17, 24; for the horns of the enemy in signaling defeat, see Ps 22:21.

86. Joel M. LeMon, *Yahweh's Winged Form in the Psalms: Exploring Congruent Iconography and Texts*, OBO 242 (Göttingen: Vandenhoeck & Ruprecht; Fribourg: Academic Press, 2010); Gert Kwakkel, "Under Yhwh's Wings," in *Metaphors in the Psalms*, ed. Pierre van Hecke and Antje Labahn, BETL CCXXXI (Leuven: Peeters, 2010), 141–65; and Martin, "Theriomorphismus im Alten Testament und im Alten Orient," 2–11. My thanks to Evelyne Mar-tin for these references.

87. See the important discussion of Baruch A. Levine, *Numbers 21–36: A New Translation with Introduction and Commentary*, AYB 4A (New York: Double-day, 2000), 193–96, 217–30.

88. *KTU* 1.46.6, in *RCU* 27; and del Olmo Lete, *Canaanite Religion*, 231.

89. *RCU* 276.

90. See the evidence discussed by Keel and Uehlinger, *Gods*, 144, 158. See in particu-lar the bull figurine from the so-called Bull Site in Amihai Mazar, "The 'Bull Site': An Iron Age I Open Cult Site," *BASOR* 247 (1982): 27–42; cf. Michael David Coogan, "Of Cults and Cultures: Reflections on the Interpretation of Archaeological Evidence," *PEQ* 119 (1987): 1–8. For a recently discovered ter-racotta bull statue from a temple at Iron II Khirbet 'Ataruz, see Chang-Ho Ji, "Khirbat 'Ataruz: An Interim Overview of 10 Years of Archaeological Archi-tectural Findings," *ADAJ* 55 (2011): 561–79, here 569–70.

91. See the discussion in Chapter 4.

92. Weiss, "Motives Behind Biblical Mixed Metaphors," in *Making a Difference: Essays on the Bible and Judaism in Honor of Tamara Cohn Eskenazi*, ed. David J. A. Clines, Kent Harold Richards, and Jacob L. Wright (Sheffield: Sheffield Phoenix, 2012), 317–28, here 321.

93. See Lewis, "Syro-Palestinian Iconography," 69–107. That such combination is traditional can be seen from a terracotta model "sanctuary" from Early Bronze

Vounous, containing a ritual scene with a figure that combines human and bovine attributes. See V. Karageorghis, *The Coroplastic Art of Ancient Cyprus I: Chalcolithic–Late Cypriote I* (Nicosia: A. G. Leventis Foundation, 1991), noted by David Wengrow, *The Archaeology of Early Egypt: Social Transformations in North-East Africa, 10,000 to 2650 BC,* Cambridge World Archaeology (Cambridge: Cambridge University Press, 2006), 61.

94. Othmar Keel, *Goddesses and Trees, New Moon and Yahweh: Ancient Near Eastern Art and the Hebrew Bible,* JSOTSup 261 (Sheffield: Sheffield Academic, 1998), 115–20 figures 107–9; and Lewis, "Syro-Palestinian Iconography," 76.

95. Note the inverse representation of the Phoenician smiting the anthropomorphic figure with a bull's head said to be Baal. See Izak Cornelius, *The Iconography of the Canaanite Gods Reshef and Baal,* OBO 140 (Fribourg: Fribourg University Press, 1994), figure 36b.

96. For a convenient presentation, see Philip J. King and Lawrence E. Stager, *Life in Biblical Israel,* LAI (Louisville, Ky.: Westminster John Knox, 2001), 320–21. The public aspect of this representation in the city gate may compare with imagery of deities chiseled on stone panels lining the walls of public spaces in a number of Syrian architectural complexes. See Ömür Harmanşah, *Cities and the Shaping of Memory in the Ancient Near East* (Cambridge: Cambridge University Press, 2013), 168–88.

97. *ANEP* #500, #501, #531, and #537. Cf. *ANEP* #534.

98. See the discussion of Keel and Uehlinger, *Gods,* 192–94. Keel and Uehlinger stress the temporal discontinuities between the evidence of the situation at Dan versus the Late Bronze and Iron I evidence on one side and the later Iron IIC period on the other. While the representation is surely not specific to Dan and Bethel, the evidence is suggestive of a broad representational phenomenon that includes the cases of Dan and Bethel.

99. Keel, *Studien zu den Stempelsiegeln aus Palästinas/Israel, Band 3,* OBO 130 (Freiburg: Universitätsverlag; Göttingen: Vandenhoeck & Ruprecht, 1994), 144, nos. 46–47; see also LeMon, *Yahweh's Winged Form in the Psalms,* 209 figure 8. As LeMon's study shows, the animal feature of wings on human forms is commonplace for deities in ancient Near Eastern art.

100. *CMHE* 73 n. 117; and Keel and Uehlinger, *Gods,* 172 and 192.

101. *CMHE* 73–75. Keel and Uehlinger (*Gods,* 278) rightly raise the possibility that this god at Dan and Bethel was El, which may also be the case in Num 23:22 and 24:8; see Stephen C. Russell, *Images of Egypt in Early Biblical Literature: Cisjordan-Israelite, Transjordan-Israelite, and Judahite Portrayals,* BZAW 403 (Berlin: de Gruyter, 2009), 113–19.

102. See the discussion in Chapter 6 below.

103. Cf. the depiction of a naked female above a lion on a pendant from Ugarit; see Marguerite Yon, *The City of Ugarit at Tell Ras Shamra* (Winona Lake, Ind.: Eisenbrauns, 2006), 166–67, #58.

104. Korpel, *Rift in the Clouds,* 560–69.
105. *KTU* 1.3 V 17–18, 1.4 VIII 21–22, 1.6 II 24–25, in *UNP* 116, 139, 156, respectively. Cf. *KTU* 1.23.41, in *UNP* 211. For the verb (**ṣḥr*), see Gary A. Rendsburg, "Modern South Arabian as a Source for Ugaritic Etymologies," *JAOS* 107/4 (1987): 625; and Mark S. Smith, *The Sacrificial Rituals and Myths of the Goodly Gods, KTU/CAT 1.23: Royal Constructions of Opposition, Intersection, Integration and Domination,* SBLRBS 51 (Atlanta: SBL; Leiden: Brill, 2006), 92.
106. *KTU* 1.6 IV 17–20, in *UNP* 159; 1.6 VI 22–29, in *UNP* 163. Cf. the moon-god in *KTU* 1.24.30–39, in *UNP* 217. See Steve A. Wiggins, "What's in a Name? Yariḥ at Ugarit," *UF* 30 (1998): 761–79.
107. *KTU* 1.5 V 6–11, in *UNP* 149. Cf. groups of seven winds in Akkadian literature, for example in Enuma Elish IV, lines 46, 47 (cf. four winds in line 42); see *CAD* Š/2:136a, under *šāru* A; and Wilfred G. Lambert, *Babylonian Creation Myths,* MC 16 (Winona Lake, Ind.: Eisenbrauns, 2013), 88–89.
108. This example was brought to my attention by Brent Strawn.
109. See Izaak J. de Hulster and Brent A. Strawn, "Figuring YHWH in Unusual Ways: Deuteronomy 32 and Other Mixed Metaphors for God in the Old Testament," in *Iconographic Exegesis in the Hebrew Bible/Old Testament: An Introduction to Its Method and Practice,* ed. Izaak J. de Hulster, Brent A. Strawn, and Ryan P. Bonfiglio (Göttingen: Vandenhoeck & Ruprecht, 2015), 117–33.

Chapter 4. The Calf Images at Dan and Bethel

1. Klaus Koenen, *Bethel: Geschichte, Kult und Theologie,* OBO 192 (Freiburg Schweiz: Universitätsverlag; Göttingen: Vandenhoeck & Ruprecht, 2003), 215.
2. For textual evidence, see Mark W. Bartusch, *Understanding Dan: An Exegetical Approach to a Biblical City, Tribe and Ancestor,* JSOTSup 379 (London: Sheffield Academic, 2003). See also Keith Whitelam, "Dan," *ABD* 2.10–12; and Philippe Lefebre, "Mystère et Disparition de Dan: de la Septante à l'Apocalypse," in *IX Congress of the International Organization for the Septuagint and Cognate Studies: Cambridge 1995,* ed. Bernard A. Taylor, SBLSCS 45 (Atlanta: SBL, 1997), 280–307. For the archaeology of the site, see Avraham Biran, "Dan," *ABD* 2.12–17; "Dan," *NEAEHL* 1.323–32, and *Biblical Dan* (Jerusalem: Israel Exploration Society/Hebrew Union College-Jewish Institute of Religion, 1994); and "The High Places of Biblical Dan," in *Studies in the Archaeology of the Iron Age in Israel and Jordan,* ed. Amihai Mazar, with the assistance of Ginny Mathias, JSOTSup 331 (Sheffield: Sheffield Academic, 2001), 148–55. See also Tina Haettner Blomquist, *Gates and Gods: Cults in the City Gates of Iron Age Palestine. An Investigation of the Archaeological and Biblical Sources,* ConBOT 46 (Stockholm: Almqvist & Wiksell, 1999), 57–69 and 122–23, figures 2a–b; Andrew R. Davis, *Tel Dan in Its Northern Cultic Context,* SBL Archaeology and Biblical Studies

20 (Atlanta: SBL, 2013), 17–107; and Jonathan S. Greer, *Dinner at Dan: Biblical and Archaeological Evidence for Sacred Feasts at Iron Age II Tel Dan and Their Significance,* CHANE 66 (Leiden: Brill, 2013) 7–26.

3. See Koenen, *Bethel;* and Melanie Köhlmoos, *Bet-El-Erinnerungen an eine Stadt: Perspectiven der alttestamentlichen Bet-El-Überlieferung,* FAT 1/49 (Tübingen: Mohr Siebeck, 2006). Note also H. Brodsky, "Bethel," *ABD* 1.710–12; and J. L. Kelso, "Bethel," *NEAEHL* 1.192–94.

4. So also LXX 3 Reigns 12:29 (NETS): "And he set the one in Baithel, and the one he gave in Dan." See Alfred Rahlfs, *Septuaginta,* ed. Robert Hanhart, rev. ed. (Stuttgart: Deutsche Bibelgesellschaft, 2006), 664.

5. See Alan Cooper and Bernard R. Goldstein, "Exodus and *Maṣṣôt* in History and Tradition," *Maarav* 8 = *Let Your Colleagues Praise You: Studies in Memory of Stanley Gevirtz: Volume 2,* ed. Robert J. Ratner, Lewis M. Barth, Marianne Luijken Gevirtz, and Bruce Zuckerman (Rolling Hill Estates, Calif.: Western Academic, 1992), 18–38; Rainer Albertz, *A History of Israelite Religion in the Old Testament Period: Volume I: From the Beginnings to the End of the Monarchy,* trans. J. Bowden, OTL (Louisville, Ky.: Westminster John Knox, 1994), 143; and Karel van der Toorn, *Family Religion in Babylonia, Syria and Israel: Continuity and Change in the Forms of Religious Life,* Studies in the History and Culture of the Ancient Near East VII (Leiden: Brill, 1996), 287–302. Elizabeth Bloch-Smith informs me that this view was anticipated by Julian Morgenstern, *Rites of Birth, Marriage, Death, and Kindred Occasions Among the Semites* (Cincinnati: Hebrew Union College Press, 1966), 166–78. The plural verb for the deity "that brought you up from Egypt" in Exod 32:4b, 8b and 1 Kgs 12:28 remains a debated matter. Joel S. Burnett proposes to see a head warrior-god with his divine retinue in this plural formulation. See Burnett, *A Reassessment of Biblical Elohim,* SBLDS 183 (Atlanta: SBL, 2001), 82–86. See below.

6. Burnett, *Reassessment of Biblical Elohim,* 82–84. See also Greer, *Dinner at Dan,* 25 n. 90.

7. Shemaryahu Talmon, *King, Cult and Calendar in Ancient Israel: Collected Studies* (Leiden: Brill, Magnes, 1986), 115 n. 1; *CMHE* 73–74; Albertz, *History of Israelite Religion,* 144; Othmar Keel and Christoph Uehlinger, *Gods, Goddesses, and Images of God in Ancient Israel,* trans. Thomas H. Trapp (Minneapolis: Fortress, 1998), 191 n. 9, 192, 194; Wesley I. Toews, *Monarchy and Religious Institution Under Jeroboam I,* SBLMS 47 (Atlanta: Scholars, 1993), 43–45, 67; Burnett, *Reassessment of Biblical Elohim,* 79–119, esp. 82–86; Koenen, *Bethel,* 129, 131–32.

8. For the physical evidence of the cultic complex at Dan, see Davis, *Tel Dan in Its Northern Cultic Context;* and Greer, *Dinner at Dan.*

9. Montgomery and Gehman, *A Critical and Exegetical Commentary on the Books of Kings,* International Critical Commentary (Edinburgh: T & T Clark, 1951), 260; Toews, *Monarchy,* 100–101. See also C. F. Burney, *Notes on the Hebrew Text of the Book of Kings* (Oxford: Clarendon, 1903), 178–79.

10. Julio Trebolle Barrera rejects *BHS*'s proposals to omit two pieces here: first, in v. 32, "and he ascended the altar; thus he did in Bethel" (*wayya'al 'al-hammizbēaḥ kēn 'āśâ bēbêt-'ēl*), deleted by *BHS* as a variant of somewhat similar-looking material in v. 33; and second, in v. 33, "and he ascended the altar that he had made" (*wayya'al 'al-hammizbēaḥ 'ašer-'āśâ*), deleted as a variant of "and he ascended the altar to offer incense" (*wayya'al 'al-hammizbēaḥ lēhaqṭîr*). See his "The Text-Critical Use of the Septuagint in the Books of Kings," in *VII Congress of the International Organization for the Septuagint and Cognate Studies: Leuven 1989*, ed. C. E. Cox, SBLSCS 31 (Atlanta: Scholars, 1989), 290.

11. Trebolle Barrera, "Text-Critical Use of the Septuagint," 290.

12. E.g., Mordechai Cogan, *1 Kings: A New Translation with Introduction and Commentary*, AYB 10 (New York: Doubleday, 2000), 361.

13. So *BDB* 94: "devise, invent (bad sense)."

14. Barrick, *The King and the Cemeteries: Toward a New Understanding of Josiah's Reform*, VTSup 88 (Leiden: Brill, 2002), 64. See also P. Joüon and T. Muraoka, *A Grammar of Biblical Hebrew*, Subsidia biblica 14/II (Rome: Pontifical Biblical Institute, 1991), para. 119z.

15. Burney, *Notes on the Hebrew Text of Kings*, 179; Montgomery and Gehman, *Critical and Exegetical Commentary*, 263.

16. See also Toews, *Monarchy*, 88.

17. Albertz, *History of Israelite Religion*, 144.

18. See Richard C. Steiner, "The Aramaic Text in Demotic Script," in *COS* 1.309–27, esp. 309; "Papyrus Amherst 63: A New Source for the Language, Literature, Religion, and History of the Arameans," in *Studia Aramaica: New Sources and New Approaches*, ed. M. J. Geller, J. C. Greenfield, and M. P. Weitzman (Oxford: Oxford University Press, 1995), 199–207, esp. 199. See also Steiner, "The Aramaic Text in Demotic Script: The Liturgy of a New Year's Festival Imported from Bethel to Syene by Exiles from Rash," *JAOS* 111 (1991): 362–63; Charles F. Nims and Richard C. Steiner, "A Paganized Version of Ps 20:2–6 from the Aramaic Text in Demotic Script," *JAOS* 103 (1983): 261–74; Steiner and Nims, "You Can't Offer Your Sacrifice and Eat It Too: A Polemical Poem from the Aramaic Text in Demotic Script," *JAOS* 43 (1984): 89–114, and "Ashurbanipal and Shamash-shum-ukin: A Tale of Two Brothers from the Aramaic Text in Demotic Script," *RB* 92 (1985): 60–81. For some of the vocabulary in the text, see R. C. Steiner and A. Moshavi, "A Selective Glossary of Northwest Semitic Texts in Egyptian Script," in *DNWSI* 1249–66. Note also S. P. Vleeming and J. W. Wesselius, *Studies in Amherst Papyrus 63: Essays on the Aramaic Text in Aramaic/Demotic Papyrus Amherst 63. Volume I* (Amsterdam: Juda Palache Instituut, 1985), and *Studies in Amherst Papyrus 63: Essays on the Aramaic Text in Aramaic/Demotic Papyrus Amherst 63. Volume II* (Amsterdam: Juda Palache Instituut, 1990). For further bibliography, see Steiner, "Aramaic Text in Demotic Script," 327; and Vleeming and Wesselius, *Studies in Amherst Papyrus 63 I*, 97.

19. The following information derives from the works of Steiner cited in the preceding note, esp. Steiner, "Papyrus Amherst 63: A New Source," 203–7, and "Aramaic Text in Demotic Script," 310. In addition, I wish to acknowledge access provided to me by Professor Steiner to his unpublished transliteration of part of this text (see below) as well as the help that he has so kindly and generously provided to me (including a review of a draft of the current study). My debt to his published and unpublished work marks my discussion of this text.

20. It is noted below that most of these references are to the god Bethel, a north Syrian deity of the first millennium. For discussion, see K. van der Toorn, "Anat-Yahu, Some Other Deities and the Jews of Elephantine," *Numen* 39/1 (1992): 80–101. For a critique of Steiner's proposal, see Vleeming and Wesselius, *Studies in Amherst Papyrus 63 I*, 9, 45–46, and 55. Steiner compares the exile of residents of Rashu/Arashu to Samaria by the Assyrians to the situation described in 2 Kgs 17:33. For further information, see also Nadav Na'aman and Ran Zadok, "Assyrian Deportations to the Province of Samerina in the Light of Two Cuneiform Tablets from Tel Hadid," *TA* 27 (2000): 159–88, esp. 179.

21. See Nims and Steiner, "Paganized Version," 261–74; Vleeming and Wesselius, *Studies in Amherst Papyrus 63 I*, 50–60; Moshe Weinfeld, "The Pagan Version of Psalm 20, 2–6: Vicissitudes of a Psalmodic Creation in Israel and Its Neighbors," *EI* 18 (1985): 130–40; Ingo Kottsieper, "Anmerkungen zu Pap. Amherst 63," *ZAW* 100 (1988): 217–44; Ziony Zevit, "The Common Origin of the Aramaicized Prayer to Horus and of Psalm 20," *JAOS* 110 (1990): 213–28, and *The Religions of Ancient Israel: A Synthesis of Parallactic Approaches* (London: Continuum, 2001), 669–74. For criticism of Bethel as the setting for Psalm 20, see Koenen, *Bethel*, 76–79. For further discussion, see M. Delcor, "Remarques sur la datation du Ps 20 comparée à celle du psaume araméen apparenté dans le papyrus Amherst 63," in *Mesopotamia–Ugaritica–Biblica: Festschrift für Kurt Bergerhof zur Vollendung seines 70. Lebensjahres am 7. Mai 1992*, ed. Manfried Dietrich and Oswald Loretz, AOAT 232 (Kevelaer: Butzon und Bercker; Neukirchen-Vluyn: Neukirchener, 1993), 25–43; and K. A. D. Smelik, "The Origins of Psalm 20," *JSOT* 31 (1985): 75–81.

22. Steiner, "Aramaic Text in Demotic Script," 310.

23. See Koenen, *Bethel*, 48–64.

24. Nims and Steiner, "Paganized Version," 261–74; Zevit, "Common Origin," 213–28, and *Religions of Ancient Israel*, 669–74.

25. Vleeming and Wesselius, *Studies in Amherst Papyrus 63 I*, 59; Delcor, "Remarques sur la datation du Ps 20," 25–43; and Koenen, *Bethel*, 78.

26. So Koenen, *Bethel*, 78 n. 51, citing VIII, line 13; IX, lines 9, 13; X, line 9; and XVII, line 15.

27. For the sake of clarification, it is to be noted that *r2* in the transliteration system of Vleeming and Wesselius is the same sign as *r* with macron used by Steiner

and Nims. Similarly, the former team's *w2* is the same sign as the *w* with the dot above used by the latter team.

28. Nims and Steiner, "Paganized Version," 268.

29. Steiner, personal communication dated 20 August 2003.

30. Vleeming and Wesselius, *Studies in Amherst Papyrus 63 I*, 59, citing Ps 79:11; and see also pp. 44, 51, followed by Koenen, *Bethel*, 78.

31. As stated by Steiner and Nims, "Paganized Version," 262.

32. The line over the letters *tw* indicates that the two letters represent a single bi-consonantal sign.

33. Koenen, *Bethel*, 77 n. 45.

34. For this word, see Steiner and Moshavi, "A Selective Glossary of Northwest Semitic Texts in Egyptian Script," in *DNSWI* 1266.

35. I thank Professor Steiner for drawing this reference to my attention in connection to this question.

36. Cf. "calf," *ʿēgel*, parallel with "wild ox," *ben-rĕʾēmim*, in Ps 29:6; cf. *[wšb' (?)] swrh yhynqn 'gl* in *KAI* 222 I 23; and *wm'h swr lhynqn 'gl* in Tel Fekheriyeh, lines 20–21.

37. Fleming, "If El Is a Bull, Who Is a Calf? Reflections on Religion in Second-Millennium Syria-Palestine," *EI* 26 (1999 = Frank M. Cross Festschrift): 23*–27*.

38. Gruber, *Aspects of Nonverbal Communication in the Ancient Near East*, Studia Pohl 12/I (Rome: Pontifical Biblical Institute, 1980), 257–91, esp. 274–75; also *CAD* N/2:58–59.

39. Gruber, *Aspects of Nonverbal Communication*, 285–86 n. 4; see also pp. 334, 345.

40. The act would then not be to "blow kisses," as suggested by Albertz, *History of Israelite Religion*, 145.

41. See Koenen, *Bethel*, 101–6, 112–19, and 122–27.

42. Francis I. Andersen and David Noel Freedman (*Hosea: A New Translation with Introduction and Commentary*, AYB 24 [Garden City, N.Y.: Doubleday, 1980], 548) comment: "There is no proof of theriomorphism, in statuary or mythology: epithets such as 'bull' could be honorifics (used for humans also), turned to derogation for polemical purposes by the Israelite prophet." It is true that "bull" served as an honorific, but it was not restricted to this usage. Among other iconography, the Bethsaida stele militates against this. For a useful discussion and depiction, see Othmar Keel, *Goddesses and Trees, New Moon and Yahweh: Ancient Near Eastern Art and the Hebrew Bible*, JSOTSup 261 (Sheffield: Sheffield Academic, 1998), 114–20 and figures 106 and 107. Many commentators accept the depiction in rather "straightforward" terms as the image of a god combining his bovine and anthropomorphic representations (e.g., "Baal-Hadad," in P. J. King and L. E. Stager, *Life in Biblical Israel*, LAI [Louisville, Ky.: Westminster John Knox, 2001], 321). Keel argues against this view and suggests that the horns represent lunar iconography and hence symbolize the moon-god. In the end, though, Keel hedges; speaking of the Bethsaida and Hauran steles, he comments: "the stelae shows a moon god interpreted as a weather god or a

lunarized weather god" (followed by Blomquist, *Gates and Gods,* 51, 54–55). If I understand Keel correctly, he acknowledges the influence of the weather-god's iconography. In short, we are back to the influence of a bovine weather-god, at least to some degree. See also Tallay Ornan, "The Bull and Its Two Masters: Moon and Storm Deities in Relation to the Bull in Ancient Near Eastern Art," *IEJ* 51 (2001): 1–26. For some consideration of this evidence, see also Chapter 3, Section 1.

43. I thank Susan Ackerman for drawing my attention to this relief. See O. R. Gurney, *Some Aspects of Hittite Religion,* Schweich Lectures of the British Academy 1976 (Oxford: Oxford University Press, 1977), plate III; and Michael B. Hundley, *Gods in Dwellings: Temples and Divine Presence in the Ancient Near East,* WAWSup 3 (Atlanta: SBL, 2011), 297. For bull iconography more generally, see the summary in Irit Ziffer, "Iconography," in Raz Kletter, Irit Ziffer, and Wolfgang Zwickel, *Yavneh I: The Excavation of the "Temple Hill" Repository Pit and the Cult Stands,* OBO, Series Archaeologica 30 (Fribourg: Academic Press; Göttingen: Vandenhoeck & Ruprecht, 2010), 71–73.

44. So Keel and Uehlinger, *Gods,* 192, 193, nos. 207a and 207b.

45. See Keel and Uehlinger, *Gods,* 194.

46. See Amihai Mazar, "The 'Bull Site': An Iron Age Open Cult Place," *BASOR* 247 (1982): 27–42; Michael D. Coogan, "Cults and Cultures: Reflections on the Interpretation of Archaeological Evidence," *PEQ* 119 (1987): 1–8; Albertz, *History of Israelite Religion,* 143–44; King and Stager, *Life in Biblical Israel,* 322.

47. For discussion, see Mark S. Smith, *The Early History of God: Yahweh and the Other Deities in Ancient Israel,* 2nd ed. (Grand Rapids, Mich.: Eerdmans; Dearborn, Mich.: Dove, 2002), 53–54.

48. See Avraham Biran, "Two Bronze Plaques and the Ḥuṣṣot of Dan," *IEJ* 49/1–2 (1999): 43–54.

49. Ziffer ("Iconography," 78 n. 30) also suggests a goddess.

50. See *KTU* 1.18 IV 27–33, in *UNP* 66; 1.108.6–9, in *RCU* 194, and Gregorio del Olmo Lete, *Canaanite Religion According to the Liturgical Texts of Ugarit,* trans. Wilfred G. E. Watson, 2nd ed., AOAT 408 (Münster: Ugarit-Verlag, 2014), 151; see also *KTU* 1.13.8. Cf. the bird as an Aegean symbol possibly connected with the seated goddess, according to A. Yasur-Landau, "A Message in a Jug: Canaanite, Philistine and Cypriote Iconography and the 'Orpheus Jug,'" in *Bene Israel: Studies in the Archaeology of Israel and the Levant During the Bronze and Iron Ages in Honor of Israel Finkelstein,* ed. A. Fantalkin and A. Yasur-Landau, CHANE 31 (Leiden: Brill, 2008), 216–18.

51. I thank Susan Ackerman for bringing this point to my attention.

52. Uehlinger, "Introduction," in *Images as Media: Sources for the Cultural History of the Near East and the Eastern Mediterranean (1st millennium BCE),* ed. Christoph Uehlinger, OBO 175 (Fribourg: University Press; Göttingen: Vandenhoeck & Ruprecht, 2000), xxix.

53. Uehlinger, "Introduction," xxix.

54. *KTU* 1.46.6, in *RTU* 27–28.

55. Keel and Uehlinger, *Gods*, 195.

56. Keel and Uehlinger, *Gods*, 195. See also Izaak Cornelius, *The Iconography of the Canaanite Gods Reshef and Baal*, OBO 140 (Fribourg: University Press, 1994), 166 figure 38.

57. Harold W. Attridge and Robert A. Oden, Jr., *Philo of Byblos: Introduction, Critical Text, Translation, Notes*, CBQMS 9 (Washington, D.C.: Catholic Biblical Association of America, 1981), 56–57 and 92 n. 138; and noted by Keel and Uehlinger, *Gods*, 197 n. 14.

58. See William P. Brown, *Seeing the Psalms: A Theology of Metaphor* (Louisville, Ky.: Westminster John Knox, 2002), 20–23; Joel M. LeMon, *Yahweh's Winged Form in the Psalms: Exploring Congruent Iconography and Texts*, OBO 242 (Fribourg: Academic Press; Göttingen: Vandenhoeck & Ruprecht, 2010); and Evelyne Martin, "Theriomorphismus im Alten Testament und im Alten Orient: Eine Einführung," in *Tiergestaltigkeit der Göttinen und Götter zwischen Metapher und Symbol*, ed. Evelyne Martin, Biblischer-theologische Studien 129 (Neukirchener-Vluyn: Neukirchener, 2012), 16–25.

59. Greer, *Dinner at Dan*, 22.

60. For this evidence, see Hayim Tadmor, *The Inscriptions of Tiglath-Pileser III King of Assyria: Critical Edition, with Introductions, Translations and Commentary* (Jerusalem: Israel Academy of Sciences and Humanities, 1994), 212–13.

61. See Douglas R. Frayne, *Old Babylonian Period (2003–1595 BC)*, Royal Inscriptions of Mesopotamia, Early Periods 4 (Toronto: University of Toronto Press, 1990), 178–79.

62. For military contexts of "horn" (*qrn*), often associated with Yahweh, see also 1 Sam 2:1, 10; Lam 2:17; Pss 75:10; 89:17, 24; 92:10; 112:9 (*BDB* 902, sub *qrn*, #2).

63. For this passage and its cultic setting at the city gate, see Blomquist, *Gates and Gods*, 203–4.

64. For discussion, see J. Gerald Janzen, "The Character of the Calf and Its Cult in Exodus 32," *CBQ* 52 (1990): 597–607. For a later Levantine analogue, see Robert Turcan, *The Cults of the Roman Empire*, trans. Antonia Nevill (Oxford: Blackwell, 1996), 149–50.

65. My thanks go to Ziony Zevit for suggesting the possibility of a diachronic solution to the problem.

66. Attridge and Oden, *Philo of Byblos*, 54, 55.

67. Bloch-Smith, "Archaeological and Inscriptional Evidence for Phoenician Astarte," in *Transformations of a Goddess: Ishtar—Astarte—Aphrodite*, ed. David T. Sugimoto, OBO 263 (Fribourg: Academic Press; Göttingen: Vandenhoeck & Ruprecht, 2014), 170. For the information on Cypriote masks, Bloch-Smith cites Vassos Karageorghis, "Notes on Some Cypriote Priests Wearing Bull-Masks," *Harvard Theological Review* 64 (1971): 261–70.

68. See the discussions of Glenn Markoe, "The Emergence of Phoenician Art," *BASOR* 279 (1990): 13–26; and Shelby Brown, "Perspectives on Phoenician Art," *Biblical Archaeologist* 55 (1992): 6–24. Note also the discussions of David Ben-Shlomo, *Philistine Iconography: A Wealth of Style and Symbolism*, OBO 241 (Fribourg: Academic Press; Göttingen: Vandenhoeck & Ruprecht, 2010), 78–79; and Dominik Elkowicz, "Herkunft und Verwendung anthropomorpher und zoomorpher Gesichtsmasken in Palästina," *UF* 43 (2011): 85–97.

69. *CAD* R:362, h.

Chapter 5. Gods and Their City Sites

An early version of this chapter was presented at Harvard University in October 2010 and at New York University on 8 November 2010. On the latter occasion Jeffrey Tigay informed me of Spencer L. Allen's dissertation. Completed in 2011, it was published as *The Splintered Divine: A Study of Ištar, Baal, and Yahweh Divine Names and Divine Multiplicity in the Ancient Near East*, Studies in Ancient Near Eastern Records 5 (Berlin: de Gruyter, 2015). For the data surveyed, the book will become a standard work on the subject. I thank Allen for providing me with his dissertation and book as well as his article "An Examination of Northwest Semitic Divine Names and the *Bet*-locative," *Journal for the Evangelical Study of the Old Testament* 2 (2013): 61–82. I also thank him for corresponding with me, especially in September 2013.

1. Robertson Smith, *Lectures on the Religion of the Semites: Second and Third Series*, ed. John Day, JSOTSup 183 (Sheffield: Sheffield Academic, 1995), 64.

2. Day, "Introduction," in Robertson Smith, *Lectures*, 23.

3. Georg Fohrer, *History of Israelite Religion*, trans. David E. Green (Nashville, Tenn.: Abingdon, 1972), 63; *CMHE* 49; Johannes de Moor, *An Anthology of Religious Texts*, Nisaba 16 (Leiden: Brill, 1987), 168 n. 5; Rainer Albertz, *A History of Israelite Religion in the Old Testament Period: Volume I: From the Beginnings to the End of the Monarchy*, trans. John Bowden, OTL, (Louisville, Ky.: Westminster John Knox, 1994), 183; Othmar Keel and Christoph Uehlinger, *Gods, Goddesses, and Images of God in Ancient Israel*, trans. Thomas H. Trapp (Minneapolis: Fortress, 1998), 228; and *RCU* 274–77, 283. Cf. "localization" in Helmer Ringgren, *Israelite Religion*, trans. David E. Green (Philadelphia: Fortress, 1966), 72.

4. Emerton, "New Light on Israelite Religion," *ZAW* 94 (1982): 2–28.

5. Barré, *The God-List in the Treaty Between Hannibal and Philip V of Macedonia: A Study in Light of the Ancient Near Eastern Treaty Tradition* (Baltimore: Johns Hopkins University Press, 1983), 186 n. 472.

6. McCarter, "Aspects of the Religion of the Israelite Monarchy," in *Ancient Israelite Religion: Essays in Honor of Frank Moore Cross*, ed. P. D. Miller, Jr., Paul D. Hanson, and S. Dean McBride (Philadelphia: Fortress, 1987), 137–55.

7. McCarter, "Aspects," 139.

8. McCarter, "Aspects," 140.

9. McCarter, "Aspects," 141. Allen (*Splintered Divine*, 306–7, and "An Examination," 68–69) rejects DN "in" (*b*-)GN as a divine title. Allen also states (*Splintered Divine*, 307): "Just because a deity is worshiped in or associated with one or more temples in a city, that deity is not necessarily known by that location." It seems to me that precisely because a deity is worshipped in such a place, the deity is known by that location even if not only by that location. Second Kings 14:23 provides a human analogy with Jeroboam in Samaria where he is said to reign "in" (**mlk . . . b*-). Even if DN *b*-GN is not a name (and on this point Allen makes a reasonable case), DN *b*-GN still seems to be a marker of divine manifestation in a specific locale (cf. "David of/in Hebron" in 2 Sam 3:22 and 4:8 and "Absalom in Hebron" in 2 Sam 15:10); for this reason DN "in" (*b*-)GN is included in this discussion.

10. The two expressions appear in poetic parallelism (e.g., Judg 5:17; Ps 68:16).

11. See McCarter, "Aspects," 141, where he includes Baal-perazim (2 Sam 5:20) as DN of GN and translates "the lord of [Mt.] Perazim." For the various Baals + GN, see also their listings in *DDD* 140–56. See Klaus Koch, *Studien zur alttestamentichen und altorientalischen Religionsgeschichte: Zum 60. Geburstag von Klaus Koch*, ed. Eckart Otto (Göttingen: Vandenhoeck & Ruprecht, 1988), 189–205, here 201 and 202. Koch views Baal as a kind of expression of divine power, "ein besondere *Innewerden der numinosen Kraft von Autorität*" (Koch's italics). This power appears under different rubrics of *b'l* + GNs. While this view offers a broad understanding of the etymological background of *b'l* as "lord," Baal also functions sometimes as a divine name. As a result, it is not always clear when *b'l* functions as a name and when it is a title meaning "lord." See further below.

12. Sommer, *The Bodies of God and the World of Ancient Israel* (Cambridge: Cambridge University Press, 2009), 75: "at any moment many objects in many places could host the presence of a particular deity."

13. Hutton, "Local Manifestations of Yahweh and Worship in the Interstices: A Note on Kuntillet 'Ajrud," *Journal of Ancient Near Eastern Religions* 10 (2010): 177–210.

14. Allen, *The Splintered Divine: A Study of Ištar, Baal, and Yahweh Divine Names and Divine Multiplicity in the Ancient Near East*, Studies in Ancient Near Eastern Records 5 (Berlin: de Gruyter, 2015).

15. Leuenberger, "Jhwh, 'der Gott Jerusalems' (BLay 1,2): Konturen der Jerusalemer Tempeltheologie aus religions-und theologiegeschichtlicher Perspektive," *EvT* 74 (2014): 245–60.

16. McCarter, "Aspects," 150 n. 11, citing Barré, *God-List*, 186 n. 472. See also the evidence cited by Hutton, "Local Manifestations," 177–210; and Allen, *Splintered Divine*.

17. For further Mesopotamian listings, see Knut Tallqvist, *Akkadische Götterepitheta* (Helsinki: Societas Orientalis Fennica, 1938), 331–32; Hutton, "Local Manifestations," 181–82; and Allen, *Splintered Divine.*

18. For Ishtar, see Allen, *Splintered Divine,* 141–99. Note also Elizabeth Knott, "The Construction of Ishtar-Type Goddesses in Syria and Iraq During the Ages of Internationalism (ca. 2000–1200 B.C.)," Ph.D. diss., New York University, in preparation. For Hittite and Hurrian evidence, see Allen, *Splintered Divine,* 71–93 and 355–68. Cf. the special class of deities named for peoples of areas discussed by Paul-Alain Beaulieu, "The God Amurru as Emblem of Ethnic and Cultural Identity," in *Ethnicity in Ancient Mesopotamia: Papers Read at the 74th Rencontre Assyriologique Internationale, Leiden 1–4 July 2002,* ed. W. H. van Soldt (Leiden: Nederlands Instituut voor het Nabije Oosten, 2005), 31–46.

19. For *yhwh tmn* on Pithos B, see Zeev Meshel, *Kuntillet ʿAjrud (Horvat Teman): An Iron Age II Religious Site on the Judah–Sinai Border* (Jerusalem: Israel Exploration Society, 2012), 92–97, Inscription 3.5/3.6. For *yhwh tymn* on a plaster inscription found in the "bench room," see Meshel, *Kuntillet ʿAjrud,* 105–7, Inscription 4.1.1; and F. W. Dobbs-Allsopp, J. J. M. Roberts, C. L. Seow, and R. E. Whitaker, *Hebrew Inscriptions: Texts from the Biblical Period of the Monarchy with Concordance* (New Haven, Conn.: Yale University Press, 2005), 285–86. It is in Phoenician script, but Judahite orthography and dialect, according to Hutton, "Local Manifestations," 196. Note also the syntheses in McCarter, "Aspects," 140–41; Keel and Uehlinger, *Gods,* 226–28; Dobbs-Allsopp et al., *Hebrew Inscriptions,* 293–96; Hutton, "Local Manifestations," 189; and Nadav Naʾaman, "The Inscriptions of Kuntillet ʿAjrud Through the Lens of Historical Research," *UF* 43 (2011): 299–324, esp. 303–4, 306, 308, and 316 n. 10.

20. Meshel, *Kuntillet ʿAjrud,* 98–100, Inscription 3.9, and 105–7, Inscription 4.1.1 (line 2). The apparent definite article is said to be puzzling; it is perhaps a reference to a region or possibly a dittography; see Meshel (*Kuntillet ʿAjrud,* 100). It is to be noted that in line 1 of Inscription 4.1.1 (see n. 19), the form appears without the definite article.

21. See Meshel, *Kuntillet ʿAjrud,* 87–89, Inscription 3.1. The initial publication appeared in Zeev Meshel, *Kuntillet ʿAjrud: A Religious Centre from the Time of the Judaean Monarchy on the Border of Sinai,* Catalogue no. 175 (Jerusalem: Israel Museum, 1978), illustration 12. Meshel and others originally read "Yahweh our guardian," but in light of "Yahweh of Teman" also at the site, they read "Yahweh of Samaria." See also McCarter, "Aspects," 139; Keel and Uehlinger, *Gods,* 225–26 and 228; Dobbs-Allsopp et al., *Hebrew Inscriptions,* 289–92; Hutton, "Local Manifestations," 190; and Naʾaman, "Inscriptions of Kuntillet ʿAjrud," 304.

22. Cf. *KAI* 48:2, read as *[ ]rt šmrn* in *PPD* 392–93, reconstructed as either "[Ashe]rah of Samaria" or "[Asht]art of Samaria" or "[Melq]art of Samaria."

23. The reading is controversial. See Johannes Renz, *Handbuch der althebräischen Epigraphik Band I: Teil I. Text und Kommentar* (Darmstadt: Wissenschaftliche Buchgesellschaft, 1995), 245–46; Dobbs-Allsopp et al., *Hebrew Inscriptions*, 128–29; and Leuenberger, "Jhwh, 'der Gott Jerusalems,'" 252–56.

24. *UNP* 19. Apparently this is the place-name with enclitic-*m* despite the possibly incongruent second term in the parallel expression, *'ilt ṣdynm*, in lines 35–36 and 39.

25. The rendering Sapan is standard, but it may be Sapun based on Akkadian texts from Ras Shamra and other evidence. See N. Wyatt, "The Significance of ṢPN in West Semitic Thought: A Contribution to the History of a Mythological Motif," in *Ugarit: Ein ostmediterranes Kulturzentrum im Alten Orient. Ergebnisse und Perspektiven der Forschung. Band I: Ugarit und seine altorientalische Umwelt*, ed. Manfried Dietrich and Oswald Loretz, Abhandlungen zur Literatur Alt-Syren-Palästinas und Mesopotamiens 7 (Münster: Ugarit-Verlag, 1995), 212–15, 228, 230, followed by *RCU* 284. For Baal Sapan at Ugarit, see the survey of Richard J. Clifford, *Cosmic Mountain in Canaan and the Old Testament*, HSM 4 (Cambridge, Mass.: Harvard University Press, 1972), 57–79.

26. Often thought to be Baal of Aleppo or of some town in the kingdom of Ugarit. See Francesco Pomponio and Paolo Xella, *Les dieux d'Ebla: Étude analytique des divinités éblaïtes à l'époque des archives royales du IIIe millénaire*, AOAT 245 (Münster: Ugarit-Verlag, 1997), 42–48 and 53. Halab also appears as a theophoric element in Ebla texts; see Pomponio and Xella, *Les dieux d'Ebla*, 417. See also "gods of the land of Aleppo" in *KTU* 1.148.42–43, as reconstructed in *RCU* 46–47, 49, and 278.

27. For this god at Emar, see Alfonso Archi, "Kizzuwatna amid Anatolian and Syrian Cults," in *Anatolia Antica: Studi in memoria di Fiorelli Imparati*, ed. Stefano de Martino and Franca Pecchioli Daddi (Florence: LoGisma, 2002), 50.

28. "When 'Athtart *ḫr* enters the mound of the palace of the king" (for such a procession, see also line 9; cf. lines 23–26; *RCU* 69, 70–71, and Gregorio del Olmo Lete, *Canaanite Religion According to the Liturgical Texts of Ugarit*, trans. Wilfred G. E. Watson, 2nd ed., AOAT 408 (Münster: Ugarit-Verlag, 2014), 237–38.

29. See also below in the Akkadian listing, ᵈištar *ḫur-ri* at Ugarit (RS 16.273.9, in *PRU III* p. 171): a person placed in administrative service is given to the goddess. The identity of 'Athtart *ḫr* has received a number of proposals: "Hurrian Ishtar" (Pardee, *RCU* 275, among many commentators); "'Athtartu of the tomb(s)" (del Olmo Lete, *Canaanite Religion*, 202); "'Athtartu of the grotto/cavern" (Andrée Herdner, "Nouveaux textes alphabétiques de Ras Shamra—XXIVe champagne 1961," in *Ugaritica VII*, ed. Claude F. A. Schaeffer, Mission de Ras Shamra XVIII [Paris: Mission Archéologique de Ras Shamra/Collège de France/Librairie orientaliste Paul Geuthner/Brill, 1978], pp. 21–26); or, "Athtart of the window" (Emile Puech, "Le vocable d'*Attart ḫurri—ʿštrt ḫr* à Ugarit et en Phénicie," *UF* 25 [1993]: 327–30). The first remains the most prominent in the scholarly litera-

ture. See Frank M. Cross, *Leaves from An Epigrapher's Notebook: Collected Papers in Hebrew and West Semitic Paleography and Epigraphy*, HSS 51 (Winona Lake, Ind.: Eisenbrauns, 2003), 273–75; Dennis Pardee, *Les textes rituels*, RSO XII, 2 vols. (Paris: Éditions Recherche sur les Civilisations, 2000), 1.233–36; Corrine Bonnet, *Astarté: Dossier documentaire et perspectives historiques*, Contributi alla storia della religione fenicio-punica II (Rome: Consiglio nazionale delle ricerche, 1996), 127–31, and plate X. For Puech, there is no -*y* gentilic; thus it does not mean "Hurrian" (as in 1.40.29, 37; cf. "Kassite Yarihu" [*yrḫ kty*] in 1.39.19, 1.102.14, in *RCU* 21, 69). Puech expects final -*t* for the goddess as "Hurrian"? See further del Olmo Lete, "The Ugaritic Ritual Texts: A New Edition and Commentary. A Critical Assessment," *UF* 36 (2004): 577. Puech's view assumes a feminine adjectival form rather than a construct "Astarte of Hurri." Moreover, Puech's own proposal takes *ḫr* as "window," which would otherwise be unattested in Ugaritic. See below n. 47 for Phoenician *štrt ḫr*.

30. *RCU* 283. Cf. below "Resheph at Bbt" in *KTU* 1.100.31, identified as an Anatolian city.

31. *RCU* 283. Pardee identifies Gn as a Syrian city. For this Resheph and his manifestations at Ebla, see Maciej M. Münnich, *The God Resheph in the Ancient Near East*, ORA 11 (Tübingen: Mohr Siebeck, 2013), 48–58.

32. For examples from Ebla, see Pomponio and Xella, *Les dieux d'Ebla*, 64–65. For seventy-two more examples of DN + GN at Ebla, see Pomponio and Xella, *Les dieux d'Ebla*, 527–33.

33. Amanda H. Podany, *The Land of Hana: Kings, Chronology, and Scribal Tradition* (Bethesda, Md.: CDL, 2002), 53, 108.

34. Lluís Feliu, *The God Dagan in Bronze Age Syria*, trans. Wilfred G. E. Watson, CHANE 19 (Leiden: Brill, 2003), 130–31. See also Wilfred G. Lambert, "The Pantheon of Mari," *Mari, Annales de Recherches interdisciplinaires* 4 (1985): 525–39.

35. Martti Nissinen, *Prophets and Prophecy in the Ancient Near East*, WAW 12 (Atlanta: SBL, 2003), 28, with further examples on 31 and 83.

36. Nissinen, *Prophets and Prophecy*, 44.

37. Feliu, *God Dagan*, 134–36, 139.

38. Feliu, *God Dagan*, 136–39, with additional examples on pp. 139–42.

39. Daniel E. Fleming, "'The Storm God of Canaan' at Emar," *UF* 26 (1994): 127–30, and *Time at Emar: The Cultic Calendar and the Rituals from the Diviner's Archive*, MC 11 (Winona Lake, Ind.: Eisenbrauns, 2000), 169–70. As Fleming notes, the primary storm-god of Emar in this text is also mentioned, and the two are equated.

40. *Ugaritica V* p. 321, #170:19. See *DULAT* 206.

41. *PRU III* p. 171.

42. RS 18.01.3, 6 in *PRU IV* p. 230. See Silvie Lackenbacher, *Textes Akkadiens d'Ugarit: Textes provenant des vingt-cinq premières campagnes*, LAPO 20 (Paris:

Cerf, 2002), 141; and John McLaughlin, *The marzēaḥ in the Prophetic Literature,* VTSup 86 (Leiden: Brill, 2001), 17.

43. See Simo Parpola and Kazuko Watanabe, *Neo-Assyrian Treaties and Loyalty Oaths,* SAA 2 (Helsinki: Helsinki University Press, 1988), 29. This goddess and Ishtar of Arbela are commonly paired in Neo-Assyrian sources. For a comprehensive survey, see Allen, *Splintered Divine,* 141–99. The two goddesses commonly appear together in Neo-Assyrian prophecies and annals; see Nissinen, *Prophets and Prophecy,* 137, 139, 144, 158 ("According to what Ishtar of N[ineveh] and Ishtar of Arbela have said to me [*iqban(ni)*]," a singular verb); and 144–45, #100, column ii, line 128, and column iii, lines 13–14. In standard blessings in royal correspondence, the two Ishtars appear, in Mikko Luukko and Greta Van Buylaere, *The Political Correspondence of Esarhaddon,* SAA 16 (Helsinki: Helsinki University Press, 2002), 31, #33, lines 6–7; 44, #49, lines 4–5; 52, #59, line 3; 54, #60, lines 2–3; 56, #61, line 3; 95, #105, lines 4–5; see also Nissinen, *Prophets and Prophecy,* 131 n. a, with further examples on 97, #106, lines 6–7; 112, #126, lines 5–6 (the two Ishtars combined also with Ishtar of the Kidmuri temple); #127, lines 5–6; 114, #128, line 5; 159, #108, line 3; 170, #115, line 3; 172, #116, line 3. For further discussion, see the following note.

44. See Parpola and Watanabe, *Neo-Assyrian Treaties,* 29; see also Jacob Lauinger, "Esarhaddon's Succession Treaty at Tell Tayinat: Text and Commentary," *JCS* 64 (2012): 93 (T i 33). In addition to the references to Ishtar of Arbela in the preceding note, see the "weavers of Ishtar of Arbela," in Luuko and Van Buylaere, *The Political Correspondence of Esarhaddon,* 79, #84, lines 8–9. See Ishtar of Arbela in Nissinen, *Prophets and Prophecy,* 102; see also 105, 106, 109, 110, 115, 121, 122–23, 126, 127, 130, 169. Ishtar is represented as Ishtar of Arbela: "Ishtar heard my desperate sighs. . . . The very same night as I implored, a visionary lay down and had a dream. When he woke up, he reported to me the nocturnal vision shown to him by Ishtar: 'Ishtar who dwells in Arbela entered'" (Nissinen, *Prophets and Prophecy,* 147, #101, lines 46–53). The accent on Ishtar of Arbela in many of these texts may be tied to the place of her prophetic words, as suggested by this text (Nissinen, *Prophets and Prophecy,* 113–14). There seems to be a ritual component as well. In a word from "Ishtar of Arbela," she says to Esarhaddon: "You say to yourself: 'Ishtar—she is small beer!' Then you go into your cities and your districts, eat your own bread and forget this covenant. But every time when you drink this water, you will remember me and keep this covenant which I have made on behalf of Esarhaddon" (Nissinen, *Prophets and Prophecy,* 122–23). For these Ishtars, see further Martti Nissinen, "Gender and Prophetic Agency in the Ancient Near East and Greece," in *Prophets Male and Female: Gender and Prophecy in the Hebrew Bible, the Eastern Mediterranean, and the Ancient Near East,* ed. Jonathan Stökl and Corrine L. Carvalho, AIL 15 (Atlanta: SBL, 2013), 50–54; and note the discussion below in Section 5.

45. Ali Abou-Assaf, Pierre Bordreuil, and Alan R. Millard, *La statue de Tell Fekherye et son inscription bilingue assyro-araméenne*, Études Assyriologiques (Paris: Éditions Recherche sur les civilisations, 1982), 23, line 1. See also *DNWSI* 475. No place-name is attached to Adad in the parallel Akkadian text. See Abou-Assaf, Bordreuil, and Millard, *La statue de Tell Fekherye*, 61.

46. See below for the parallel Akkadian text in this bilingual.

47. The meaning is disputed; see Puech, "Le vocable," 327–30; Cross, *Leaves from an Epigrapher's Notebook*, 273–75; Pardee, *Les textes rituels*, 1.233–36; Bonnet, *Astarté*, 127–33 and plate X; and Robert M. Kerr, "Notre-Dame-de-la-Huronie?," *WO* 43 (2013): 206–12. Note also n. 29 above.

48. *PPD* 392.

49. Frank L. Benz, *Personal Names in the Phoenician and Punic Inscriptions*, Studia Pohl 8 (Rome: Biblical Institute Press, 1972), 386; *PPD* 392.

50. Cf. Paphian Venus in Apuleuis's *Metamorphoses*. For discussion, see Mark S. Smith, *God in Translation: Deities in Cross-Cultural Discourse in the Biblical World*, FAT 1/57 (Tübingen: Mohr Siebeck, 2008; republ., Grand Rapids, Mich.: Eerdmans, 2010), 244.

51. So *PPD* 391.

52. Benz, *Personal Names*, 386.

53. Cf. the element **zu-* in Amorite PNs, in Herbert Bardwell Huffmon, *Amorite Personal Names in the Mari Texts: A Structural and Lexical Study* (Baltimore: Johns Hopkins University Press, 1965), 186; Ignace J. Gelb, *Computer-Aided Analysis of Amorite*, Assyriological Studies 21 (Chicago: Oriental Institute of the University of Chicago, 1980), 130; and Michael P. Streck, "Remarks on Two Recent Studies on Amorite," *UF* 44 (2013): 312. Note also "Karib'il, he (*d̲*) of Raydân," in Albert Jamme, *Sabaean Inscriptions from Maḥram Bilqîs (Mârib)* (Baltimore: Johns Hopkins University Press, 1962), 83, 84, #578.22, 26, 28; 93, #586.9; and 96, #589.9–10. For this construction, see Na'ama Pat-El, *Studies in the Historical Syntax of Aramaic*, Perspectives on Linguistics and Ancient Languages 1 (Piscataway, N.J.: Gorgias, 2012), 125–26.

54. So most commentators. Cf. Israel Knohl, "Psalm 68: Structure, Composition and Geography," *JHS* 12, Article 15 (2012): 16–17.

55. For these inscriptions, see Jamme, *Sabaean Inscriptions*.

56. See Joan Copeland Biella, *Dictionary of Old South Arabic: Sabaean Dialect*, HSS 25 (Chico, Calif.: Scholars, 1982), 89. Note also the interesting example in Maria Höfner, *Sabäische Inschriften (Letze Folge)* (Vienna: Österreichischen Akademie der Wissenschaften, 1981), 29: *ʿttr ddbn mwtb*, "'Attar *d*-DBN den Göttersitz."

57. Cf. *bʿl (b)ṣrrt ṣpn* (*KTU* 1.3 I 21–22, in *UNP* 106; 1.6 VI 12, in *UNP* 162); and *bʿl mrym ṣpn* (*KTU* 1.3 IV 37, in *UNP* 114; 1.4 V 23, in *UNP* 130; 1.5 I 10, in *UNP* 141; and 1.100.9, in *RCU* 174). For this subtype, see Allen, "An Examination," 61–82.

58. De Moor (*Anthology of Religious Texts*, 150 n. 13) notes: "Apparently this goddess (cf. lines 20 and 41) is Ishtar who had a large temple in Mari."

59. Pomponio and Xella, *Les dieux d'Ebla*, 14–15.
60. McCarter takes Tannit as the referent for *blbnn*, while *PPD* 391 suggests both "ladies."
61. *PPD* 391.
62. So *PPD* 391.
63. Karel Jongeling, *Handbook of Neo-Punic Inscriptions* (Tübingen: Mohr Siebeck, 2008), 155.
64. See Walter E. Aufrecht, *A Corpus of Ammonite Inscriptions,* Ancient Near Eastern Texts and Studies Volume 4 (Lewiston, N.Y.: Mellen, 1989), 145–48.
65. Allen, *Splintered Divine,* 303, and "An Examination," 78–80.
66. Allen, *Splintered Divine,* 303, and "An Examination," 78–80.
67. Cf. Pss 15:1; 74:2; 78:54, 60; and 1 Chr 23:25. Note also **škn b-* in Jer 7:3, 7.
68. See NRSV and NABRE; and Frank Moore Cross, Jr., and David Noel Freedman, *Studies in Ancient Yahwistic Poetry,* 2nd ed., Biblical Resource Series (Grand Rapids, Mich.: Eerdmans; Livonia, Mich.: Dove, 1997), 68, 78 nn. 53–54.
69. See *RCU* 193–94; and del Olmo Lete, *Canaanite Religion,* 150 n. 45. The initial name and title are usually translated "Rp'u, the eternal king" or the like. The rendering of *mlk* as a name or title rather than as the generic noun meaning "king" here is suggested by the address of *rp'u mlk 'lm* shared with *mlk 'ttrth* (*KTU* 1.100.41, in *RCU* 177) and *mlk b'ttrt* (*KTU* 1.107.42, in *RCU* 181, 184). While more than one deity can inhabit a location, the combination of the same place with *mlk* in *KTU* 1.108.1–2 suggests this interpretation. See Mark S. Smith, *Poetic Heroes: Warriors and Warrior Culture in the Early Biblical World* (Grand Rapids, Mich.: Eerdmans, 2014), 138 and 447–48 n. 12.
70. See Abou-Assaf, Bordreuil, and Millard, *La statue de Tell Fekherye,* 23, lines 15–16. See also *DNWSI* 47. Note also Aramaic *ysb skn* in lines 5–6, parallel to Akkadian *āšib* ᵘʳᵘ*guzana,* in Abou-Assaf, Bordreuil, and Millard, *La statue de Tell Fekherye,* 62. See below note 76.
71. Emil G. Kraeling, *The Brooklyn Museum Aramaic Papyri: New Documents of the Fifth Century B.C. from the Jewish Colony at Elephantine* (New Haven, Conn.: Yale University Press; London: Geoffrey Cumberlege, Oxford University Press, 1953; repr. Arno, 1969), 270–71, #12.2. For the wording and syntax, cf. A. E. Cowley, *Aramaic Papyri of the Fifth Century B.C.* (Oxford: Clarendon, 1923), 30, line 6 and 31, line 7: "the temple of Yahu the god which is in Yeb the fortress" (*yhw 'lh' zy byb byrt'*); see Bezalel Porten and Ada Yardeni, *Textbook of Aramaic Documents from Ancient Egypt: 1. Letters* (Jerusalem: Hebrew University, 1986), 68–71 and 72–75.
72. *CAD* A/1:397.
73. Parpola and Watanabe, *Neo-Assyrian Treaties,* 48; Lauinger, "Esarhaddon's Succession Treaty," 101. Cf. lines 459–460.
74. Unpublished, cited by Owen Jarus, "2,700-year-old royal loyalty oath discovered in Turkey," *The Independent: Archaeology,* at http://www.independent.co.uk/

news/science/archaeology/news/2700yearold-royal-loyalty-oath-discovered
-in-turkey-2107830.html.

75. Nissinen, *Prophets and Prophecy*, 145, #100, lines 4–5; 147, #101, line 52.
76. Abou-Assaf, Bordreuil, and Millard, *La statue de Tell Fekherye*, 64, lines 24–25.
    For the Aramaic parallel text, see note 70 above.
77. Cf. *b'l ṣpn* and *b'l 'ugrt*, listed above as DN + GN, and also discussed below.
    Cf. *b'l ṣdn* (*KAI* 14.18, 60.6), "lord/Baal of Sidon"; and *b'l kty* (Kition D 37; so
    DNWSI 183), "baal/Baal of Kition."
78. See also "lord/lady" + GN in Ebla texts, in Pomponio and Xella, *Les dieux
    d'Ebla*, 89–109 and 114–21. Note also DN lú GN in Ebla cases; see Pomponio
    and Xella, *Les dieux d'Ebla*, 29, 42, 48, 50, 51, 191, 311; cf. DN dinger GN, in Pom-
    ponio and Xella, *Les dieux d'Ebla*, 334.
79. See *CAD* B:194; Nissinen, *Prophets and Prophecy*, 18–19; and Fleming, *Time at
    Emar*, 114.
80. Nissinen, *Prophets and Prophecy*, 19–21.
81. *Ugaritica V* p. 44, #18.4. For this example at Mari, see *CAD* B:194.
82. Daniel E. Fleming, "The Emar Festivals: City Unity and Syrian Identity Under
    Hittite Hegemony," in *Emar: The History, Religion, and Culture of a Syrian Town
    in the Late Bronze Age*, ed. Mark W. Chavalas (Bethesda, Md.: CDL, 1996),
    86 n. 15.
83. The title is common; see Allen, *Splintered Divine*, viii, 1–4, 12–13, 24–25, 47–48,
    139–43, 154–57, 139–99; and Nissinen, *Prophets and Prophecy*, 127.
84. The title is common; see Allen, *Splintered Divine*, viii, 1–4, 12–13, 24–25, 47–48,
    104, 124, 127, 139–199.
85. Lauinger, "Esarhaddon's Succession Treaty," 87–123, here 102, 113, and 119. For
    further examples of this type of divine title, see Tallqvist, *Akkadische Götterepi-
    theta*, 236, 238; *CAD* Š/II:75b, 4'. Cf. the Luwian title, "Kubaba, queen of Karke-
    mish," in John David Hawkins, *Corpus of Hieroglyphic Luwian Inscriptions: Vol-
    ume I. Inscriptions of the Iron Age. Part 1*, Studies in Indo-European Language
    and Culture 8.1 (Berlin: de Gruyter, 2000), 119, #II.19, lines 1 and 5, 122, #II.20,
    line 3, etc. Note also "queen [*šarrat*] of Sippar" as the title of the local manifes-
    tation of Ishtar, e.g., Ira Spar and Michael Jursa, *The Ebabbar Temple Archive
    and Other Texts from the Fourth to the First Millennium B.C.*, Cuneiform Texts
    in the Metropolitan Museum of Art IV (New York: Metropolitan Museum of
    Art; Winona Lake, Ind.: Eisenbrauns, 2014), #43:11; #44:11; #45:10; #46:11, 20;
    #47:9; #48:10; #49:9; #80:5.
86. Lauinger ("Esarhaddon's Succession Treaty," 119) associates this title with
    ptgyh, attested in a seventh-century inscription from Ekron; see Seymour Gi-
    tin, Trude Dothan, and Joseph Naveh, "A Royal Dedicatory Inscription from
    Ekron," *IEJ* 47 (1997): 1–16, here 9; and Shmuel Aḥituv, *Echoes from the Past: He-
    brew and Cognate Inscriptions from the Biblical Period* (Jerusalem: Carta, 2008),
    335, 339.

87. For the following references, see *DNWSI* 183.

88. Albert Jamme, "Le pantheon sud-arabe préislamiques d'après les sources épigraphiques," *Muséon* 60 (1947): 90.

89. Jamme, "Le pantheon sud-arabe préislamiques," 91, with more examples.

90. Jamme, "Le pantheon sud-arabe préislamiques," 101, with more examples.

91. Cf. *'ily 'ugrt*, "the gods (deities) of Ugarit," in *KTU* 2.16.4–5; *'il špn*, "the gods (deities) of Sapan" in *KTU* 1.47.1; *kl 'il 'alty*, "all the gods of Alashiya" (*KTU* 2.42.8); and "the gods of the land of Aleppo" (*KTU* 1.148.42–43, as reconstructed in *RCU* 46–47, 49, 278). Cf. "the gods of Gubla" in EA 137:31 and "the gods of y[our] land" in EA 74:14–18, in William L. Moran, *The Amarna Letters* (Baltimore: Johns Hopkins University Press, 1992), 218 and 143, respectively. For further listings, see *CAD* I/J:92b–93a, #2".

92. Note also for groups of workers in *KTU* 4.214 I 4, III 1; 4.230.1; 4.683.1; 4.728.1–2 (?).

93. The syntax has also been understood as expressing a locative, "David at Hebron" (so NRSV).

94. Note the variant in *KTU* 4.54.1 and 4.542.1.

95. See this idiom also in several series of *b*-GN in *KTU* 4.625. Note **ytb* for "residence" in *KTU* 1.49.12 and 5.11.5 (*DULAT* 979).

96. See also "the kingdom of Og in Bashan" in Deut 3:4.

97. For **škn b-* (noted above in connection with **ytb b-*) for the deity, see *DCH* VIII:357–58, and for people dwelling in a locale, see *DCH* VIII:356.

98. See also *KAI* 26A ii 18f.//26C iii 15f.; 214:19, "I made this/my god dwell [**yšb*] in it" (see *DNWSI* 475). For Akkadian *ašābu* also used for gods in temples or shrines, see *CAD* A/2:396–97.

99. For Ugaritic, see the parade case of the eight instances of **ytb b-*GN for residence in *KTU* 4.382.23–34 (*DULAT* 970). For Hebrew examples, see *DCH* IV:321.

100. For Ugaritic **ytb* in this meaning, see *KTU* 1.23.8 (in *UNP* 208). Cf. *KTU* 1.10 III 13–14, in *UNP* 185, and 1.16 VI 22–25, in *UNP* 40. The usage in 1.101.1 is "to sit" ("Baal sits like the sitting of the mountain"), with the connotation of enthronement (see below for this text). For BH **yšb* for sitting on a throne, see Amos 1:5, 8 and Exod 15:15, so *CMHE* 130 n. 65; note also Deut 3:2 and 4:46 for "Sihon, king of the Amorites, who was dwelling/enthroned in Heshbon." The meaning is also evident in Phoenician, in *KAI* 24.9, in *PPD* 216; see also *KAI* 214.19. Note Akkadian *ašābu ina* with respect to royal enthronement, see *CAD* A/1:390–92, *CAD* Š/3:135, #2'c', and Moran, *Amarna Letters*, 131 n. 2. This formulation also denotes the location of the army in Judg 4:2.

101. See *CAD* B:191, 196–98; Moran, *Amarna Letters*, 175–76 n. 5.

102. For *ba'ălê* + GN, see also Num 21:28; Josh 24:11; 1 Sam 23:11; 2 Sam 21:12. Cf. *ba'al habbayit*, "owner of the house," in Exod 22:7; Judg 19:22–23; and 2 Chr 23:17.

103. Cowley, *Aramaic Papyri*, cited in *DNWSI* 1.183.
104. J. David Schloen, *The House of the Father as Fact and Symbolic: Patrimonialism in Ugarit and the Ancient Near East*, Studies in the Archaeology and History of the Levant 2 (Winona Lake, Ind.: Eisenbrauns, 2001), 327.
105. *KTU* 1.6 VI 58, in *UNP* 164. See Pardee, *COS* 1.273, esp. n. 283; *UBC* 2.727; cf. *DULAT* 918. Note also *b'l* in *KTU* 2.81.3 and 30–31, "lord (*b'l*) of the whole land of Egypt" used for "[the Sun], great king, king of Egypt" (lines 1 and 10) by the king of Ugarit. Cf. *'lmqh b'l 'wm* (Jamme, *Sabaean Inscriptions*, #559.7, 20 = #561.7, 20; #562.3; cf. #562.3, 9, 12, 20–21; etc.), "'Ilumquh, lord of 'Awwâm" (thought to be a temple; see Biella, *Dictionary of Old South Arabic*, 50).
106. *CAD* B:190.
107. For this plural usage, see *UBC* 2.568. See also S. Tamar Kamionkowski, "The Erotics of Pilgrimage: A Fresh Look at Psalms 84 and 63," in *Gazing on the Deep: Ancient Near Eastern, Biblical, and Jewish Studies in Honor of Tzvi Abusch*, ed. Jeffrey Stackert, Barbara Nevling Porter, and David P. Wright (Bethesda, Md.: CDL, 2010), 469–74.
108. McCarter, "Aspects," 141–42, though without any particular evidence for such difference.
109. McCarter, "Aspects," 143.
110. Huffmon, "Name," *DDD* 610–11.
111. Abusch, "Ishtar," *DDD* 453.
112. Allen, *Splintered Divine*, 203–21, and "An Examination," 61–82. It is unclear in many instances whether **b'l* GN entails a title ("lord") or a virtual name ("Baal"). The latter is the case for Baal of Sapan and Baal of Ugarit. Cf. Koch, *Studien*, 200–201. Note the parallel difficulty with **ba'alat* + GN, noted in Chapter 5, Section 4.
113. Sommer, *Bodies of God*.
114. According to Sommer, any given deity could have "many bodies located in sundry places" (*Bodies of God*, 1; see also pp. 12 and 192 n. 126). Sommer (p. 13) sees these various manifestations as "a type of fluidity we might call fragmentation. Some divinities have a fluid self in the sense that there are several divinities with a single name who somehow are and are not the same deity" (for "fluidity" and "fragmentation," see also pp. 14, 25, 26, 27, 55, 67; labeled as "splitting" on p. 36; note also "fluidity model" on p. 38 and "fluidity tradition" on p. 79). He sometimes refers to divine presence as an "incarnation" (as on p. 47, writing on the asherah as "an incarnation of Yhwh"). He also says that the divine "self seems to be fragmented" (p. 14; see also p. 25: "the Baal of Canaanite myth seems to have fragmented into a great number of baal-gods who could be worshipped and addressed separately"). Such local manifestations involve "a certain diminution" of the god (p. 15).
115. Sommer, *Bodies of God*, 44, 75.
116. Sommer, *Bodies of God*, 44.

117. *KTU* 1.4 VII, in *UNP* 135–38.
118. See Gen 11:5 noted in Sommer, *Bodies of God*, 2; and Num 11:17 mentioned on p. 82; note also p. 99.
119. Sommer, *Bodies of God*, 41.
120. See the discussion of Genesis 18 in Chapter 1, Section 2.
121. Alisdair Livingstone, *Court Poetry and Literary Miscellanea*, SAA 3 (Helsinki: Helsinki University Press, 1989), 11–12, text 3, lines 1–13; reference courtesy of Beate Pongratz-Leisten.
122. Nissinen, *Prophets and Prophecy*, 130–31, #94.
123. Nissinen, *Prophets and Prophecy*, 130 n. b.
124. See Billie Jean Collins, *COS* 1.164–65.
125. Cf. Ishtars of various locales in an incantation bowl, in Dan Levene and Gideon Bohak, "A Babylonian Jewish Aramaic Incantation Bowl with a List of Deities and Toponyms," *JSQ* 19 (2012): 56–72.
126. Cf. temporal manifestations of "Triple Inanna/deity of Unug," "none other than the three forms of Inanna to whom offerings were regularly made in archaic Uruk," namely "morning Inanna," "evening Inanna," and "princely (?) Inanna" according to Piotr Steinkeller, "Archaic City Seals and the Question of Early Babylonian Unity," in *Riches Hidden in Secret Places: Ancient Near Eastern Studies in Memory of Thorkild Jacobsen*, ed. Tzvi Abusch (Winona Lake, Ind.: Eisenbrauns, 2002), 253–54.
127. *KUB* 32.133, obv. I, lines 1–3 in Jared L. Miller, *Studies in the Origins, Development and Interpretation of the Kizzuwatna Rituals*, Studien zu den Boğazköy-Texten 46 (Wiesbaden: Harrassowitz, 2004), 312.
128. *KUB* 29.4/*KBo* 24.86, A iii 25–29 in Miller, *Studies in the Origins*, 290 (see also pp. 273–74). My attention was first drawn to these rituals by Aaron Tugendhaft (personal communication, 9 November 2010), with my gratitude. See also Allen, *Splintered Divine*, 71–72, 90.
129. Sommer, *Bodies of God*, 26.
130. This is not always the case. *KTU* 1.27 mentions Baal of Ugarit in line 4, and Sapan has been reconstructed for line 11. See Meindert Dijkstra, "The Ritual *KTU* 1.46 (= RS 1.9) and Its Duplicates," *UF* 16 (1984): 69–76; Pardee, *Les textes rituels*, 265 n. 2; and Juan-Pablo Vita, "Les scribes des texts rituels d'Ougarit," *UF* 39 (2007 = In Memoriam Kurt Bergerhof): 651–53.
131. *RCU* 56–65; and del Olmo Lete, *Canaanite Religion*, 107–25.
132. As noted by commentators, *inter alia*, Clifford, *Cosmic Mountain*, 61.
133. See *RCU* 64; and del Olmo Lete, *Canaanite Religion*, 87.
134. Dijkstra, "The Weather-God on Two Mountains," *UF* 23 (1991): 136–37. Cf. *KTU* 1.42.10–11, a Hurrian text in alphabetic writing, translated by Meindert Dijkstra, "Please (?), let my supplication be heard, o Teshub of Halab, Teshub of Hazi, Teshub of Ugarit, Nanni-Hazi." Note Teshub of Hazi before Teshub of Ugarit. Cf. Hazi and Nanni in Emar 472.58' (Emar 460, 463), 473.9 (Emar

466, 467), and 476.20' (Emar 470). See Doris Preschel, "Hethitische Rituale in Emar?," in *The City of Emar Among the Late Bronze Age Empires. History, Landscape, and Society,* Proceedings of the Konstanz Emar Conference 25–26.04.2006, ed. Lorenzo d'Alfonso, Yoram Cohen, and Dietrich Sürenhagen, AOAT 349 (Münster: Ugarit-Verlag, 2008), 248–49.

135. *RCU* 41–43.

136. Pardee, *Les textes rituels,* 1.587.

137. Cf. the "two-mule loads of earth" that Naaman takes from Israel in order to make on it offerings to Yahweh (2 Kgs 5:17); comparison courtesy of Heath Dewrell.

138. *RCU* 29–33; and del Olmo Lete, *Canaanite Religion,* 226–30.

139. Pardee (*Les textes rituels,* 1.608 n. 22) sees these different Baals as deities. For criticism, see del Olmo Lete, "Ugaritic Ritual Texts," 609.

140. *RCU* 50–53; and del Olmo Lete, *Canaanite Religion,* 245–57. See also Joel M. LeMon, "The Power of Parallelism in *KTU*² 1.119: Another 'Trial Cut,'" *UF* 37 (2005): 375–94.

141. *KTU* asks about reading "*mgdl?*"

142. *RCU* 32–33; and del Olmo Lete, *Canaanite Religion,* 232–35.

143. Note also this order in *KTU* 1.65.10–11, in *RCU* 23.

144. *ANET* 249 and *ANEP* #485, pp. 167, 306. See Marguerite Yon, *The City of Ugarit at Tell Ras Shamra* (Winona Lake, Ind.: Eisenbrauns, 2006), 134–35, #17; and Herbert Niehr, "Baal-Zaphon," *DDD* 152.

145. RS 16.157.27, in *PRU III* p. 84; and RS 16.238.18, in *PRU III* p. 108. See further Dennis Pardee, "RS 94.2168 and the Right of the Firstborn at Ugarit," in *Society and Administration in Ancient Ugarit,* ed. Wilfred H. van Soldt (Leiden: Nederlands Instituut voor hert Nabije Oosten, 2010), 102–3.

146. RS 16.276.21–24, in *PRU III* p. 70; Michael Heltzer, *COS* 3.201. For the sanctuary at Cassios in Philo of Byblos (PE 1.10.20), see Harold W. Attridge and Robert A. Oden, Jr., *Philo of Byblos. The Phoenician History: Introduction, Critical Text, Translation, Notes,* CBQMS 9 (Washington, D.C.: Catholic Biblical Association of America, 1981), 50–51.

147. For a layout in parallel columns, see *RCU* 14–15.

148. Pardee, *RCU* 23 n. 3, and *Les textes rituels,* 1.294–95.

149. Del Olmo Lete, *Canaanite Religion,* 58.

150. For different possibilities, see Pardee, *Les textes rituels,* 1.300–302.

151. A translation of Pardee's phrase in *Les textes rituels,* 1.295.

152. See the layout in parallel columns by Pardee, *Les textes rituels,* 2.796, and *RCU* 17–19.

153. Generally thought to be Baal of Aleppo. See above.

154. Cf. "Baali-Zaphon" in Papyrus Sallier IV (I 5–6), which may be a plural form (hence rendered "the Baals of the North" in *ANET* 250 n. 12) or a plural of majesty (so also *ANET* 250 n. 12).

155. Cf. RS 17.429.2, in *PRU IV* p. 227.
156. Clifford, *Cosmic Mountain*, 64.
157. There is a question about the reading. *KTU* reads *b'l ṣp[n]*. A. Bernard Knapp has *b'ly x* and translates "Ba'al." See Knapp, "An Alashiysan Merchant at Ugarit," *TA* 10 (1983): 39 and 40.
158. See Alan Cooper, "MLK 'LM: 'Eternal King' or 'King of Eternity'?" in *Love and Death in the Ancient Near East: Essays in Honor of Marvin H. Pope*, ed. John H. Marks and Robert M. Good (Guilford, Conn.: Four Quarters, 1987), 2; and A. Bernard Knapp, "An Alashiysan Merchant at Ugarit," 38–45.
159. Silvie Lackenbacher, "Une letter d'Égypte," in *Études ougaritiques I: Travaux 1985–1995*, ed. Marguerite Yon and Daniel Arnaud, RSO XIV (Paris: Éditions Recherche sur les Civilisations, 2001), 240.
160. RS 17.340.21', in *PRU IV* p. 52; RS 17.237.15', in *PRU IV* p. 65; RS 18.06.7, in *PRU IV* p. 137; see also RS 17.79.56 (?), in *PRU IV* p. 99.
161. RS 16.144.12, in *PRU III* p. 76; RS 16.157.27, in *PRU III* p. 84; cf. RS 16.238.18, in *PRU III* p. 108.
162. *KTU* 1.1 V 5, 18; 1.3 I 22; 1.3 III 29; 1.3 IV 1, 19, 38; 1.4 IV 19; 1.4 V 23, 55; 1.4 VII 6; 1.5 I 11; 1.6 I 16, 57, 62; 1.6 VI 13; see *UNP* 87, 106, 110, 112, 113, 114, 127, 130, 132, 135, 141, 152, 154, and 162, respectively. Cf. Niehr ("Baal-Zaphon," 152): "mythological texts never speak of Baal-Zaphon."
163. As noted by commentators, e.g., Clifford, *Cosmic Mountain*, 61–62.
164. See Joan Goodnick Westenholz, "The Theological Foundation of the City, the Capital City and Babylon," in *Capital Cities: Urban Planning and Spiritual Dimensions*, Proceedings of the Symposium Held on May 27–29, 1996, Jerusalem, Israel, ed. Joan Goodnick Westenholz (Jerusalem: Bible Lands Museum, 1998), 49.
165. Dijkstra, "Weather-God," 137. See also N. Wyatt, "Making Sense of the Senseless," *UF* 39 (2007 = In Memoriam Kurt Bergerhof): 758–59.
166. For text and translation, see Chapter 3, Section 2.
167. Heffelfinger ("Like the Sitting of the Mountain: The Significance of Metaphor in *KTU* 1.101's [recto] Description of Ba'l," *UF* 39 [2007 = In Memoriam Kurt Bergerhof]: 380–82, 390–97) views the text as negotiating between the pair of metaphors, "Baal is a mountain" and "Baal is a storm."
168. Cf. the "Berggott" type of deity in Mesopotamian iconography, discussed by Elisabeth von der Osten-Sacken, "Aššur, grosser Berg, König von Himmel und Erde: Darstellungen des assyrischen Hauptgottes im Wandel von *numen loci* zum Götterherrn," *UF* 42 (2010): 770–74.
169. See Heffelfinger, "Like the Sitting of the Mountain," 395.
170. See also Michael B. Hundley, *Gods in Dwellings: Temples and Divine Presence in the Ancient Near East*, WAWSup 3 (Atlanta: SBL, 2013), 354–55. Cf. Allen, *Splintered Divine*, 212.
171. Pomponio and Xella, *Les dieux d'Ebla*, 418.

172. See Edith Porada, "The Cylinder Seal from Tell el-Dabʻa," *American Journal of Archaeology* 88 (1984): 485–88, plate 65, figure 1; Manfred Bietak, "Zur Herkunft des Seth von Avaris," *Ägypten und Levante* 1 (1990): 9–16; Dijkstra, "Weather-God," 127–40; Niehr, "Baal-Zaphon," 152; Aaron Jed Brody, *"Each Man Cried Out to His God": The Specialized Religion of Canaanite and Phoenician Seafarers,* HSM 58 (Atlanta: Scholars, 1998), 18–19.

173. *ANET* 250. See also Brody, *"Each Man,"* 17–18.

174. Pierre Bordreuil, "Attestations inédités de Melqart, Baal Hamon et Baal Saphon à Tyr," in *Religio Phoenicia,* ed. C. Bonnet, E. Lipiński, and P. Marchetti, Studia Phoenicia 4 (Namur: Peeters, 1986), 177–86; Niehr, "Baal-Zaphon," 153.

175. Otto Eissfeldt, *Baal Zaphon, Zeus Kasios und der Durchzug der Israeliten durchs Meer,* Beiträge zur Religionsgeschichte des Alterums Heft 1 (Halle: Max Niemeyer, 1932), 6–16; W. Fauth, "Das Kasion-Gebirge und Zeus Kasios," *UF* 22 (1990): 105–18; Klaus Koch, *Der Gott Israels und die Götter des Orients: Religionsgeschichtliche Studien II. Zum 80. Geburstag von Klaus Koch,* ed. Friedhelm Hartenstein and Martin Rösel, FRLANT 216 (Göttingen: Vandenhoeck & Ruprecht, 2007), 133; and Niehr, "Baal-Zaphon," 152–53. See also Gregorio del Olmo Lete and Joaquín Sanmartín, "ks (Kásios/Casius) = Hazzi = ḫš," *Aula Orientalis* 13 (1995): 259–61. For the name of Sapan in Egyptian sources, see James Hoch, *Semitic Words in Egyptian Texts of the New Kingdom and Third Intermediate Period* (Princeton, N.J.: Princeton University Press, 1994), 384, #576; see also Donald B. Redford, *Egypt, Canaan, and Israel in Ancient Times* (Princeton, N.J.: Princeton University Press, 1992), 410 and 457. Note also Exod 14:2, 9 and Num 33:7, as well as Kassios in Philo of Byblos (PE 1.10.9), in Attridge and Oden, *Philo of Byblos,* 42–43; and Albert I. Baumgarten, *The Phoenician History of Philo of Byblos: A Commentary,* Études préliminaires aux religions orientales dans l'empire romain 89 (Leiden: Brill, 1981), 153–54.

176. See Steiner, "The Aramaic Text in Demotic Script," in *COS* 1.313, 318; and Charles F. Nims and Richard C. Steiner, "A Paganized Version of Psalm 20:2–6 from the Aramaic Text in Demotic Script," *JAOS* 103 (1983): 264, 266; cf. S. P. Vleeming and J. W. Wesselius, *Studies in Amherst Papyrus 63: Essays on the Aramaic Text in Aramaic/Demotic Papyrus Amherst 63. Volume I* (Amsterdam: Juda Palache Instituut, 1985), 46, 55; and Niehr, "Baal-Zaphon," 153. For this papyrus, see Chapter 4. For Phoenician PNs with **spn* possibly as the theophoric element, see Frauke Gröndahl, *Die Personennamen der Texte aus Ugarit,* Studia Pohl 1 (Rome: Pontifical Biblical Institute, 1967), 111, 189, cited by Clifford, *Cosmic Mountain,* 62.

177. See Parpola and Watanabe, *Neo-Assyrian Treaties,* 27, column IV, line 10ʼ. See also *ANET* 534; and Brody, *"Each Man,"* 10–19, 35, and 95.

178. A "rather elusive figure," according to Barré, *God-List,* 55, and 84–86.

179. See Sommer, *Bodies of God,* 24.

180. Barré, *God-List,* 55. For putative maritime evidence for Baal Sapan, see Brody, *"Each Man,"* 17–18.

181. See also Beelsamen in Phoenicia, in PE 1.10.7, in Attridge and Oden, *Philo of Byblos,* 40–41.

182. See Oswald Loretz, "Ugaritisch-hebräische Symbiose Gottesberge ṣapānu und Zion in Psalm 48,2c–3c," *UF* 40 (2008): 489–505. As noted by Loretz, commentators differ over a preexilic or postexilic dating for the psalm.

183. See already Eissfeldt, *Baal Zaphon,* 15–16. See Allen, *Splintered Divine,* 287.

184. Steiner, "The Aramaic Text in Demotic Script," in *COS* 1.318; and Nims and Steiner, "Paganized Version," 264 and 266.

185. For the correspondence, see Nims and Steiner, "Paganized Version," 266.

186. McCarter, "Aspects of the Religion," 141. See also Abraham Malamat, *Mari and the Early Israelite Experience,* Schweich Lectures of the British Academy 1984 (Oxford: Oxford University Press, 1989), 112–21. See also Giovanni Mazzini, "The Defeat of the Dragon in *KTU* 1.83,4–10: Ugaritic ŠBM and the South Arabian Root ŚBM," *UF* 35 (2003): 400. Mazzini refers to Lebanon as the "Garden of God," a notion with a long scholarly lineage; see W. Robertson Smith, *The Religion of the Semites: The Fundamental Institutions* (New York: Schocken, 1972), 113; note also P. Kyle McCarter, "The Garden of Eden: Geographical and Etymological Ruminations on the Garden of God in the Bible and the Ancient Near East," unpublished paper presented to the Colloquium for Biblical Research, Duke University, 19 August 2001 (cited with permission).

187. For Lebanon in *Gilgamesh,* see Andrew R. George, *The Babylonian Gilgamesh Epic: Introduction, Critical Edition and Cuneiform Texts,* 2 vols. (Oxford: Oxford University Press, 2003), 1.94, 225–26, 263, 266, 456, 467, 589, 591, 593, 595, 609 (cf. Psalm 114); and 2.818–19. For the splitting of the Lebanon and Anti-Lebanon, see Victor A. Hurowitz, "Splitting the Sacred Mountain: Zechariah 14,4 and Gilgamesh V ii 4–5," *UF* 31 (1999): 241–45.

188. George, *Babylonian Gilgamesh Epic,* 1.602, 603; 2.822. See also W. G. Lambert, "Interchange of Ideas Between Southern Mesopotamia and Syria-Palestine as Seen in Literature," in *Mesopotamien und seine Nachbaren,* ed. H. J. Nissen and J. Renger, Berliner Beiträge zum Vorderen Orient 1, Comptes rendues de la rencontre assyriologique internationale 25 (Berlin: Dietrich Reimer, 1982), 113–14; and Abraham Malamat, *Mari and the Bible,* Studies in the History and Culture of the Ancient Near East XII (Leiden: Brill, 1998), 22.

189. *KTU* 1.4 VI 18, in *UNP* 133; 1.17 VI 21, in *UNP* 60; 1.22 I 20, in *UNP* 204; 1.22 I 25, in *UNP* 204; cf. 4.65.4.

190. See *RCU* 18, 46–48.

191. Note also the parallel Akkadian text, RS 92.2004.35, in *RCU* 18. See also RS 26.142, a fragmentary syllabic list of deities, which includes "the gods of Lebanon" in line 4' (*Ugaritica V* p. 321, #170). See Daniel Arnaud, "Relecture de la liste sacrificielle RS 26.142," *SMEA* 34 (1994): 107–9.

192. For the Lebanon in later classical sources, see Edward Lipiński, *Dieux et déesses de l'univers phénicien et punique,* Orientalia Lovaniensia Analecta 64 (Leuven: Uitgeverij Peeters and Departement Oosterse Studies, 1995), 105–7. See also Mikko Luukko, *The Correspondence of Tiglath-Pileser III and Sargon II from Calah/Nimrud,* SAA XIX, Publications of the Foundation for Finnish Assyriological Research 6 (Helsinki: Neo-Assyrian Text Corpus Project, 2012), 28.

193. For convenient translations, see *KAI* 2.49–50 and John C. L. Gibson, *Textbook of Syrian Semitic Inscriptions,* 3 vols. (Oxford: Oxford University Press, 1971, 1975, 1982; repr., Oxford: Oxford University Press, 2002), 3.67–68. *KAI* 2.50 also notes Tannit of Lebanon in *KAI* 81 and the mountain of Baal Hermon in Judg 3:3. See also Baumgarten, *Phoenician History,* 154.

194. S. P. Vleeming and J. W. Wesselius, *Studies in Papyrus Amherst 63: Essays on the Aramaic Text in Aramaic/Demotic Papyrus Amherst 63. Volume II* (Amsterdam: Juda Palache Instituut, 1990), 55, 56. I thank Karel van der Toorn for bringing this reference to my attention. Cf. column X, lines 1–2, in Richard C. Steiner, "The Aramaic Text in Demotic Script (1.99)," in *COS* 1.316.

195. McCarter, "Aspects of the Religion," 139.

196. McCarter, "Aspects of the Religion," 139. For the goddess at Sidon, see also *KAI* 13.1 and 14.15, 16, 18, translated in *ANET* 662.

197. Ginsberg, "A Phoenician Hymn in the Psalter," in *Atti del XIX Congresso Internazonale degli Orientalisti: Roma, 23–29 Settembre 1935—XIII* (Rome: Tipografia del Senato, 1938), 472–76, esp. 473–74.

198. Pardee, "Gods of Glory Ought to Thunder: The Canaanite Matrix of Psalm 29," in *Psalm 29 Through Time and Tradition,* ed. Lowell K. Handy (Eugene, Ore.: Pickwick, 2009), 121.

199. Michael L. Barré has suggested that the best parallels for Ps 29:11 are Phoenician (esp. *KAI* 26 A III 2–7 = C III 16–IV 4); Barré, "A Phoenician Parallel to Psalm 29," *HAR* 13 (1991): 25–32. See also Ginsberg, "A Phoenician Hymn in the Psalter," 472–76. For this psalm, see also *Psalm 29 Through Time and Tradition,* esp. Pardee, "Gods of Glory Ought to Thunder," 115–25.

200. For Baal on Carmel, see the evidence laid out by Lipiński, *Dieux et déesses de l'univers phénicien et punique,* 284–88.

201. See the baalim mentioned in Hos 2:15 and 11:2, which here may refer to other gods in general but may go back to the notion of Baal cult sites in the north; cf. Baal mentioned in 2:10 and 13:1. Some scholars have thought that Hos 2:18 may reflect a prior compatibility of the Yahweh cult and the Baal cult in the north. According to McCarter ("Aspects of the Religion," 139), Baal-perazim in 2 Sam 5:20 would be an example of a cult place named originally for another god that had been taken over by Yahweh.

202. For his discussion and the following quotations, see McCarter, "Aspects of the Religion," 139–41.

203. Hutton, "Local Manifestations," 177–210.

204. Hutton, "Local Manifestations," 178.

205. *CMHE* 86, 102–3, and 150.

206. For this tradition, see Mark S. Smith, "God in Israel's Bible: Divinity Between the World and Israel, Between the Old and the New," *CBQ* 74 (2012): 1–27.

207. For the storm imagery, see Aloysius Fitzgerald, F.S.C., *The Lord of the East Wind*, CBQMS 34 (Washington, D.C.: Catholic Biblical Association of America, 2002), 83–88.

208. For the book's Neo-Babylonian setting, see Francis I. Andersen, *Habakkuk: A New Translation with Introduction and Commentary*, AYB 25 (New York: Doubleday, 2001), 24–27; Robert D. Haak, *Habakkuk*, VTSup 44 (Leiden: Brill, 1992), 107–49; J. J. M. Roberts, *Nahum, Habakkuk, and Zephaniah: A Commentary*, OTL (Louisville, Ky.: Westminster John Knox, 1991), 82–84. See also David Stephen Vanderhooft, *The Neo-Babylonian Empire and Babylon in the Latter Prophets*, HSM 59 (Atlanta: Scholars, 1999), 152–63; and Reinhard Achenbach, "Monotheistischer Universalismus und frühe Formen eines Völkerrechts in prophetischen Textten Israels aus achämendischer Zeit," in *Monotheism in Late Prophetic and Early Apocalyptic Literature*, ed. Nathan MacDonald and Ken Brown, Studies of the Sofja Kovalevskaja Research Group on Early Jewish Monotheism III, FAT 2/72 (Tübingen: Mohr Siebeck, 2014), 155–66.

209. Dion, personal communication, in Walter E. Aufrecht, *A Corpus of Ammonite Inscriptions*, Ancient Near Eastern Texts and Studies 4 (Lewiston, N.Y.: Mellen, 1989), 147.

210. The translation largely follows Aufrecht, *A Corpus of Ammonite Inscriptions*, 145. See Aufrecht, *A Corpus of Ammonite Inscriptions*, 147, for the spelling of the DN.

211. *KTU* 1.14 IV 35, in *UNP* 19.

212. McCarter, "Aspects of the Religion," 138–39. For examples for Jerusalem/Zion, see Barré, *God-List*, 186 n. 473.

213. Conroy, *Absalom Absalom!*, AnBib 81 (Rome: Biblical Institute, 1978), 111 n. 58. For recent analyses of 2 Sam 15–20, see Mahri Leonard-Fleckman, "The House of David: Between Political Formation and Literary Revision," Ph.D. diss., New York University, 2014, 136–86; and Seth Sanders, "Absalom's Audience (2 Sam 15–19)," *JBL* (in press).

214. See further Saul Olyan, "Zadok's Origins and the Tribal Politics of David," *JBL* 101 (1982): 177–93.

215. Jorg Jeremias (personal communication) suggests that Samaria (Amos 3:9, 12; 4:1; 8:14; Hos 4:15; 8:5–6; 10:5; 14:1) may stand in some sort of relationship to the older site of Bethel. He sees a great animus against Bethel in Amos 3:14; 4:4; and 5:5–6 (note also Gilgal in Hos 4:15, 9:15, 12:12; Amos 4:4, 5:5). Note also the joint condemnation of Samaria and Bethel in Amos 3:9, 12, and 14.

216. The passage is raised by a number of scholars, e.g., McCarter, "Aspects," 142–43.

217. See Simeon Chavel, "The Literary Development of Deuteronomy 12: Between Religious Ideal and Social Reality," in *The Pentateuch: International Perspectives on Current Research*, ed. Thomas B. Dozeman, Konrad Schmid, and Baruch J. Schwartz, FAT 78 (Tübingen: Mohr Siebeck, 2011), 303–26; and Rannfrid I. Thelle, *Approaches to the "Chosen Place": Accessing a Biblical Concept*, LHB/OTS 564 (London: T & T Clark, 2012), 57–80.

218. See Stefan Schorch, "The Samaritan Version of Deuteronomy and the Origin of Deuteronomy," in *Samaria, Samarians, Samaritans: Studies on Bible, History and Linguistics*, ed. József Zsengellér, Studia Samaritana 6 (Berlin: de Gruyter, 2011), 23–37.

219. Note Nebo in *KAI* 181:14, with reference to Yahweh's cult vessels in lines 17–18 (Aḥituv, *Echoes*, 392, 394), suggesting an old Yahwistic shrine there; see Frank Moore Cross, *From Epic to Canon: History and Literature in Ancient Israel* (Baltimore: Johns Hopkins University Press, 1998), 57; and Baruch A. Levine, *Numbers 21–36: A New Translation with Introduction and Commentary*, AYB 4A (New York: Doubleday, 2000), 116, 233. The place is attested as Reubenite in Num 32:3, 38, subsequently passing to the Moabites (Num 33:47; Isa 15:2; Jer 48:1, 22; see Levine, *Numbers 21–36*, 484–85).

220. Early Cisjordanian sanctuaries may have been largely forgotten, for example, at Mount Tabor in Deut 33:18–19, denounced in Hos 5:1 and perhaps preserved in later Greek sources. See Otto Eissfeldt, *Kleine Schriften: Zweiter Band*, ed. Rudolf Sellheim and Fritz Maass (Tübingen: Mohr [Paul Siebeck], 1963), 29–54; and Hans Wolter Wolff, *Hosea: A Commentary on the Book of the Prophet Hosea*, ed. Paul D. Hanson, trans. Gary Stansell, Hermeneia (Philadelphia: Fortress, 1974), 98–99 n. 31.

221. A cultic tradition at Hermon is suggested by the name Baal Hermon (Judg 3:3; 1 Chr 5:23). For cultic references about Hermon in Latin writers, see Rami Arav, "Hermon, Mount," *ABD* 3.159, and for mythic associations with the Watchers at Hermon, see 1 Enoch 6:6; 13:9 and 2 Enoch 18:4; 19:4, discussed by Edward Lipiński, "El's Abode: Mythological Traditions Related to Mt. Hermon and the Mountains of Armenia," *OLP* 2 (1971): 13–69. A cult site is perhaps suggested also by the meaning of the site's name, "consecrated" or "sacred" (see *BDB* 356); cf. 1 Enoch 6:6, in Miryam Brand, in *Outside the Bible: Ancient Jewish Writings Related to Scripture*, ed. Louis H. Feldman, James L. Kugel, and Lawrence H. Schiffman, 3 vols. (Philadelphia: Jewish Publication Society, 2013), 2.1368–69.

222. See Schorch, "Samaritan Version," 23–37. Schorch argues for Gerizim as the original referent of the formulary in Deuteronomy 12. See the more cautious treatment of Gary N. Knoppers, *Jews and Samaritans: The Origins and History of Their Early Relations* (Oxford: Oxford University Press, 2013), 194–216.

223. See John A. Emerton, "The 'Mountain of God' in Psalm 68:16," in *History and Traditions of Early Israel: Studies Presented to Eduard Nielsen May 8th 1993*, ed. André Lemaire and Benedikt Otzen, VTSup 50 (Leiden: Brill, 1993), 24–37; and Israel Knohl, "Psalm 68: Structure, Composition and Geography," *JHS* 12, Article 15 (2012): 11–12.

224. See Thelle, *Approaches to the "Chosen Place,"* 41–56.

225. Ahituv, Eshel, and Meshel in Meshel, *Kuntillet 'Ajrud (Horvat Teman)*, 130; Hutton, "Local Manifestations," 179–80, 185, and 206; Sommer, *Bodies of God*, 67. Note also Brian Peckham, "Phoenicia and the Religion of Israel: The Epigraphic Evidence," in *Ancient Israelite Religion: Essays in Honor of Frank Moore Cross*, ed. P. D. Miller, Jr., Paul D. Hanson, and S. Dean McBride (Philadelphia: Fortress, 1987), 88 n. 1; J. Andrew Dearman, *Religion and Culture in Ancient Israel* (Peabody, Mass.: Hendrickson, 1992), 145; Robert Karl Gnuse, *No Other Gods: Emergent Monotheism in Israel*, JSOTSup 241 (Sheffield: Sheffield Academic, 1997), 183; Patrick D. Miller, *The Religion of Ancient Israel*, LAI (London: SPCK; Louisville, Ky.: Westminster John Knox, 2000), 79, 213 n. 3; Ahituv, *Echoes*, 317. Note the earlier study of Peter Höffken, "Eine Bemerkung zum religionsgeschichtlichen Hintergrund von Dtr 6,4," *Biblische Notizen* 28 (1984): 88–93; and Georg Braulik, "Das Deuteronomium und die Geburt des Monotheismus," in *Gott, der Einzige: Zur Entstehung des Monotheismus in Israel*, ed. H. Haag, Quaestiones disputatae 104 (Freiburg: Herder, 1985), 115–59, here 119–22.

226. See McCarter, "Aspects," 142.

227. For the meaning of "one" here as well as other translation issues, see Jeffrey H. Tigay, *The JPS Torah Commentary: Deuteronomy* (Philadelphia: Jewish Publication Society, 1996), 439–40; and Smith, *God in Translation*, 143–46.

228. The original setting for Deut 6:4 may predate its present context. See Norbert Lohfink, *Das Hauptgebot: Eine Untersuchung literarischer Einleitungsfragen zu Dtn 5–11*, AnBib 20 (Rome: Pontificio Istituto Biblico, 1963), 164; Juha Pakkala, *Intolerant Monolatry in the Deuteronomistic History*, Publications of the Finnish Exegetical Society 76 (Helsinki: Finnish Exegetical Society; Göttingen: Vandenhoeck & Ruprecht, 1999), 74; and Smith, *God in Translation*, 143–44. If so, then the original setting is unknown.

229. Lev 19:30; 20:3; and 26:2. Ezekiel refers only to the one sanctuary: 5:11; 8:6; 9:6; 23:38; 24:21; 25:3; 37:26, 28; and 44:7–9, 11, 15–16 (the plural in 28:18 concerns the sanctuaries of Tyre).

230. See Matthew Lynch, *Monotheism and Institutions in the Book of Chronicles: Temple, Priesthood, and Kingship in Post-Exilic Perspective*, Studies of the Sofja Kovalevskaja Research Group on Early Jewish Monotheism I, FAT 2/64 (Tübingen: Mohr Siebeck, 2014).

231. Carr, *The Erotic Word: Sexuality, Spirituality, and the Bible* (Oxford: Oxford University Press, 2003), 4 (Carr's italics). Ariel Bloch and Hanna Bloch are critical of allegorical interpretations, including the political interpretation of

Luis Stadelmann, *Love and Politics: A New Commentary on the Song of Songs* (New York: Paulist, 1992), 2, 16, and 23. See Bloch and Bloch, *The Song of Songs: A New Translation with an Introduction and Commentary* (Berkeley: University of California Press, 1995), 31–32.

232. Carr, *Erotic Word,* 145 (Carr's italics).

233. Note Ellen F. Davis, "Romance of the Land in the Song of Songs," *Anglican Theological Review* 80/4 (1998): 533–46.

234. So George A. F. Knight and Friedemann W. Golka, *Revelation of God: A Commentary on the Books of the Song of Songs and Jonah* (Grand Rapids, Mich.: Eerdmans; Edinburgh: Handsel, 1988), 5.

235. For the usage, see Num 21:25, 32; 32:42; Josh 15:45, 47; 17:11, 16; Judg 1:27; 11:26; Jer 49:2; Ezek 26:8; Neh 11:25–31; and 1 Chr 2:23; 18:1. See *BDB* 123, #4; and I. W. J. Hopkins, "The 'Daughters of Judah' Are Really Satellites of an Urban Center," *Biblical Archeology Review* 6/5 (1980): 44–45.

236. For these two words, see Bloch and Bloch, *Song of Songs,* 24–27; F. W. Dobbs-Allsopp, "Late Linguistic Features in the Song of Songs," in *Perspectives on the Song of Songs—Perspektiven der Hoheliedauslegung,* ed. Anselm C. Hagedorn, BZAW 346 (Berlin: de Gruyter, 2005), 65–71; and Scott B. Noegel and Gary A. Rendsburg, *Solomon's Vineyard: Literary and Linguistic Studies in the Song of Songs,* AIL 1 (Atlanta: SBL, 2009), 174–80. The Blochs suggest a Hellenistic date, while Noegel and Rendsburg entertain a Persian period date for the accumulated work. Dobbs-Allsopp ("Late Linguistic Features," 27–77) points to many other grammatical features suggesting a postexilic date.

237. See Gerson D. Cohen, "The Song of Songs and the Jewish Religious Mentality," in *The Samuel Friedland Lectures 1960–1966* (New York: Jewish Theological Seminary, 1966), 1–21; and David Stern, "Ancient Jewish Interpretation of the Song of Songs in a Comparative Context," in *Jewish Biblical Interpretation and Cultural Exchange: Comparative Exegesis in Context,* ed. Natalie B. Dohrmann and David Stern (Philadelphia: University of Pennsylvania Press, 2008), 87–107, 263–72. For the analogous argument that the Song of Songs was meant to evoke the love of the god and goddess, see Marvin H. Pope, *Song of Songs: A New Translation with Introduction and Commentary,* AYB 7C (New York: Doubleday, 1977). I have also entertained the notion that the woman evoking the north and the king and male lover evoking the south might signal a hope in the reunification of the old northern and southern kingdoms (cf. Jer 30–31). See Mark S. Smith, *The Memoirs of God: History, Memory, and the Experience of the Divine in Ancient Israel* (Minneapolis: Fortress, 2004), 80.

Chapter 6. The Royal City and Its Gods

1. See 2 Kgs 19:21//Isa 37:22; Lam 1 and 4:22; Ezek 16 and 23. See also "daughter Zion" (Isa 1:8; 10:32; 16:1; 52:2; 62:11; Mic 1:13; 4:10, 13; Jer 6:2, 23; Lam 1:6; 2:1, 4, 8, 10, 13; Zech 2:14; 3:14; Ps 9:14). The secondary literature on this subject is

immense. See William F. Stinespring, "No Daughter of Zion: Study of the Appositional Genitive in Hebrew Grammar," *Encounter* 26 (1965): 133–41; Aloysius Fitzgerald, F.S.C., "Mythological Background for the Presentation of Jerusalem as a Queen and False Worship as Adultery in the OT," *CBQ* 34 (1972): 403–16, and "BTWLT and BT as Titles for Capital Cities," *CBQ* 37 (1975): 167–83; John J. Schmitt, "The Gender of Ancient Israel," *JSOT* 26 (1983): 115–25, "The Motherhood of God and Zion as Mother," *RB* 92 (1985): 557–69, and "The Virgin of Israel: Reference and Use of the Phrase in Amos and Jeremiah," *CBQ* 53 (1991): 365–87; Elaine R. Follis, "The Holy City as Daughter," in *New Directions in Biblical Hebrew Poetry,* ed. Elaine R. Follis, JSOTSup 40 (Sheffield: JSOT, 1987), 173–84; Mark Biddle, "The Figure of Lady Jerusalem: Identification, Deification and Personification of Cities in the Ancient Near East," in *The Biblical Canon in Comparative Perspective,* ed. K. Lawson Younger, Jr., William W. Hallo, and Bernard F. Batto, Ancient Near Eastern Texts and Studies 11 (Lewiston, N.Y.: Mellen, 1991), 173–94; F. W. Dobbs-Allsopp, *Weep, O Daughter of Zion: A Study of the City-Lament Genre in the Hebrew Bible,* Biblica et orientalia 44 (Rome: Pontificio Istituto Biblico, 1993), 75–90, and "The Syntagma of *bat* Followed by a Geographical Name in the Hebrew Bible: Reconsideration of Its Meaning and Grammar," *CBQ* 57 (1995): 451–70; F. W. Dobbs-Allsopp and Tod Linafelt, "The Rape of Zion in Lam 1:10," *ZAW* 113 (2001): 77–81; and Christl M. Maier, "Daughter Zion as Queen and the Iconography of the Female City," in *Images and Prophecy in the Ancient Eastern Mediterranean,* ed. Martti Nissinen and Charles E. Carter, FRLANT 233 (Göttingen: Vandenhoeck & Ruprecht, 2009), 147–62, and *Daughter Zion, Mother Zion: Gender, Space, and the Sacred in Ancient Israel* (Minneapolis: Fortress, 2008).

2. De Geus, *Towns in Ancient Israel and in the Southern Levant,* Palaestina Antiqua 10 (Leuven: Peeters, 2003), 1, 161, 170. See also Michael Patrick O'Connor, "The Biblical Notion of the City," in *Constructions of Space II: The Biblical City and Other Imagined Spaces,* ed. Jon L. Berquist and Claudia V. Camp, LHB/OTS 490 (New York: T & T Clark, 2008), 23.

3. De Geus, *Towns in Ancient Israel,* 170.

4. De Geus, *Towns in Ancient Israel,* 161. Note also John Woodhead, "Royal Cities in the Kingdom of Israel," in *Capital Cities: Urban Planning and Spiritual Dimensions,* Proceedings of the Symposium Held on May 27–29, 1996, Jerusalem, Israel, ed. Joan Goodnick Westenholz (Jerusalem: Bible Lands Museum, 1998), 111–16; and Avi Faust, "City, Villages, and Towns, Bronze and Iron Age," *Oxford Encyclopedia of Bible and Archaeology,* ed. D. Master, B. Alpert-Nakhai, L. M. White, and J. K. Zangenberg (New York: Oxford University Press, 2013), 203–11.

5. Tappy, *The Archaeology of Israelite Samaria: Volume II: The Eighth Century BCE,* HSS 50 (Winona Lake, Ind.: Eisenbrauns, 2001), 170 n. 633.

6. Marguerite Yon, *The City of Ugarit at Tell Ras Shamra* (Winona Lake, Ind.: Eisenbrauns, 2006), 9.

7. Juan-Pablo Vita, "The Society of Ugarit," in *Handbook of Ugaritic Studies*, ed. W. G. E. Watson and N. Wyatt, HdO I/39 (Leiden: Brill, 1999), 455.

8. Schloen, *The House of the Father as Fact and Symbol: Patrimonialism in Ugarit and the Ancient Near East*, Studies in the Archaeology and History of the Levant 2 (Winona Lake, Ind.: Eisenbrauns, 2001), 160, 196. For this view, Schloen draws on the work of Marc Van de Mieroop, *The Ancient Mesopotamian City* (Oxford: Clarendon, 1997), 10.

9. Fleming, *Democracy's Ancient Ancestors: Mari and the Early Collective Governance* (Cambridge: Cambridge University Press, 2004), 21.

10. Fleming, *Democracy's Ancient Ancestors*, 109.

11. Fleming, *Democracy's Ancient Ancestors*, 116. For a recent archaeological examination of ancient Near Eastern cities, see Ömür Harmanşah, *Cities and the Shaping of Memory in the Ancient Near East* (Cambridge: Cambridge University Press, 2013).

12. Fleming, "'House'/'City': An Unrecognized Parallel Word Pair," *JBL* 105 (1986): 689–93.

13. Gzella, "Some Penciled Notes on Ugaritic Lexicography," *Bibliotheca Orientalis* 64 (2007): 537. Note also BH *qrt* in the poetic corpus of Prov 8:3; 9:3, 14; and 11:11, discussed by H. L. Ginsberg, "Ugaritico-Phoenicia," *Journal of the Ancient Near Eastern Society of Columbia University* 5 (1973 = The Gaster Festschrift): 134 n. 19; and *The Israelian Heritage of Judaism*, Texts and Studies of the Jewish Theological Seminary of America XXIV (New York: Jewish Theological Seminary of America, 1982), 36.

14. *KTU* 1.14 II 28, IV 9, in *UNP* 14, 18. For the forms, see Huehnergard, *Ugaritic Vocabulary in Syllabic Transcription*, rev. ed., HSS 32 (Winona Lake, Ind.: Eisenbrauns, 2008), 58, 175.

15. *DULAT* 702 takes some usages as "capital."

16. Cf. the Moabite GN *Qîr-ḥereś/-ḥăreśet* attested in 2 Kgs 3:25; Isa 16:7, 11; and Jer 48:31, 36.

17. For examples, see *DCH* II.317.

18. Jonas C. Greenfield, *'Al Kanfei Yonah: Collected Studies of Jonas C. Greenfield on Semitic Philology*, ed. Shalom M. Paul, Michael E. Stone, and Avital Pinnick, 2 vols. (Leiden: Brill; Jerusalem: Hebrew University Magnes Press, 2001), 2.898–900.

19. For this information, see James E. Hoch, *Semitic Words in Egyptian Texts of the New Kingdom and Third Intermediate Period* (Princeton, N.J.: Princeton University Press, 1994), 204 #277; and Kevin A. Wilson, *The Campaign of Pharaoh Shoshenq I into Palestine*, FAT 2/9 (Tübingen: Mohr Siebeck, 2005), 106.

20. *DULAT* 717; *AHw* 964; *CAD* R:26.

21. Cf. the plural translation "the forsaken places are many," in H. G. M. Williamson, *The Book Called Isaiah: Deutero-Isaiah's Role in Composition and Redaction* (Oxford: Clarendon, 1994), 51. However, the passive participle, "forsaken," is singular and may be the predicate of *rabbâ* (see Zion compared to a "forsaken woman" in Isa 54:6).

22. *DNWSI* 1.67. P. Kyle McCarter, Jr. (*II Samuel: A New Translation with Introduction and Commentary*, AYB 9 [Garden City, N.Y.: Doubleday, 1984], 243) also notes the usage. See also *PPD* 57, which notes the usage of the word for the mother-city of a colony.

23. It might also underlie the expression *meteg-hā'ammâ* in 2 Sam 8:1, translated "(authority of) mother-city" in *BDB* 52. For other views, see McCarter, *II Samuel*, 243.

24. For further discussion, see Carey Walsh, "The Social Functions of City-Gates in Biblical Memory," in *Memory and the City in the Hebrew Bible*, ed. Diana V. Edelman and Ehud Ben Zvi (Winona Lake, Ind.: Eisenbrauns, 2014), 43–59.

25. See *KTU* 1.119.27, 36: "if a powerful one attacks your walls," along with "its gates," in *RCU* 149–50; and Gregorio del Olmo Lete, *Canaanite Religion According to the Liturgical Texts of Ugarit*, trans. Wilfred G. E. Watson, 2nd ed., AOAT 408 (Münster: Ugarit-Verlag, 2014), 256–57, 394. Cf. "walls of Ugarit" in 1.40.18, 36, in *RCU* 80–83; see also *KTU* 1.161.34, in *RCU* 85–89, cited below.

26. Cf. the house of Baal of Ugarit, see *KTU* 1.105.6, in *RCU* 42–43, and del Olmo Lete, *Canaanite Religion*, 208; 1.109.11, in *RCU* 29, 31; and 1.119.3, 9–10, in *RCU* 149–50. See further below.

27. See the Introduction, Section 2, for details. For biblical material, see Maier, *Daughter Zion*, 10–14. For the relevant Ugaritic locales, see del Olmo Lete, *Canaanite Religion*, 21–25, 112, 236–37. Note also the discussion of Assyrian and Syro-Hittite cities as religious spaces in Harmanşah, *Cities*, 102–52.

28. Cf. "the god(s) of the city" in Akkadian texts, in *CAD* I/J:93a–b, #3"; and Karel van der Toorn, "God (I)," *DDD* 355 and 357. Cf. Luwian "Hebat of the city," in John David Hawkins, *Corpus of Hieroglyphic Luwian Inscriptions: Volume I. Inscriptions of the Iron Age. Part 1*, Studies in Indo-European Language and Culture 8.1 (Berlin: de Gruyter, 2000), 305, #V.5, line 6.

29. Cf. "city" used for "citadel" (so NRSV) or perhaps "precinct" of the house of Baal in 2 Kgs 10:25. For the latter use for "city," see Loren Fisher, "The Temple Quarter," *Journal of Semitic Studies* 8 (1963): 34–41.

30. See also RS 15.33.5, in *PRU III* p. 15; RS 15.24 + 50, lines 5–7, in *PRU III* p. 18. See also RS 17.116.1–2, in *PRU IV* p. 132; and the unusual case in RS 20.178.5–11, in *Ugaritica V* pp. 147–48. "The gods of the city" are probably to be reconstructed in the ritual text, *KTU* 1.148.40. See Pardee, *Les textes rituels*, RSO XII, 2 vols. (Paris: Éditions Recherche sur les Civilisations, 2000), 2.786, 803–4; *RCU* 18.

31. Emar 604, in Daniel Arnaud's listing of the colophons, in *Recherches au pays Aštata VI.4: Textes de la bibliothèque. Transcriptions et traductions* (Paris: Éditions Recherche sur les Civilisations, 1987), 199. For diviners at Emar, see Daniel E.

Fleming, *Time at Emar: The Cultic Calendar and the Rituals from the Diviner's House*, MC 11 (Winona Lake, Ind.: Eisenbrauns, 2000), 26–35. Among these, note also "the diviner of the gods of Emar," discussed by Fleming, *Time at Emar*, 26; and "the diviner of the king and of the city," discussed by Fleming, *The Installation of Baal's High Priestess at Emar: A Window on Ancient Syrian Religion*, HSS 42 (Atlanta: Scholars, 1992), 88.

32. Démare-Lafont, "The King and the Diviner at Emar," in *The City of Emar Among the Late Bronze Age Empires: History, Landscape, and Society*, Proceedings of the Konstanz Emar Conference, 25–26.04.2006, ed. Lorenzo d'Alfonso, Yoram Cohen, and Dietrich Sürenhagen, AOAT 349 (Münster: Ugarit-Verlag, 2008), 213–16.

33. See the discussion of Fleming, *Time at Emar*, 146–73.

34. See Chapter 5, and also below.

35. *KTU* 2.19.7, 8; 2.20.2; 2.35.17; 2.38.1; 2.44.1; 2.46.2; cf. "king of (the land of) Ugarit," in RS 16.03.3, in *PRU III* p. 3; RS 13.7B, in *PRU III* p. 6, etc. The Ugaritic expression also occurs in other genres: legal documents (*KTU* 3.1.14, 25; 3.2.4; 3.5.4), a royal seal (*KTU* 6.23.3), administrative records (*KTU* 4.17.18; 6.29.4), and colophons on the Baal Cycle (*KTU* 1.4 VIII 49, 1.6 VI 57, in *UNP* 141 and 164).

36. *KTU* 2.21.2, 9; and Akkadian letters RS 15.86.4–5, in *PRU III* p. 51; RS 12.33.2, in *PRU III* p. 14.

37. RS 16.146 + 161, line 4: 1, in *PRU III* pp. 182–83.

38. This type of crown is also known from rabbinic sources, m. Kelim 11:8, m. Shabbat 6:1; bt. Shabbat 59b, etc., cited in Shalom Paul, *Divrei Shalom: Collected Studies of Shalom Paul on the Bible and the Ancient Near East 1967–2005*, CHANE 23 (Leiden: Brill, 2005), 333–42. As Paul notes, the crown is called "Jerusalem of gold" in rabbinic literature (e.g., bt. Ned. 50a).

39. For this concern, I have been influenced by Daniel E. Fleming, *The Legacy of Israel in Judah's Bible: History, Politics, and the Reinscribing of Tradition* (Cambridge: Cambridge University Press, 2012).

40. See Timothy M. Willis, *The Elders of the City: A Study of the Elders-Laws in Deuteronomy*, SBLMS 55 (Atlanta: SBL, 2001).

41. Schloen (*House of the Father*, 256 n. 1 and 326–28) suggests that the word refers to "(house-)owners," in part on the basis of the use of the related Ugaritic word *b'lm*.

42. BDB 127; and Schloen, *House of the Father*, 160. See also Num 21:28 for "lords of the heights of Arnon"; cf. Baale-goiim in Isa 16:8.

43. RS 17.424 C + 397 B.25, in *PRU IV* p. 219.

44. See Itamar Singer, "A Political History of Ugarit," in *Handbook of Ugaritic Studies*, 672 n. 217, following Daniel Arnaud, "Études sur Alalaḫ et Ougarit à l'âge du Bronze Récent," *SMEA* 37 (1996): 63 n. 94.

45. For the commercial context, see Arnaud, "Études sur Alalaḫ," 63; cf. Michael Heltzer, *The Rural Community of Ugarit* (Wiesbaden: Dr. Ludwig Reichert, 1976), 79, and "The Economy of Ugarit," in *Handbook of Ugaritic Studies*, 444.

For such a body of elders, see also Mario Liverani, "Ras Shamra II. Histoire," in *Supplément au dictionnaire de la Bible* (Paris: Letouzey et Ané, 1978), 1342; and Heltzer, *Rural Community of Ugarit,* 79, noted by Juan Pablo Vita, "The Society of Ugarit," in *Handbook of Ugaritic Studies,* 483.

46. Heltzer, *Rural Community of Ugarit,* 79.

47. See Michael Heltzer, "The Political Institutions of Ancient Emar as Compared with Contemporary Ugarit (13.–Beginning of the 12. Century B.C.E.)," *UF* 33 (2001): 219–36; here 231–34, 236. Note also for the Emar evidence, Démare-Lafont, "King and the Diviner at Emar," 207–17.

48. See, for example, RS 20.239.21, in *Ugaritica V* p. 142; Silvie Lackenbacher, *Textes akkadiens d'Ugarit,* LAPO 20 (Paris: Cerf, 2002), 200–201. For evidence from Mari, see Jean-Marie Durand, *Les documents épistolaires du palais de Mari: Tome I,* LAPO 16 (Paris: Cerf, 2002), 458–59; and Fleming, *Democracy's Ancient Ancestors,* 68–70, 190–200.

49. For example, RS 20.04.1, in *Ugaritica V* p. 193. If in the letter the word does not denote elders but ancestors, the verb used in this context would refer to posing an oracle (as to deities; see *CAD* Š/1:278). In Ugaritic the cognate verb (*š'l) is used for consulting the eponymous ancestor Ditanu in *KTU* 1.124.1–3, in *RCU* 171–72.

50. *KTU* 2.72.19; see also line 22. For this letter, see George J. Brooke, "The Textual, Formal and Historical Significance of Ugaritic Letter RS 34.124 (= *KTU* 2.72)," *UF* 11 (1979 = Claude Schaeffer Festschrift): 69–87; and Pierre Bordreuil and Dennis Pardee, "Les textes en cuneiforms alphabétiques," in *Une bibliothèque au sud de la ville: Les textes de la 34e campagne (1973),* RSO VII (Paris: Éditions Recherche sur les Civilisations, 1991), 143–50.

51. Walter Mayer, *Tall Munbāqa—Ekalte II: Die Texte,* Wissenschaftliche Veröffentlichungen der deutschen Orientgesellschaft 102 (Saarbrücken: Saarbrücker Druckerei und Verlag, 2001), 73 (MBQ-T 49, lines 1–3).

52. For the text and discussion, see Démare-Lafont, "King and the Diviner at Emar," 209. It is text 6 in Marcel Sigrist, "Seven Emar Tablets," in *kinattūtu ša dārâti: Raphael Kutscher Memorial Volume,* ed. A. F. Rainey, Institute of Archaeology Occasional Publications 1 (Tel Aviv: Institute of Archaeology of Tel Aviv University, 1993), 165–84.

53. For some thoughts in this direction for what he calls the "Jerusalemer Tempeltheologie," see Martin Leuenberger, "Jhwh, 'der Gott Jerusalems' (BLay 1,2): Konturen der Jerusalemer Tempeltheologie aus religions- und theologiegeschichtlicher Perspektive," *EvT* 74 (2014): 245–60.

54. See Bernard Lang, *The Hebrew God: Portrait of an Ancient Deity* (New Haven, Conn.: Yale University Press, 2002), 9–11 and 55–56.

55. For these oracles recontextualized in this psalm, see Scott R. A. Starbuck, *Court Oracles in the Psalms: The So-Called Royal Psalms in the Ancient Near Eastern Context,* SBLDS 172 (Atlanta: SBL, 1999), 161–67.

56. The nature of the ritual activity entailed is unclear. Ziony Zevit associates this verse with rooftop ritual in Zeph 1:4–7. See Zevit, *The Religions of Ancient Israel: A Synthesis of Parallactic Approaches* (London: Continuum, 2001), 472, 581. He also believes that it was for a non-Yahwistic cult, though he provides no evidence. For another view, see Mordecai Cogan and Hayim Tadmor, *II Kings: A New Translation with Introduction and Commentary*, AYB 11 (New York: Doubleday, 1988), 256.

57. See Francesca Stavrakopoulou, "Exploring the Garden of Uzza: Death, Burial and Ideologies of Kingship," *Bib* 87 (2006): 1–21.

58. See Pierre Bordreuil and Dennis Pardee, *A Manual of Ugaritic*, Linguistic Studies in Ancient West Semitic 3 (Winona Lake, Ind.: Eisenbrauns, 2008), 113, 215–17. See also *RCU* 85–88, and Pardee, *Les textes rituels*, 2.816–25, based largely on his study "Poetry in Ugaritic Ritual Texts," in *Verse in Ancient Near Eastern Prose*, ed. Johannes C. de Moor and Wilfred G. E. Watson, AOAT 42 (Kevelaer: Bercker und Butzon; Neukirchen-Vluyn: Neukirchener, 1993), 208–10; and Wayne T. Pitard, "RS 34.126: Notes on the Text," *Maarav* 4/1 (1987): 75–86, 111–55 (photographs by Wayne T. Pitard and drawings by Bruce Zuckerman). See also del Olmo Lete, *Canaanite Religion*, 156–61.

59. Cf. the blessing in *KTU* 1.108.23b–27 for the city of Ugarit associated with the eponymous ancestor of the dead leaders, in *RCU* 195; and del Olmo Lete, *Canaanite Religion*, 154.

60. For a proposed archaeological scenario for this ritual, see Schloen, *House of the Father*, 345. Schloen notes some evidence for a shrine suggested by two cavities in wall 1006 of room 1045 in House B of the "Centre de la Ville." This room is also the location of the *dromos* (corridor) of tomb 1068. Schloen detects fittings for wooden beams for benches as well as pottery suggesting possible food remains. The evidence is suggestive of ritual pertaining to the dead, but perhaps not the royal dead, given the location in the "Centre de la Ville" rather than within the massive compound of the royal palace. What Schloen detects may be evidence for elite emulation of royal ritual of the sort that *KTU* 1.161 details.

61. This form of translation avoids adding any expressed direct object (e.g., "Tell *it* not . . . ,//Do not proclaim *it* . . ."; NJPS, my italics). The implied object of these verbs in v. 20 is the death of Saul and Jonathan; the form it might have taken might be vv. 21–23. If so, this may affect also the understanding of the corresponding v. 24. This verse would in turn suggest a possible picture of the women weeping and lamenting with the words of vv. 21–23. For the verbal expression, compare *pen-yaggīdû* ("lest they tell") in 1 Sam 27:11, which also involves communication about conflict with the Philistines. There, any man or woman is thought to be able to pass on the news, which may be the case here as well.

62. Noting the imbalance of these first two lines in this verse, Stanley Gevirtz would emend to *brḥbwt gt*, since *rḥbwt* and *ḥwṣwt* are paired nine times elsewhere.

Gevirtz especially notes Amos 5:16, with its lament context. It is true that the first line of the couplet is quite short relative to the parallel line following it. See Gevirtz, *Patterns in the Early Poetry of Israel*, Studies in Ancient Oriental Civilization 32 (Chicago: University of Chicago Press, 1963), 83. Note also Baruch A. Levine, *Numbers 21–36: A New Translation with Introduction and Commentary*, AYB 4A (New York: Doubleday, 2000), 102.

63. For Iron II streets in Ashkelon, see *Ashkelon 1: Introduction and Overview (1985–2006)*, ed. Lawrence E. Stager, J. David Schloen, and Daniel M. Master, Leon Levy Expedition to Ashkelon (Winona Lake, Ind.: Eisenbrauns, 2008), 284, 288, 307, 310. For city planning in other Philistine sites, see Ze'ev Herzog, *Archaeology of the City: Urban Planning in Ancient Israel and Its Social Implications*, Sonia and Marco Nadler Institute of Archaeology Monograph 13 (Tel Aviv: Tel Aviv University, 1997), 201–4.

64. See Alan Millard, "Oral Proclamation and Written Record: Spreading and Preserving Information in Ancient Israel," in *Michael: Historical, Epigraphical and Biblical Studies in Honor of Prof. Michael Heltzer*, ed. Yitzhak Avishur and Robert Deutsch (Tel Aviv: Archaeological Center, 1999), 237–41.

65. Literally, "outsides," presumed to be outside of houses or other habitations in space shared by people of multiple houses or habitations. See *BDB* 299.

66. See William P. Brown and John T. Carroll, "The Garden and the Plaza: Biblical Images of the City," *Interpretation* 54 (2000): 3–11. Cf. Inanna and her lover in the square in "Love by the Light of the Moon," in *COS* 1.542–43.

67. Cf. *BDB* 300; see also Punic evidence noted in *DNWSI* 398. For streets and plazas for Iron Age Israel, see Yigal Shiloh, "Elements in the Development of Town Planning in the Israelite City," *IEJ* 28 (1978): 36–51. Herzog (*Archaeology of the City*, 216, 232–33, and 245) mentions streets in the city design of tenth-century Tell el-Far'ah (North), ninth/eighth-century Tell es-Sa'idiyeh, and eighth-century Beersheba.

68. Millard, "Oral Proclamation and Written Record," 237. Millard compares Wisdom to "hawkers" of wares. See below for the business side of such communal spaces. Cf. Akkadian *maḫīru*, "market place," in *CAD* M/1:93.

69. Note *rĕḥôb* in Deut 13:17 and Judg 19:15. Cf. the reading of torah in the *rĕḥôb* at the Water Gate in Neh 8:13, and the rabbinic evidence for prayer in the town square, in Sidney B. Hoenig, "Historical Inquiries: I. Heber Ir II. City-Square," *JQR* 48 (1958): 123–39.

70. For extensive discussion, see Tina Haettner Blomquist, *Gates and Gods: Cults in the City Gates of Iron Age Palestine. An Investigation of the Archaeological and Biblical Sources*, ConBOT 46 (Stockholm: Almqvist and Wiksell, 1999).

71. Yohanan Aharoni compared a so-called gate shrine at Megiddo, but according to Ziony Zevit (*Religions of Ancient Israel*, 231), there is no archaeological evidence to support a cultic interpretation. For 2 Kgs 23:8, Zevit (*Religions of*

Ancient Israel, 191–95) instead compares the standing stones around the city gate at the site of Dan.

72. For further discussion of this iconography, see Chapter 4.

73. See Rami Arav, Richard A. Freund, and John F. Shroder, Jr., "Bethsaida Rediscovered," *Biblical Archaeology Review* 26/1 (2000): 44–56, esp. 48–50. See also the plan and photographs in Zevit, *Religions of Ancient Israel,* 148–53, esp. figures 3.11–3.13.

74. Note also the metonymic use of gates for settlements where ritual activity takes place, in Deut 12:15, 17, 21; 15:22; 16:5; 26:12.

75. *KTU* 1.14 II–IV, esp. II 20–22, 26–27, in *UNP* 14; and IV 2–4, 8–9, in *UNP* 18.

76. *KTU* 1.119.26–36, in *RCU* 149–50; and del Olmo Lete, *Canaanite Religion,* 256–57, 394.

77. See Jeremias, *Theophanie: Die Geschichte einer alttestamentlichen Gattungen,* WMANT 10 (Neukirchen-Vluyn: Neukirchener, 1965).

78. *CMHE* 147–77.

79. See Eric Nels Ortlund, *Theophany and Chaoskampf: The Interpretation of Theophanic Imagery in the Baal Epic, Isaiah, and the Twelve,* Gorgias Ugaritic Studies 5 (Piscataway, N.J.: Gorgias, 2010).

80. See Chapter 5 for Teman as one name for the southern home of Yahweh.

81. For this motif's background, see Victor A. Hurowitz, "Splitting the Sacred Mountain: Zechariah 14,4 and Gilgamesh V ii 4–5," *UF* 31 (1999): 241–45. Compare also Ps 114. In view of the geographical setting, the "mythology" (Hurowitz's term), as it were, seems to belong to Baal of Lebanon (see also the discussion of Ps 29 in Chapter 3).

82. Richard J. Clifford, *Cosmic Mountain in Canaan and the Old Testament,* HSM 4 (Cambridge, Mass.: Harvard University Press, 1972), 142–53; and *UBC* 2.150–51. See also Moshe Weinfeld, "Jerusalem—A Political and Spiritual Capital," in *Capital Cities: Urban Planning and Spiritual Dimensions,* Proceedings of the Symposium Held on May 27–29, 1996, Jerusalem, Israel, ed. Joan Goodnick Westenholz (Jerusalem: Bible Lands Museum, 1998), 33.

83. *UBC* 2.674.

84. Fitzgerald, *The Lord of the East Wind,* CBQMS 34 (Washington, D.C.: Catholic Biblical Association of America, 2002), 121–25.

85. Fitzgerald, "Mythological Background" and "BTWLT and BT as Titles"; cf. Dobbs-Allsopp, "Syntagma of *bat.*" For some support for Fitzgerald's approach, see Maier, *Daughter Zion,* 235 n. 15. As Fitzgerald notes, the grammatical gender of "city" in West Semitic languages would comport with female personification. For a confirmation of West Semitic "city" as feminine in grammatical gender even in peripheral Akkadian, see Hazor 3: "The city, its (feminine) gods (URU DINGER.MEŠ-*ša*) will return there." See Wayne Horowitz and Takayoshi Oshima, *Cuneiform in Canaan: Cuneiform Sources from the Land of Israel in*

Ancient Times (Jerusalem: Israel Exploration Society/Hebrew University of Jerusalem, 2006), 68.

86. See Hans-Jürgen Hermisson, "Die Frau Zion," in *Studies in the Book of Isaiah: Festschrift Willem A. M. Beuken,* ed. J. van Ruiten and M. Vervenne, BETL 132 (Leuven: Leuven University Press, 1997), 19–39; and Peggy L. Day, "The Personification of Cities as Female in the Hebrew Bible: The Thesis of Aloysius Fitzgerald, F.S.C.," in *Reading from This Place. Volume 2: Social Location and Biblical Interpretation in Global Perspective,* ed. F. F. Segovia and M. A. Tolbert (Minneapolis: Fortress, 1995), 283–302, both noted by Maier, *Daughter Zion,* 235 n. 7. See also the review by Adele Berlin, *Lamentations,* OTL (Louisville, Ky.: Westminster John Knox, 2002), 10–12. See Maier, *Daughter Zion,* 60–93, esp. 63–64.

87. Maier, *Daughter Zion,* 64. The word *b'lt* commonly but not always applies to a goddess; see *DULAT* 208; *KAI* 56 (*DNWSI* 184); cf. *PPD* 120. Note also "master (f.) of the house" (1 Kgs 17:17; cf. 1 Sam 28:7; Nah 3:4).

88. Paul, *Divrei Shalom,* 333–42; and Maier, *Daughter Zion,* 64–69.

89. For this letter, see above note 50.

Epilogue

1. Kawashima, "*Homo Faber* in J's Primeval History," *ZAW* 116 (2004): 496. Note also Rebecca's initiative in making an inquiry of the deity in Gen 25:22.

2. Cf. Kawashima's remarks on religion in Gen 1–11 ("*Homo Faber,*" 496): "What is surprising is that according to J, God does not instruct humans how to worship, or even, to worship at all. Like civilization itself and the epic quest for fame, religion is a human invention." Kawashima also notes Cain and Abel in Gen 4:3–4 as inventors of "sacrificial worship" ("*Homo Faber,*" 497).

Subject Index

Absalom, 77, 92, 93, 94, 95, 160, 176
Absalom-in-Hebron, 77, 160
Adad, 165. *See also* Hadad
Adad at Sikan, 76. *See also* Hadad of Sikan
Adad of Aleppo, 76
Adad of Hazi, 85. *See also* Baal (of) Sapan
Adad of Kallassu, 76
Adad of Ugarit, 85. *See also* Baal of Ugarit
'Ain Dara temple, 19, 26–27, 127
Alaca Höyük, 55, 64
Aleppo, 82, 162
analogy, 7, 9, 31, 37, 50, 51, 52–53, 64, 65, 76, 96, 109, 111, 122, 133, 158, 160. *See also* anthropomorphism; correlation; homology; metaphor; simile
Anat, 41, 48, 49, 50, 51, 52, 54, 65, 74, 82, 138, 143, 144, 149, 150
Anat of Sapan, 73, 82, 83
Anat-Yahu, 155
ancestor(s), 17, 103, 104, 131, 184, 185. *See also* family god(s)
angels, 15, 17, 18, 25, 123, 125, 132
animals, 48, 51, 52, 54, 55, 56, 57, 64, 68, 144, 151. *See also* theriomorphism
anthropomorphism, 2, 3, 5–10, 13, 14, 25, 26, 28, 29, 44, 47, 48–57, 66, 68, 108, 110, 112, 115, 118, 119, 121, 123, 134, 143, 147, 148, 149, 156. *See also* analogy

Aqhat, 24, 25, 48, 49, 123, 130, 144
asherah, 35, 40, 169
Asherah, 32, 35, 40, 142. *See also* Athirat
Asherah of Samaria, 73, 161
Ashtart, 75. *See also* Astarte; Athtart
Ashtart in Sidon, 75, 93
Ashtart of Eryx, 74
Ashtart of Hurri, 74. *See also* Athtart of Hurri
Ashtart of Kition, 74
Ashtart of Nineveh, 74
Ashtart of Paphos, 74. *See also* Venus
Ashtart of Samaria, 161
assembly, 103. *See also* divine assembly
Astarte, 49, 50, 52, 67, 68, 143. *See also* Athtart
Athirat, 32. *See also* Asherah; Athirat of Tyre
Athirat of Tyre, 73, 93
Athtar, 54, 74, 76
Athtart, 41, 54, 55, 73, 74, 75. *See also* Astarte
Athtart at Mari, 75
Athtart of Hurri, 73, 162, 163. *See also* Ashtart of Hurri
attribute animal(s), 54. *See also* animals; birds; bull; calf; emblem-animal(s); lion; panther; theriomorphism

Baal, 36, 37, 38, 40, 41, 42, 48, 49, 52, 53, 54, 55, 63, 65, 71, 72, 76, 78, 81,

Index of Modern Authors

Index of Ancient Sources